1991

EDUCAȚII

EDUCATING THE RESPECTABLE

THE WOBURN EDUCATION SERIES

General Series Editor: Professor Peter Gordon

EDUCATING
THE RESPECTABLE

A Study of Fleet Road
Board School, Hampstead,
1879–1903

W. E. MARSDEN

Reader in Education
University of Liverpool

THE WOBURN PRESS

First published 1991 in Great Britain by
THE WOBURN PRESS
Gainsborough House, Gainsborough Road,
London E11 1RS, England

and in the United States of America by
THE WOBURN PRESS
c/o International Specialized Book Services, Inc.
5602 N.E. Hassalo Street, Portland, OR 97213

Copyright © 1991 William E. Marsden

British Library Cataloguing in Publication Data

Marsden, W.E. (William Edward) *1932–*
  Educating the respectable : a study of Fleet Road Board
  School, Hampstead, 1879–1903
  1. London. (London Borough) Camden. Hampstead. Primary
  schools. Fleet Road Board School, history
  I. Title
  372.942142

ISBN 0-7130-0184-4

Printed in Great Britain by
Antony Rowe Ltd, Chippenham

Contents

List of Plates

List of Maps

Abbreviations

BFSS	British and Foreign School Society
BPP	British Parliamentary Papers
GLC	Greater London Council
HHE	*Hampstead and Highgate Express*
LCC	London County Council
LSB	London School Board
MCCE	Minutes of the Committee of Council on Education
PRO	Public Record Office
RCCE	Reports of the Committee of Council on Education
SBC	*School Board Chronicle*
SBL	School Board for London records in GLC archives

Acknowledgements

My thanks are first due to librarians, curators and archivists who have been so supportive and helped to make research time such a pleasure. They include John Vaughan and the library staff in the University of Liverpool Department of Education; the staffs of the British Library, Camden Local History Library, the Greater London Record Office, the Public Record Office, and the National Society. In particular, I owe a huge debt to George Bartle, Archivist of the British and Foreign School Society, who has been assiduous well beyond the call of duty in searching out material on the Adams family. Not for the first time, I am grateful to Bob Hunt, for drawing most of the maps, and to him and the University of Liverpool photographic service for processing many of the illustrations. Similarly, I appreciate the help of my colleague Robin Betts, who has picked up some crucial leads I might well have missed. I also wish to thank Merfyn Jones, for translating the Welsh extract in Chapter 5; David Reeder for his support; Wilfred Harrison, for information on J.W.B. Adams's period at Tenby; Anna Davin, for useful references; and of course Peter Gordon, for his editorial skills and encouragement.

In Hampstead, I gained valuable contacts first through Ruth Merttens, and then Susan Doyle of the *Hampstead Advertiser*. Her article on my research brought letters from old pupils of Fleet Road: Miss D.J. Armstrong, Mr. L.H. Dewar, and from Mr. H.J. Newcombe and his brother Mr. A. Newcombe. The recollections of the Newcombe family have proved particularly useful.

The critical link has of course been with Fleet Primary School, still flourishing. I am very grateful for the cooperation and hospitality of the late Edith Kahn, the former Headteacher, and her successor, Pat Hollister. I have particularly enjoyed a spin-off benefit of the research, working with the Fleet Road staff and children on a project on the Victorian period, making use of some of the materials collected for this book. I shall certainly not forget the reenactment for a 1989 Fleet Road 'entertainment' of two of Louisa Walker's action songs, 'Model Laundry Maids' and 'A Case of Toys'. Most significant of all was meeting Mr. John Jones at this entertainment. He still lives round the corner from the school, was a pupil in Mrs. Walker's Department towards the end of her time there, and had an aunt who was one of Mrs. Walker's assistants. He was able to recapitulate the words and actions of Louisa Walker's 'A Silly Fish': a truly historic experience. He also provided two photographs which I have used, showing him as an infant in fancy dress for two of Mrs. Walker's occasions. He gave me the cues which led to contact with grandchildren or grandchildren-in-law of Mrs. Walker – Mrs Kay Taylor, Mrs. Pax Lohan, and Mrs Mary Fryett – who have been very open and informative in supplying family detail, photographs and memorabilia, including a copy of a book of Louisa Walker's not in the British Library catalogue. I have valued meeting them.

Completion of this book has been heavily reliant on a Nuffield Social Science Research Fellowship, and on continuing support from the University of Liverpool's Research Fund. I also thank Janet Marsden for help in preparing the index.

More formally, I wish to acknowledge the permission of the following for the reproduction of maps and photographs: Aerofilms for Plates 7, 8 and 9; British Library for Map 8, the timetables on pages 137 and 192–3, the musical extract on page 223, and Plates 1, 4, 15, 19a/b, 21a/b, 25, 26, 27, 30, 31; Camden Local History Library for Plate 2; Greater London Record Office for Map 7, and Plates 3, 5, 6, 16, 28, 29.

W.E. Marsden

PREFACE

'The Eton of the Board Schools'

> After spending a day with Mr. Adams, the head-master
> of Fleet Road Schools, I do not wonder at this strange
> enthusiasm (for attending school). Here we have a very Eton
> for nothing a week ... I make no apology to Eton for using
> her famous name in this connection. No, rather I should beg
> Fleet Road to forgive me, for I would back a picked dozen of
> its ex-7th standard boys and girls against as many Etonians –
> 'weight for age', of course, to borrow a metaphor from the
> turf ... Our 'Eton for Nothing a Week' I have taken as a type
> of the best, the very aristocracy of Board schools.[1]
>
> Morley, 1897

The above quotation is from Charles Morley's *Studies in Board
Schools*, the source which probably first drew my attention to
Fleet Road. The Eton tag is also mentioned in Stuart Maclure's
much later *One Hundred Years of London Education, 1870–1970*
(1970). More unusually, Fleet Road is referred to as the 'Harrow
of the Board Schools' in F.M.L. Thompson's invaluable *Hampstead; Building a Borough 1650–1964* (1974), though the source
noted by Thompson, F.E. Baines' history of Hampstead (1890),
does not mention Harrow.[2] Maclure ascribes the Eton metaphor
to Fleet Road's 'academic success and the way it began to attract a
middle class clientele'.[3] Thompson refers to 'the enviable regularity with which Fleet Road children carried off a large number
of the School Board's scholarships to secondary schools'.[4]

Within a few years of W.B. Adams assuming the headship of
Fleet Road School in 1879 the London School Board was aware
that it had a success story on its hands. By the late 1880s Fleet
Road was well established as a scholarship school and by the late
1890s its reputation was at its peak. But to attach the Eton epithet
to a scholarship school seems conceptually inappropriate, for the
scholarship system was not about privilege and connection, but

about making progress on merit. Fleet Road was to do with social mobility, not the more rigid divides of an earlier period. While the upper middle classes had by the end of the nineteenth century gained access to the great public schools, they had then helped to seal them off from the social groups below. And while schools like Fleet Road provided a ladder of opportunity, it was not realistically directed towards the heights of Eton.

The linking of the two names had a much looser basis than this. It was rather a matter of image. Comparisons were being made with Eton at Fleet Road annual prize-givings in the early 1890s, if not before.[5] There was frequent jocular and popular reference to 'Old Fleetonians'. The motto 'Semper Floreat Fleetonia' appeared in school magazines of the 1890s. The Eton reference was therefore emblematic, intended to convey the image of Fleet Road as an elite, if not the top, school of its type. It was clearly beneficial to the London School Board to have such visibly successful schools, to help to counter the allegations of extravagance heaped upon it. Fleet Road and its peer scholarship schools became a kind of metropolitan Ivy League. A more generally applicable explanation of the Eton label was the widely-held view in official circles that it was important to transplant the public school ethos into the elementary sector as a means of upgrading the social image of board schools, long characterized as providing for less than respectable groups in the population.

Fleet Road therefore presented itself as an elect school of its type. Its prime purpose was the education of the respectable. Respectability was a key social concept in the late nineteenth century.[6] The need to be seen to be respectable was a vital issue for the expanding social cohort between the rich and the rough. While Fleet Road was often tagged, chiefly by its opponents, as a middle-class school, it was certainly not this in any strict sense. As we shall find, while it avoided taking more than a small quota of deprived children, neither did it cater for the well-to-do. Its main role lay in defining and meeting the requirements of economically comfortable and socially respectable lower-middle- and upper-working class children who, prior to the 1870 Education Act, had been badly provided for. In the 1869 debates preceding the Act, W.E. Forster referred to these as 'a large and interesting class of children', one having 'occupied our attention more than any other'.[7]

In addition to the Eton title, Fleet Road's influential supporters were prone to refer to it as 'the finest elementary school in' either London, England or even Europe. This was a doubly dubious accolade, for few of its rivals would have accepted it was the best, and in any case it was not strictly an elementary school. As an institution committed to extending the boundaries of elementary education, it strove to keep large numbers of children in Standards VI, VII and Ex-VII. The Senior Mixed Department contained many pupils over 13 years of age. Though in part a secondary school, it was still working under the provisions of the Elementary Education Acts. The very publicity it sought and gained worked to its disadvantage, and to that of the larger system, in this context. Fleet Road was one of the examples used in the late 1890s by the Education Department to attack the London School Board, a confrontation which led to the demise of the school board system.

Fleet Road's spectacular successes were consistently recorded and have left a richer legacy of sources for research than are available for most board schools. They are rather dangerous materials, however, in tending to present an unbalanced picture of high achievement. Fleet Road was also a normal elementary school. It was a large minority of children that won the scholarships and sang in the choirs which brought the school so much of its fame. The solid foundation work, of the Junior Mixed Department in particular, was relatively little recognised.

While its peers would hardly have conceded that Fleet Road was the finest of the London board schools, they might well have accepted that it was the most famous. Its pre-eminence was in large measure the fortunate consequence of the concurrent appointments of William Bateman Adams and Louisa Walker, who quickly established their reputations, and were to become the most charismatic and media-conscious of all the London School Board's staff. It is particularly as a result of their endeavours that so wide-ranging an historical record remains. The major gap in these materials is the scantness of the school records themselves. Even without these, a substantial recreation of the social and educational experience of people associated with Fleet Road schools is possible. The case study illustrates vividly a number of the cross-currents impinging on society and schooling in the late nineteenth century. An inter-disciplinary methodology is used, the nature of which is outlined in an earlier

earlier book,[8] to which this one can be regarded as complementary. But it additionally takes us further into the significant
connections between the socio-economic context of the school
and its curricular and extra-curricular offerings.

No doubt personal bias has crept into the account and the
associated judgements. Some may feel that less than justice is
done to the voluntary cause, for example. I cannot, however,
take too seriously the view, one that was strongly advanced in
Hampstead during the School Board period, and is present in the
later historiography, that had the 1870 Act allowed it, and with a
little bit of help from on high, church schools could have met the
quantitative, and still less the qualitative, needs of tertiary
society in late Victorian times. The Fleet Road case suggests that
what took place in the urban school board sector was nothing less
than the Second Educational Revolution in mass education,
taking the First as being the implementation of the monitorial
system by the churches. Had the school boards not been, it would
seem that continuity rather than change would have been the
hall-mark of the system. Consider the following. The British and
Foreign School Society's archives contain the copy books of
Jamaican children, some of them slave children, from the 1820s.
The children were required to write out a number of times in their
best hand-writing precepts such as: 'Cautiously avoid sin'; 'Aim
at Improvement'; and 'Happy are the just'.[9] Jumping forward
nearly one hundred years later to a Church of England school in
Southport in 1909, my father, then a nine-year-old, was solemnly
signing away his freedoms in a juvenile declaration in which he
promised 'by God's help, to Abstain from the use of all Intoxi-
cating Liquors': in his best hand-writing. Thirty years later the
author of this book, also at a Church of England School, at the
age of eight, was equally earnestly writing in his exercise book:
'Sin is naughtiness' and 'the Holy Spirit makes us good'. Much
of the practice in writing consisted of copying out the Ten
Commandments.

Fleet Road certainly did not neglect religious instruction, and
indeed gained commendation for its efforts in this sphere.
Nor did its children escape moral pressure that on occasions
amounted to indoctrination, not least in the kindergarten offerings of the Infant Department. But the fundamentalist rigidities
which had long reinforced an unchanging social order were in
retreat. It has to be said that many parents at the time did

not approve this trend. Such judged the scholastic value of attendance at a distinguished board school like Fleet Road to be less important than the perceived moral benefits of a church school education. The process of educating the respectable, however, meant catering for change: implementing occupational and social uplift. For those who conceived of popular education as being the 'education of the poor', these were not comfortable ideas. The significance of the secularization process that followed the Revised Code and the 1870 Act has been conceded by some educational historians, such as John Hurt, but by few others. Aside from the superficial gloss of accomplishment that was sufficient to earn Fleet Road its title of 'the Eton of the Board Schools', its achievement was to be measured more profoundly against the social problematic of the unleashing of the meritocracy, and also against the yardstick of what might have happened if schools like it had proved to be unsuccessful.

REFERENCES AND NOTES

1. C. Morley, *Studies in Board Schools* (London, 1897), pp.85–6. Morley's 'Studies' had first appeared in the *Daily News*.
2. F.E. Baines (ed.), *Records of the Manor, Parish and Borough of Hampstead in the County of London to December 1st 1889* (London, 1890), pp.324–5.
3. S. Maclure, *One Hundred Years of London Education 1870–1970* (London, 1970), p.57.
4. F.M.L. Thompson, *Hampstead: Building a Borough 1650–1964* (London, 1974), note on p.416.
5. For example, *HHE*, 17 Jan. 1891.
6. See F.M.L. Thompson, *The Rise of Respectable Society: a Social History of Victorian Britain, 1830–1900* (London, 1988), pp.140–1 and 360–1. Also G. Crossick, *An Artisan Elite in Victorian Society: Kentish London 1840–1880* (London, 1978), p.135.
7. *Hansard*, 3rd Series, vol. 194 (1969), Co. 1357.
8. W.E. Marsden, *Unequal Educational Provision in England and Wales: the Nineteenth-century Roots* (London, Woburn Press, 1987), Chapter 1.
9. I am grateful to George Bartle, Archivist of the British and Foreign Schools Society, for access to this unique record.

CHAPTER ONE

The Fringes of Hampstead

It may well be that small pox, trams and trains between them
settled the social character of the Fleet Road district, there-
by confirming the general proposition that the working
classes were permitted to set up house where no one else
wanted to live ...[1]
(Thompson, 1974)

The late nineteenth century was a germinal period in the
development of, on the face of it, three barely connected social
and economic phenomena: popular education, urban transport
systems, and domestic music. But these, with other influences,
converged to shape the early fortunes of a London board school,
Fleet Road, located on the south-eastern fringe of Hampstead.

Just over 20 years before the school was built, the Newcastle
Commission had been established (1858) to report on the state of
popular education. At that time it was still characterized as 'the
education of the poor', a very broad mass of the population
regarded as generally negative in attitude towards schooling.
The Commissioners were soon made aware not only of the
inexactness of this notion, but also of a burgeoning demand from
much less than poor groups in the population for adequate
educational provision for their children. Perhaps HMI Morell
jumped the gun when he claimed, in a paper read to the United
Association of Schoolmasters of Great Britain in 1859:

I think, my friends, that it should be a subject of special gratification,
particularly to a company of teachers, that we live in what may be emphatically
termed *the age of popular education*.[2]

But he was certainly not much more than ten years premature. By
the 1870s the social forces demanding educational expansion
were in full flow. The 1870 Education Act, which established the
school boards, made practicable, through drawing on local rates,

1

a stupendous increase in accommodation, particularly designed to plug the gaps in large towns and cities, whose school boards, and not least London's, became the pace-setters in educational development.

At the same time, rapid urban population growth and associated suburbanization demanded the expansion of transport systems. The fringes of Hampstead were caught up in railway development as lines from Broad Street, St. Pancras, Euston and Marylebone stations converged to tunnel under its slopes, turning huge expanses into railway land.[3] Fleet Road's catchment area included a fair share of this development, particularly in West Kentish Town (Map 1).

Kentish Town was also the new heartland of a rapidly growing piano-manufacturing industry. This had spread from its Tottenham Court Road origins north-westwards into Camden Town, then on into Kentish Town, on the one hand because of the congestion and rising land prices in the city centre, and on the other because of the huge rise in demand for pianos as the pleasures of domestic music were diffused down the social ladder. As a member of the famous Brinsmead piano-making family put it:

The social importance of the piano is, beyond question, far greater than that of any other musical instrument ... This influence of the piano extends to all classes; and while considerable towns often have no orchestras, families possess the best possible substitute, making them familiar with the finest compositions ...[4]

Piano-makers, like railway workers, made up an upwardly-mobile cohort in the Kentish Town labour force, and their children too were a significant element in the Fleet Road School intake. The infant department, through the initiative of its headmistress, is said to have introduced the first piano into a London board school (Chapter 6), while the choral prowess achieved by the senior mixed department was one of the most potent contributions to the school's public image (Chapter 9). As domestic music-making expanded, so did lower-middle-class and artisan participation in amateur musical activity and concert-going.[5] School concerts became regular and locally popular extra-curricular activities.

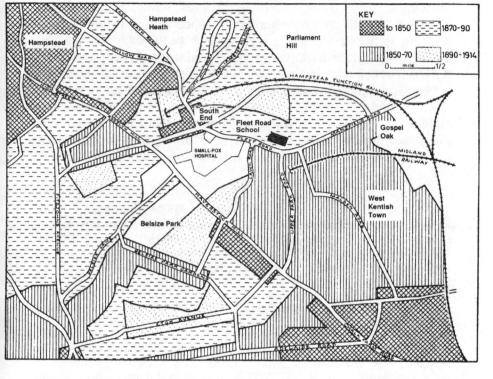

Map 1. Hampstead and Environs: Urban Growth to 1914

THE PHYSICAL SETTING OF THE FLEET ROAD AREA

The Fleet River, the largest of London's 'lost rivers', had
two headwaters, separated by Parliament Hill. The western or
Hampstead headwater was represented by Hampstead Ponds,
and was to run underground near Hampstead Heath Station. Its
line on the surface became that of Fleet Road, pointing towards
Kentish Town, then on to Camden Town, the King's Cross
district, Farringdon Road and, finally, the Thames. In Barton's
words, the Fleet declined from 'a river to a brook, from a
brook to a ditch, and from a ditch to a drain'.[6] Its valley was
shallow, bounded on the west by Primrose Hill, on the north by
Hampstead Heath and Parliament Hill, and on the east by the
more gently rising ground of Camden Town. Above this physical
bowl the heights of Hampstead were geologically of Bagshot

3

sands and gravels, as against the damper London clay of the valley. From Hampstead Heath a spur of land ran south-eastwards, down the eastern side of which the thoroughfares of Rosslyn Hill and Haverstock Hill were built (Map 1). On the more gentle western slopes of the spur, the affluent suburb of Belsize Park was developed.

Hampstead itself had grown as a spa with the opening of mineral springs in the late seventeenth century. By the late eighteenth, it had consolidated its function as a select residential town, beyond the built-up area of London. Its physical location reinforced its social situation: a kind of 'hill-station'.[7]

... the Northern Heights were destined by topography for upper-class occupation. The slopes gave advantages of drainage, water supply, and fresh air which the wealthier sort were prepared to pay for, thus driving property values beyond the reach of the lower ranks; while in any case the terrain discouraged industry and therefore the chance of work on the spot for the poorer sort, for whom daily journeys to work from a purely residential encampment on the hill would have been punishing either to the feet or to the pocket. It is therefore inconceivable that the Heights could in any circumstances have been occupied by a working-class suburb, and in a broad sense the contour lines provided Hampstead's defences against any such encroachment ... along most of the south-eastern and eastern front the mixed-character force from Camden Town and Gospel Oak was halted and contained before its advance reached the hill proper, and before the gradient sharpened enough to slow its momentum ... something more than a simple natural frontier was involved.[8]

It was in this social buffer zone that Fleet Road School was located.

POPULATION, URBAN GROWTH AND HOUSING

Map 1 shows urban growth in the Hampstead and West Kentish Town areas prior to 1914. Before 1850 there had been some south-eastward expansion from Hampstead itself into the Rosslyn Hill and South End districts, while from the other direction the north-westward extension of housing from the centre had reached Chalk Farm, with an outlier on Haverstock Hill. West Kentish Town was largely built up in the 1850–1870 period. This was mostly artisan housing with some higher-priced property in the Upper Park Road–Lawn Road district. More prestigious developments were taking place in these decades in the Adelaide Road area and in the southern part of Belsize Park.

By 1890 Hampstead was fully caught up in the sprawl of north-west London, though protected from encirclement by the Heath. The hugely prosperous Fitzjohn's Avenue district was the social apogee, but high quality residences spread towards the Heath and Parliament Hill in the Downshire Hill and South Hill Park districts. A socially intermediate development, from 1870 to beyond the turn of the century, was the predominantly lower-middle-class quarter which arose on the boundary of Hampstead and Gospel Oak to the north of Fleet Road and Mansfield Road. This was to be critical to the fortunes of Fleet Road School.

The 60 years between 1841 and 1901 saw the population of Hampstead Registration District increase eight-fold, with a particularly large increment during the 1880s. Table 1.1 shows the growth during Fleet Road School's early stages of development, on the basis of rounded figures.

TABLE 1.1

Census Year	Population	Inhabited Houses
1871	32,000	4,300
1881	45,000	5,800
1891	68,000	9,500
1901	82,000	11,000

Kentish Town had similarly grown apace, though its population spurt was slowing down by the 1890s. Not all of Kentish Town lies within the study area, but the figures for its Registration District (Table 1.2) are still a useful guide.

TABLE 1.2

Census Year	Population	Inhabited Houses
1861	14,000	6,000
1871	68,000	8,500
1881	87,000	10,000
1891	95,000	11,000

A major and enduring distinction between Hampstead and Kentish Town was the ratio of females to males in the population. Thus in 1881, of Hampstead's 45,452 inhabitants, 27,883 were female. In contrast, of 87,487 in Kentish Town, 45,756, not a great deal over half, were female. The preponderance of females in Hampstead was clearly linked with its social status. Of its 41,639 females in 1891, 28,940 were unmarried, 9,769 married, and 1,930 widowed. The greatest discrepancy between the sexes was in the 25–34 age range: 1,964 males and 5,345 females, reflecting the large proportion of women in domestic service. By 1901 Hampstead had 16,998 families or separate occupiers, and no fewer than 13,579 domestic servants, the highest proportion in London. The next most important female occupations in the district were dressmaking (874) and teaching (795). The presence of many unmarried females combined with a socially high status population clearly reduced the demand for public provision of schooling. But the opposite circumstances, as demonstrated in Kentish Town, equally led to the reverse.

Of Hampstead's 13,169 households in 1891, only 5,393 had less than five rooms. There were problems, but overall Hampstead was ranked low on Booth's poverty criteria, based on the 1891 census,[9] with only 16.5 per cent crowding, the lowest figure in London apart from Lewisham. Of the 27 divisions of the metropolis, Hampstead was rated as 'alpha plus' on the combined criteria which Booth worked out as connected indices of social disadvantage. St. Pancras, in which Kentish Town was placed, had a much more mixed profile than Hampstead, though its disadvantage was experienced more severely in terms of overcrowding than of poverty (Table 1.3).

TABLE 1.3

Indices	Ranking (out of 27)	
	Hampstead	St. Pancras
Poverty scale	27th	12th
Domestic crowding scale	26th	7th
Proportion of young married females	27th	12th
Surplus unmarried males	27th	14th
Birth rate (low)	27th	19th
Death rate (low)	27th	13th
Combined order	27th	11th

By 1901, Hampstead had 36.7 persons and 5.4 houses per acre. St. Pancras, which included more disadvantaged areas of course than West Kentish Town, had figures of 88.0 and 9.4 respectively. Focusing down to the lower-middle- and upper-working-class areas of Hampstead, that is the West Hampstead and Fleet Road districts, the densities increased to 53 persons and 8 houses to the acre, as against 28 and $3\frac{1}{2}$ respectively in the upper-middle-class parts of Hampstead.[10]

On the more detailed scale provided by Booth's later survey,[11] and based on only four of the earlier criteria, Hampstead again comes out near the top, with Kentish Town considerably lower down. But by this stage Hampstead was being overtaken on the social advantage scale by parts of south London. The high level of crowding for Kentish Town was in part explained by the absorption of building land for railway development (Table 1.4).

TABLE 1.4

| | Ranking (out of 50) | |
Indices	Hampstead	Kentish Town
Poverty	48th	33rd
Crowding	42nd	19th
Birth rate	47th	28th
Death rate	49th	30th

Booth's various surveys of life and labour in London illuminate the social fabric of particular districts. Particularly valuable in the context of the urban history of education is the breakdown of poverty/comfort ratios on the basis of London School Board blocks. As Map 2 illustrates, there was great variation in these ratios in Hampstead and Kentish Town. As the 1887–89 survey found, poverty levels ranged from 35 per cent and over in the Kentish Town blocks (36a and b on Map 2) to negligible amounts in the Belsize Park district. Surprisingly, old Hampstead was acquainted with quite serious poverty, affecting from one-quarter to one-third of its population. Of Kentish Town, Booth remarked that the majority of the people lived from 'hand to mouth' but there was 'not much distress'. Of Hampstead proper, he merely commented that most inhabitants were well-to-do, but that there was some very old property.[12]

The 1890s surveys, culminating in the Third Series volumes entitled *Religious Influences*, extended the very detailed street-by-street coverage into the suburbs. They were marvellously illustrated by a series of coloured maps, offering a social kaleidoscope coded in black for dire distress, dark and light blue for serious degrees of poverty, purple for mixed poverty and comfort, pink for comfort, and red and yellow for affluence. The pattern in Hampstead and West Kentish Town is depicted on Map 3, which is summarized from the information on Booth's coloured maps of the area.

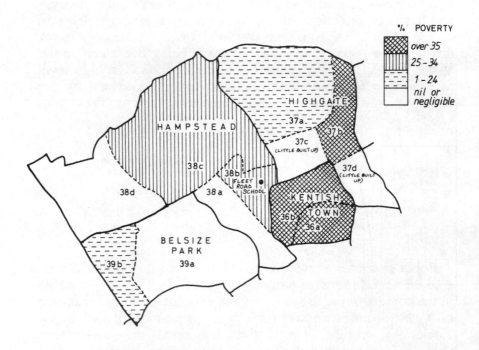

Map 2.   North Marylebone: Ratios of Poverty in School Board Blocks, 1887–89 (after C. Booth)

In no part of the map area were large tracts of serious poverty, the blue and black streets, to be found. Only Litcham Street, near Kentish Town Station, was shown as very poor. Apart from odd pockets, the only other area designated as light blue, that is in moderate poverty, was the south side of Fleet Road itself. For West Kentish Town as a whole, the social mix is ambivalently but appropriately presented as a pattern of mingled comfort and poverty, with the majority of streets coloured purple.

At the other social extreme there was a large expanse of red (well-to-do) and yellow (wealthy) districts west of Chalk Farm Road and Southampton Road, at first mostly red but culminating in the social heights of Belsize Park. Hampstead High Street was shown as well-to-do, but behind it, in the old village, was hidden a complex mix of comfort and poverty in a warren of densely-packed property, containing an odd patch of light blue.

The final category, and indeed the one most significant in the

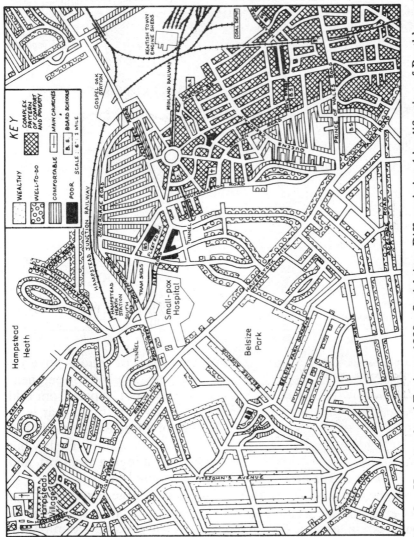

Map 3. Hampstead and Environs 1890s: Social Area Differentiation (simplification of Booth's map)

development of Fleet Road School, was the late-nineteenth-century group of streets in comfort, described by Booth as the 'best pink',[13] which lay between Fleet Road and Mansfield Road and the Hampstead Junction (North London) Railway. Streets of similar type formed the buffer zone between the mass of West Kentish Town and Haverstock Hill.

OCCUPATIONS OF THE PEOPLE

The 1871 Census provides useful evidence of the occupational contrasts between Hampstead and St. Pancras, of which Kentish Town was a part (Table 1.5).

TABLE 1.5

Classes			Hampstead		St. Pancras	
			No.	%	No.	%
I	Professional	M	1,287	19.3	7,069	12.0
		F	490	4.0	1,879	2.6
II	Domestic	M	479	7.2	2,158	3.6
		F	10,309	83.7	53,734	75.3
III	Commercial	M	1,422	21.4	11,614	19.7
		F	92	0.7	407	0.6
IV	Agricultural	M	468	7.0	1,632	2.8
		F	23	0.2	81	0.1
V	Industrial	M	2,637	35.6	31,948	54.3
		F	923	7.5	12,494	17.5
VI	Indefinite and	M	632	9.5	4,464	7.6
	Unproductive	F	483	3.9	2,776	3.9
	Total	M	6,655		58,885	
	(over 20 years)	F	12,320		71,371	

Census of Great Britain, 1871

Thus Hampstead's male population over 20 years was proportionately more heavily represented in the professional and commercial categories, and less in the industrial, than that of St. Pancras. In both areas domestic service was by far the most important female occupation, but more so in Hampstead, with a significant percentage of women working in textiles and dressmaking in St. Pancras.

The 1901 Census is more revealing, as Thompson's summary indicates (Table 1.6).[14]

TABLE 1.6

Male	Nos.	Female	Nos.
(1) Commercial clerks	2,011	(1) Domestic servants	13,579
(2) Merchants	1,314	(2) Independent gentlewomen	2,263
(3) Painters/plumbers/glaziers	659	(3) Milliners, dressmakers, etc.	1,388
(4) Bankers/bank clerks	650	(4) Teachers	848
(5) Outdoor servants/gardeners	637	(5) Nurses (not domestic)	497
(6) Artists/sculptors	626	(6) Commercial clerks/typists	487
(7) Annuitants/retired	602	(7) Art/music/drama	393
(8) Coachmen/postboys	532	(8) Washerwomen/laundresses	311
(9) Carpenters/joiners	507	(9) Charwomen	240
(10) Railway staff	504	(10) Lodging/boarding houses	187
(11) Independent gentlemen	491	(11) Annuitants/retired	174
(12) Drapers	464	(12) Barmaids/waitresses	160
(13) Barristers	447		
(14) Civil servants	439		
(15) General labourers	427		

High-status professional, commercial and artistic occupations were therefore, while important, not preponderant numerically. Of course 600 artists and 600 retired annuitants were qualitatively significant in maintaining the public image of Hampstead. But so far as quantities of people were concerned the dominant occupations, when grouped, were commercial clerks and the service trades. The main female occupation was overwhelmingly that of domestic servant. Way below in numbers, but at the other social extreme in status, were the independent gentlewomen. While millinery and dressmaking were established occupations for women, the presence of significant numbers of teachers, nurses and commercial clerks and typists was testimony to a widening range of job opportunities for career-minded lower-middle- and upper-working-class women.

Booth confirmed the local importance of these groups, describing Hampstead as the haunt of middle- and upper-class business and professional men, of merchants, authors, journalists and musicians. In the South End and Fleet Road district, he found many tram drivers and conductors, horse-keepers, railwaymen and labourers.[15] Kentish Town was characterized by large numbers of clerks and shop assistants who commuted to work in the City and the West End. The more comfortable artisan cohort included railway workers, cabinet-makers, and pianoforte-makers.[16]

URBAN TRANSPORT

The residents of the slopes of Hampstead were effectively sealed off from a considerable number of the less desirable aspects of urban living. Not the least of these were the railway developments confined to surrounding lower-lying areas. The lines necessarily and fortunately had to tunnel under Belsize Park and South Hampstead. Four railway arteries passed this way by the 1870s. Plate 1 illustrates some of the disruption caused in South Hampstead at the crossing of the London and North-western Railway by the Great Central Line at Loudoun Road station. Further north, the Midland Railway and the Hampstead Junction (North London) Railway respectively entered tunnels under Hampstead proper to the north and south of Fleet Road School (Map 3). Where the tunnels emerged at either end a series of suburban stations was located: at Loudoun Road (Plate 1) and three in the vicinity of Finchley Road on the west side; and at Hampstead Heath, Haverstock Hill and Chalk Farm on the east.

1. The Impact of Railways on Hampstead: Loudoun Street Station, South Hampstead (from *The Railway World*, 1897)

Hampstead Heath and Haverstock Hill stations were both conveniently placed for Fleet Road School.

The stations were but a small part of the land colonized for railway development. The hardest hit areas were at Finchley Road on the west, with stations on the Hampstead Junction, Midland and Great Central railway lines, and between Gospel Oak and Kentish Town stations on the east, where the land was dedicated to railway junctions and sidings, engine sheds and coal depots (Map 3). This made the area, in Thompson's words, 'a natural railwaymen's quarter' with Gospel Oak 'one of the more salubrious parts ... respectable but emphatically working class'.[17] Gillian Tindall tells that the people of West Kentish Town, across which the North London Line was carried on a roof-top-high viaduct, regarded the railway as a despoiler, disturbing once peaceful houses 'with shrill shrieks at all hours of the day ... shutting out the access of the sweet air that used to come from Highgate and Hampstead'.[18] The railway effectively limited the prospects of improving the social tone of the area, but at the same time promoted its continuity as a modestly respectable dormitory suburb for commuting lower-middle-class clerks, and provided a means of employment that was both reliable and generative of career opportunities for a significant proportion of householders within the locality.

The *Hampstead and Highgate Express* was exercised by this onslaught of the railway on the district, promoting rapid urban growth, and harming the traditional rural-fringe quality of the Hampstead area. As one reporter argued:

The convenience of the rail and the growth of population have been the means of utterly changing the entire character of our neighbourhood. South Hampstead is crowded with villas; Fleet Road and Kentish Town are linked by an intervening area of houses, crowded by tenants from basement to roof; and West Hampstead, 'ere long, will, from Finchley Road, have its shops, dwelling-houses, and public buildings, uniting old Hampstead, Belsize, Fitzjohn's Avenue and the adjacent roads, to the busy and extending population of Kilburn.[19]

The tramway was socially more dubious than the railway. Rail provision could be compartmentalized, if need be on every train. On the roads, such segregation could only be achieved by different modes of transport. Hence the horse bus, with its high fares, was a middle-class kind. But the trams, like board schools, were from the start regarded as a means of catering for the working classes.[20] Vocal opposition to the coming of the trams was epitomized in the editorial of a St. Pancras district newspaper in 1880:

In the first place, tramways have no *raison d'être* in crowded thoroughfares ... They have not fulfilled the pretended mission that was heralded of them. Altogether different from railways ... they provide accommodation only for a fraction of the populace, and, comparatively, one class only.[21]

In terms of both physical and social contours, there was manifestly only one way into Hampstead for the trams, and that was by way of Fleet Road. Thus the tramway company which had extended its route in 1880 from Kentish Town via Prince of Wales Road, Malden Road, and the less prestigious end of Southampton Road into Fleet Road, in 1887 'made a dash to the Heath'.[22] Its terminus was at South End, where the tram shown on Plate 2 is standing. This was the nearest it ever got to Hampstead proper. Whereas the higher status omnibus from Hampstead Village via Haverstock Hill to Tottenham Court Road and Oxford Street cost 5d, the trams from the Gospel Oak area to King's Cross cost only a 2d fare.[23]

The tram route was therefore another social pointer distinguishing Hampstead from West Kentish Town. The double sets of tracks down such shopping thoroughfares as Malden Road heightened the disturbance made by the 'huge, noisy, clanking, electrically driven vehicles'[24] which at the time did not enjoy the romantic glow generated by the transport historian. But the employees of the tramway company were far from a downtrodden proletariat, as the uniformed figures on Plate 2 suggest, much higher up the status ladder than the street sweepers in the background, though all are carefully posing for the picture. The children of tramway workers formed a recognisable group in the intake of Fleet Road. The school was less fortunately affected by the impact of the tramway on the urban fabric. The large tram sheds between Fleet Road and Agincourt Road (Plate 3) seriously intensified the pressure on land in the immediate vicinity of the school. The situation was worsened by the decision to take the trams on the return journey to the centre down Agincourt Road, rattling regularly past the classroom windows, and threatening the safety of the 1,800 children arriving at or leaving the school four times a day.

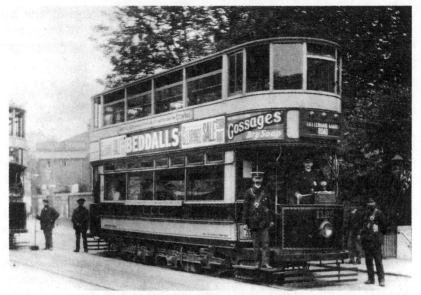

2. The Tottenham Court Road Tram at South End Green Terminus,
Hampstead, in the early years of this century

3. The construction of Cressy Road Tram-sheds, with Fleet Road
on the left

15

Fleet Road's dubious image in Hampstead was confirmed by its association with the trams. But like the railways, the trams helped to enlarge the catchment of the school, contributing to raising the overall social status of the intake, while at the same time the children of tramway employees were generally part of the solid respectable working-class base safeguarding the social repute of the school.

CONTRASTING COMMUNITIES IN HAMPSTEAD AND WEST KENTISH TOWN, 1850–1900

The public image of Fleet Road, as Hampstead's first board school, was affected by attitudes and policies prevailing outside its immediate catchment area. These reflected an entrenched but differentiated social ecology present in the contrasted neighbourhoods in which interested parties, whether influential providers or (generally) non-influential recipients of educational facilities, resided. Four·brief case studies will be used to illustrate the social range to be found in Hampstead and West Kentish Town.

Belsize Park

This was the least relevant area so far as elementary schooling was concerned. It was opened up by its landowners in the 1850s (Map 1). It was more carefully planned than any other part of Hampstead, and was specifically designed to cater for families which could afford private carriages. On Booth's map it is an almost solid phalanx of yellow. But the mews area at the junction of Belsize Lane and Belsize Crescent provided a residential core for some of the staff servicing the rich households, and became a small outlier of Fleet Road School's catchment zone (Map 9). Belsize Park was geographically distant from the controversies over the selection of new board school sites near the turn of the century. There is little evidence that its inhabitants felt the need to be concerned with the issue, while no doubt engaged in the periodic lobbying to hold at bay the dreaded prospect of financing more board schools.

Old Hampstead

On the other hand, the old Hampstead Village area was much more at risk, not least because it had an indigenous working-class population. But it was much better known for its range of attractive and historically ambient buildings and tree-lined streets, riddled with literary and artistic associations. The Heath and recollection of its heyday as a spa gave it a healthy image. The coming of the railways opened up Hampstead and its Heath to proletarian assault: 'Now and again, on high days and holidays, vulgarity makes its invasions or demonstrations.'[26] In fact the Heath was also threatened by a rash of middle-class villa development. The editor of the local newspaper interpreted this as less of a problem, however, rationalizing that the uneven terrain in itself offered protection against unseemly monotony:

Here it is impossible to build a row of houses that shall be at once regular in height and uniform in feature ... consequently there is an irregularity which has particularly favoured the artistic *penchant*, and those in search of the picturesque.[27]

Socially, old Hampstead was much nearer than Belsize Park to the educational issues of the moment. There were many children in its community requiring elementary facilities. Hampstead had indeed made voluntary provision for these children. There was thus a vested interest in education. Furthermore, the small shopkeepers and tradesmen who sent their offspring to these old-established and respectable, if educationally outmoded, schools, objected to the school board rate as a monstrous imposition. The dual system involved in their eyes dual payment. There was therefore a ready-made lobby to support local residents in opposing the building of a board school in central Hampstead towards the turn of the century, notwithstanding the manifest deficiency in provision in the Town Ward of old Hampstead (Chapter 3).

West Kentish Town

In contrast with both Belsize Park and old Hampstead, West Kentish Town was classic board school territory. As we have seen, it was an industrialized area associated on the one hand with railway development, and on the other with the craft industries such as furniture and pianoforte-making which reached Kentish Town as the growth of domestic music-making[28] justified the building of substantial factories too expensive to establish in more central locations. The most imposing of these, as already noted, was the Brinsmead plant (Plate 4). John Brinsmead had started a small piano-making business off Tottenham Court Road in 1837. He transferred to Kentish Town in the 1840s, and by the end of the century had built a huge factory in Grafton Road, near Kentish Town Station. Its railway-side location is clear in Picture 1 of the group of scenes making up Plate 4. It employed 300 and made 3,000 pianos, upright and grand, every year.[29] Booth's survey of London industries in the 1890s identified nearly 25,000 persons engaged in the manufacture of musical instruments and toys. The industry had grown steadily from the 1860s. Employment was generally regular, and 70 per cent of the workers earned over 30/- per week, well above the threshold Booth established for living in comfort. Skilled piano-makers on piece work could earn 42/-, giving them artisan elite status.[30] Nearly three-quarters lived in houses not classified as crowded. By far the major concentration of musical instrument- and toy-making was in St. Pancras.

By the late nineteenth century, Kentish Town was a classic example of an urban zone in transition. From families of coachmen, gardeners, cow-keepers and agricultural labourers emerged the employees of local workshop industries and urban transport systems. Their children were in turn sent to cheaper private schools or board schools to qualify them for the next step on the occupational ladder: office work in the City, a peak of ambition for many families.[31] But pressure on land from industrial and railway development reduced the housing stock, both driving out the well-to-do middle-class remnant, and making life more difficult for poorer groups. Booth described part of the process:

the great railway companies have brought many country folk into the district. The change in the colouring is usually from red to pink or pink-barred, and dark blue is being eliminated.[32]

More and more found themselves in straitened circumstances as rents and house prices rose. Although the houses of much of

4. Brinsmead's Pianoforte Manufactory, Kentish Town (from *Piano, Organ and Music Traders' Journal*, 1886)

the area were of reasonable quality, many streets were coloured purple (mixed comfort and poverty) by Booth.

Of those engaged as clerks Booth found only 10.8 per cent living in crowded conditions; 55 per cent were members of households averaging less than one person to a room. Six and a half per cent employed servants, as against 2 per cent in musical instrument- and toy-making occupations. The St. Pancras area was quite important for employment in clerkly occupations, although its 4.6 per cent of the total was well behind, for example, Camberwell or Hackney, with over 11 per cent each.[33] There were huge increases in numbers of clerks as tertiary employment prospects improved, from 35,500 in 1861 to 108,400 by the 1890s,[34] significant figures in creating a social dynamic for an equivalent expansion in educational opportunities.

While service on the railways provided a career ladder for some, in general those engaged in office work enjoyed better living circumstances. While, as we have seen, Booth found only 10.8 per cent of clerks living in crowded conditions, the figure for railway workers was 27.8 per cent, going up to 43 per cent for railway labourers. Only 0.5 per cent of railway families employed servants. But as in office work, there were huge increases in employment on the railways, from 8,300 in 1861 to 44,800 in 1891 in London as a whole.[35] While porters, gangers, platelayers and labourers earned only 15/- to 20/- per week, many other railway employees enjoyed much higher incomes. 13.5 per cent of London's railway workers resided in St. Pancras, the highest percentage of any district.[36]

Kentish Town was thus associated with some of the most rapidly expanding occupations in the metropolis, employment on the railways and in offices in each case increasing by over 200 per cent between 1861 and 1891. But the consequential ecological forces at work in the area, evidencing a socially fluid and equivocal situation, were viewed with some unease from the heights of Hampstead. Thompson's summary captures both the essence and the complexity of the situation:

if social character had been invariably caught by physical contact like some contagious disease, then Hampstead ought to have suffered from a bad case of shingles, if not from schizophrenia. For to the south-east and east lay areas of very mixed character in Camden Town, Chalk Farm, Kentish Town and Gospel Oak ... This is not to say that this group of neighbours was wholly innocent of good-class development. All of them, indeed, contained, and even managed to retain more or less permanently, pockets of spacious, modestly elegant, and highly respectable housing. But the important fact was that these were simply pockets, surrounded from the very first by great masses of indifferent or low-grade housing which stamped the prevailing character of these areas from a very early date.[37]

If from the ivory towers of Hampstead the social brew was unpalatable, fortunate indeed was the board school headteacher for whom this was the most difficult part of the intake.

The Fleet Road Area

Fleet Road School was literally on the border between Hampstead and Gospel Oak. The Belsize Estate swung across Haverstock Hill and ended up to the north of Fleet Road on the South End Farm sub-estate, crossed by the Hampstead Junction Railway. The social transitions can be demonstrated in the house prices – from £2,000 to £3,000 in wealthy Belsize Park, to £1,300 to £1,500 in the well-to-do Rosslyn Hill area, to £900 or so in Parliament Hill Road – and from £400 to £500 in the streets to the north of Fleet Road.[38]

The Fleet Road environs were in themselves far from socially homogeneous. Booth coloured the south side of Fleet Road, the most dubious group of houses in the area, as blue, the north side in part purple and in part pink, and most of the area to the north and east pink. Of the latter Booth reported

streets about Mansfield Road a typical group of the best pink and from them come the children who have given Fleet Road School its prestige and scholarships.[39]

But as far as Hampstead proper was concerned, Fleet Road was beyond the pale. Besant described its vicinity as 'a district very poor and slummy for such a fresh pleasant suburb as Hampstead' and Fleet Road itself as 'a dreary street'.[40] It suffered too many disadvantages to gain any social cachet from lying within the boundary of Hampstead. As Thompson stressed, for a start its location hard by the working-class districts of Kentish Town and Gospel Oak compounded its natural disadvantage of being low-lying.[41]

More specific environmental detractions included old brick workings, still present in 1885. In that year the Vestry won a suit against the owners, complaints having been made of kilns not properly enclosed, a chimney not lofty enough to disperse the smoke, and the burning of dustbin refuse 'causing evil smells'.[42] Immediately behind Fleet Road, with its entrance on Cressy Road, was also a laundry (Map 8). On the other side of Cressy Road, as we have seen, huge tram sheds were erected (Plate 3). As Thompson has graphically described, the auguries from the start were bad.

The natural destiny of Fleet Road was ... all too definite. The Fleet brook ... was an open sewer used by Downshire Hill, Pond Street and South End, and was becoming steadily more noisome when the Metropolitan Board of Works took over responsibility for London's drainage in 1856. For several years after that the Board was too preoccupied with more pressing needs ... to have time to turn to the Fleet, so that it was not tidied away into pipes until after 1860 ... Fleet Road, therefore, got off to a poor start with the area too smelly and unpleasant to attract the better class of shopkeepers aiming at middle-class trade ... The street seems to have fallen at once, in default of any other demands, into tenement and lodging houses.[43]

The later disruption of the trams and the damage done to property values had earlier been matched by that caused by the building operations, the cutting and entrance to the tunnel of the Midland Railway just to the south of Fleet Road.[44] As Booth's map shows, the only lower-grade property west of Southampton Road (Map 3) was by the tunnel approach. Nearby Lismore Circus (Map 8) was described in 1867 as a 'mud island', while the roadways around were 'dank' and 'pot-holed', marked by piles of garbage, 'puddles of dirty water, dead dogs and squads of children playing in the street'. The complainant lamented: 'we are completely isolated from the civilised world. Vehicles can only approach our dwellings by a long and roundabout detour.'[45]

Booth noted that the Fleet Road area had had an evil reputation from its origins in the 1860s and indeed was still 'going down' in the section east of Cressy Road (Map 3).[46] The local newspaper had to look no further than Fleet Road to find reports of drunken, disorderly and violent behaviour, family strife, and prostitution. A letter of 1890 suggests an entrenched stereotype:

What is Fleet Road coming to? Being a rate-payer close by for twenty-two years I find we are to have another nuisance in the shape of a music and dancing hall ... we have nuisances enough already in the form of the Fever Hospital and the fair at all holiday times.[47]

It was indeed the smallpox hospital, the North-west Fever Hospital, that was the most serious blot on the Fleet Road landscape. When the site was acquired in 1868 by the Metropolitan Asylums Board, it was destined for cases of infectious disease. In 1870 a severe epidemic of smallpox broke out and further wards were 'hastily erected'. From the start the hospital 'provoked the greatest agitation in the parish'.[48] Further outbreaks in the mid-1870s and 1884 reinforced the concern, especially in 1884 when there was a severe epidemic in Hampstead itself. The local Medical Officer of Health, Edmund Gwynn, produced a report of the epidemic, which included a map (Map 4) showing the location of the residences of people who had caught the disease. Of the 92 people recorded, only nine belonged to the higher socio-economic groups. There was a strong concentration of cases in the Fleet Road area. The scatter through Belsize Park was linked with the servant population, but no less frightening to the local inhabitants for that. There were other small pockets in Kilburn and round the workhouse in Hampstead village. A typical case in Gwynn's inventory was

a girl aged 14 ... taken ill on 29th May, and showed symptoms of Small Pox on June 1st, at a Coffee Shop, 4, Fleet Road. She had been living as servant at 60, Park Road, but coming home to sleep.[49]

The public furore centred on the debate as to whether smallpox hospitals located in crowded neighbourhoods endangered local residents. The influential middle-class residents of Hampstead proper had managed to get the route followed by the ambulances to the hospital changed from Haverstock Hill to Fleet Road.[50] They were no doubt acting on the conventional wisdom of the time that infection could be 'wafted through the atmosphere breathed by the surrounding and passing populations during the sultry season of the year now commenced'.[51]

An article in the *St. James's Gazette* entitled 'Unhealthy Hampstead' fuelled the controversy.[52] The use of Fleet Road for ambulance traffic and the concentration of smallpox cases in the district was regarded as cause and effect. It led to a memorial from Fleet Road tradesmen to the Vestry, protesting that customers were being driven away, and demanding a reduction in rates in lieu of the losses accruing.[53] A correspondent claimed that 'no worse site could have been chosen' for the hospital:

It is overlooked by houses in almost every direction, and the main road ... passes within a few feet of the dead-house, the ventilators of which slope directly on to the passers-by below. Moreover it is built on low ground, in a

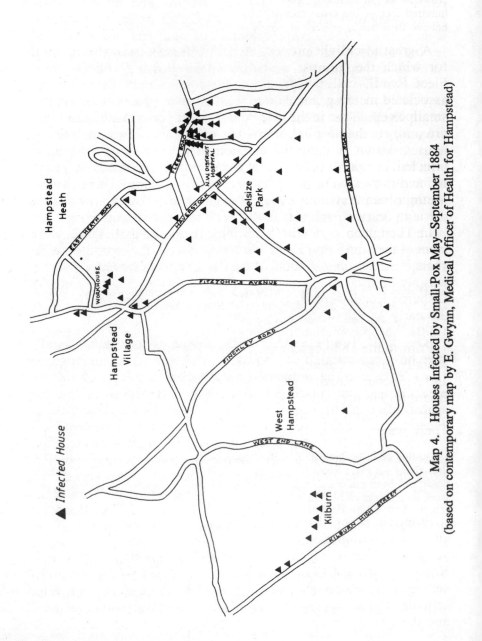

Map 4. Houses Infected by Small-Pox May–September 1884
(based on contemporary map by E. Gwynn, Medical Officer of Health for Hampstead)

▲ Infected House

Hampstead Heath

Hampstead Village

WORKHOUSE

N.W. DISTRICT HOSPITAL

Belsize Park

West Hampstead

Kilburn

EAST HEATH ROAD

FLEET ROAD

HAVERSTOCK HILL

FITZJOHN'S AVENUE

FINCHLEY ROAD

ADELAIDE ROAD

WEST END LANE

KILBURN HIGH STREET

crowded neighbourhood, close to several laundries, and within some few hundred feet, as the crow flies, of the large Fleet-road Board School, where I believe there are at present at least a thousand children in attendance.[54]

A great torchlight procession was arranged through the area, for which the 'utmost enthusiasm prevailed, especially about Fleet Road', calling for the removal of the hospital. At an associated meeting, local doctors confidently confirmed that the smallpox epidemic in the Fleet Road vicinity was indeed due to its proximity to the hospital. It was pointed out that 25 per cent of the houses within a quarter-mile radius of the wards had been infected, as against only 1 per cent beyond.[55] The dispute lingered on, and moves were made to take legal proceedings against the Metropolitan Asylums Board. But the end of the outbreak and the temporary closure of the hospital defused the situation.

In Thompson's view, the smallpox scare held back development of the South End Farm part of the Belsize Estate for up to 20 years.[56] Although Agincourt Road had been laid out in 1878 it was not built up until well into the 1880s. Constantine Road and Lisburne Road were started in the late 1880s and completed in the early 1890s, while Mackeson Road was begun only in the 1890s.[57] Map 8 indicates the later development of this district.

Prior to the 1884 epidemic, another major development with a socially suspect connotation had taken place between Fleet Road and Agincourt Road: the choice of the site by the London School Board for Hampstead's first board school. The School Board had clearly not been put off by the presence of the Fever Hospital. There were no local objections. As Thompson put it:

Up to this point nothing at all had moved on this part of the estate, except for the sale of the Fleet Road school site to the London School Board, and this no doubt had been made available most willingly because builders and developers were so uninterested in the district.[58]

From the point of view of Hampstead proper it was an ideal site, hardly competing territorially with local voluntary schools, yet bidding fair to clear working-class children off the streets of Kentish Town and Gospel Oak. Why in view of its inauspicious setting Fleet Road should have become one of the flagship schools of the London School Board is an intriguing question, and the attempt to answer it is the purpose of this book.

REFERENCES AND NOTES

1. F.M.L. Thompson, *Hampstead: Building a Borough, 1650–1964* (London, 1974), p.365.
2. J.D. Morell, *On the Progress of Society in England as Affected by the Advancement of National Education* (Edinburgh, 1859), p.3 and p.5.
3. Thompson, *op. cit.* (1974), p.72.
4. E. Brinsmead, *The History of the Pianoforte* (London, 1889 edition), pp.151–2.
5. W. Weber, *Music and the Middle Class: the Social Structure of Concert Life in London, Paris and Vienna* (London, 1975), pp.85–114.
6. N.J. Barton, *The Lost Rivers of London* (London/Leicester, 1962), p.29.
7. F.M.L. Thompson, 'Hampstead 1830–1914', in M.A. Simpson and T.H. Lloyd (eds.), *Middle Class Housing in Britain* (Newton Abbot, 1977), p.89.
8. Thompson, *op. cit.* (1974), p.73.
9. C. Booth, 'Life and Labour of the People in London: First Results of an Inquiry based on the 1891 Census', *Journal of the Royal Statistical Society*, vol. 56 (1893), p.567 and p.572.
10. Thompson, *op. cit.* (1974), pp.45–6.
11. C. Booth (ed.), *Life and Labour of the People in London: Third Series: Religious Influences, Final Volume* (London, 1902), p.12 and p.17.
12. C. Booth (ed.), *Labour and Life of the People: London, Vol. II Appendix* (London, 1891), pp.15–16.
13. C. Booth, *Police Notes, District 20* (Booth Collection, London School of Economics), Group A, vol. 38, p.22.
14. Thompson, *op. cit.* (1974), pp.438–42.
15. Booth, *op. cit.* (1902), vol. 1, p.213.
16. *Ibid.*, p.195.
17. Thompson, *op. cit.* (1974), p.72.
18. G. Tindall, *The Fields Beneath: a History of One London Village* (London, 1977), p.166.
19. *Hampstead and Highgate Express* (hereafter *HHE*), 10 Sept. 1881.
20. H. Pollins, 'Transport Lines and Social Divisions', in R. Glass *et al* (eds.), *London: Aspects of Change* (London, 1964), pp.41–6.
21. *Camden and Kentish Towns, Hampstead, Highgate, Holloway and St. Pancras Gazette*, 10 Jan. 1880.
22. Thompson, *op. cit.* (1974), p.363.
23. H. Fry, *London in 1883* (London, 1883), p.227 and p.233.
24. A. Grosch, *St. Pancras Pavements: an Autobiography* (London, 1947), p.13.
25. See, among others, M. Adams, *Some Hampstead Memories* (Hampstead, 1909).
26. Anon., *The Suburban Homes of London* (London, 1881), p.217.
27. *HHE*, 9 Dec. 1876.
28. Tindall, *op. cit.* (1977), p.146.
29. L.T. Newman, 'It all Began with J.C. Bach: the History of Piano Making in Camden', *Camden History Review*, vol. 1 (1973), pp.30–2.
30. C. Booth (ed.), *Life and Labour of the People in London: 2nd Series: Industry* (London, 1896), vol. 6, pp.4–6, p.70, and p.366; and vol. 9, p.379.
31. Tindall, *op. cit.* (1977), p.191.
32. Booth, *op. cit.* (1902), vol. 1, p.196.
33. Booth, *op. cit.* (1896), vol. 7, pp.488–9.
34. *Ibid.*, p.242 and pp.245–6.
35. *Ibid.*, pp.284–8.
36. *Ibid.*, pp.492–3.
37. Thompson, *op. cit.* (1974), p.67.
38. *Ibid.*, pp.366–7.
39. Booth, *Police Notes, District 20* (Booth Collection, London School of Economics),

Group A, vol. 38, p.22.
40. W. Besant, *London North of the Thames* (London, 1911), p.386.
41. Thompson, *op. cit.* (1977), p.100.
42. *HHE*, 30 May 1885.
43. Thompson, *op. cit.* (1974), pp.267–8.
44. *Ibid.*, p.268.
45. Quoted in Tindall, *op. cit.* (1977), p.167.
46. Booth, *Police Notes, District 20* (Booth Collection, London School of Economics), Group A, vol. 38, pp.21–2.
47. *HHE*, 4 Oct. 1890.
48. Besant, *op. cit.* (1911), p.385.
49. E. Gwynn, *Report on the Small-pox Epidemic in Hampstead* (Hampstead, 1884), p.6. I am grateful to the National Library of Medicine, Bethesda, Maryland, for a photocopy of this report.
50. G.M. Ayers, *England's First State Hospitals and the Metropolitan Asylums Board 1867–1930* (London, 1971), p.74.
51. *HHE*, 19 July 1884.
52. Quoted in *HHE*, 22 Nov. 1884.
53. *Ibid.*, 22 Nov. 1884.
54. Extract from *St. James's Gazette*, quoted in *HHE*, 22 Nov. 1884.
55. *HHE*, 6 Dec. 1884.
56. Thompson, *op. cit.* (1974), p.294.
57. C. Wade (ed.), *More Streets of Hampstead* (Camden, 1973), p.23.
58. Thompson, *op. cit.* (1974), p.357.

CHAPTER TWO

The London School Board

> Among the public buildings of the Metropolis the London Board schools occupy a conspicuous place. In every quarter the eye is arrested by their distinctive architecture, as they stand, closest where the need is greatest, each one 'like a tall sentinel at his post', keeping watch and ward over the interests of the generation that is to replace our own ... Taken as a whole, they may be said fairly to represent the high-water-mark of the public conscience in this country in its relation to the education of the children of the people.[1]
> (Tabor, 1891)

At a meeting of the London School Board in July 1871 it was resolved that 'the Statistical Committee be instructed to divide London into school districts containing a population of not less than 5,000 and not more than 10,000'. Such districts were the components of the larger divisions. The districts were in turn divided into blocks.

The committee had to take into account the social and religious condition of each district and those adjoining, existing school accommodation, and the presence of impassable barriers or dangerous thoroughfares, in drawing up the boundaries. No other boundaries but their own would suffice: 'boundaries to the schools such as careful parents of the children would approve.'[2] The divisions that were agreed were to gain wider credibility, for they provided the framework for Charles Booth's social surveys in the following decade. Indeed, Booth was to rely heavily on the experience of the school board visitors in conducting his surveys.

> They are in daily contact with the people, and have a very considerable knowledge of the parents of the school children, especially the poorest among them, and of the conditions under which they live. No one can go, as I have done, over the description of the inhabitants of street after street in this huge district, taken house by house, and family by family ... and doubt the genuine character of the information and its truth.[3]

28

FILLING IN THE GAPS

The *raison d'être* of the school boards was to plug the gaps in provision left by the voluntary agencies, particularly in the large towns and cities. The churches had been relatively but far from uniformly successful in providing for respectable populations. Here congregations were large and reasonably affluent. By the time the 1870 Act established the principle of using local rates for educational purposes, the process of suburbanization had already shifted too much of middle-class resource support from needy central areas. As was to be expected, the London School Board found that areas with higher rateable values generally had lesser problems, for these were districts with higher proportions of the people living in comfort than in poverty (Table 2.1).

TABLE 2.1

Division	Rateable Value 1884	Rank	Booth's Ratios of Poverty	Comfort	Rank
Marylebone	£4,577,241	1	25.8	74.2	8
Lambeth	£3,938,384	2	28.3	71.7	6
Westminster	£3,793,369	3	24.5	75.7	10
City	£3,592,269	4	31.5	68.5	5
Finsbury	£3,029,148	5	35.5	64.5	3
Chelsea	£2,862,761	6	24.6	75.4	9
Tower Hamlets	£1,924,825	7	36.0	64.0	2
Hackney	£1,791,784	8	34.5	65.5	4
Greenwich	£1,682,319	9	28.0	72.0	7
Southwark	£1,349,816	10	47.6	52.4	1
Average			30.7	69.3	

Source: LSB Finance Committee, 1884.

An initial survey by the London School Board revealed that only the City, Westminster, Chelsea and Marylebone came near to matching supply and demand. Each of these divisions had small surpluses of accommodation for boys. All but Westminster were deficient in places for girls, and all, without exception, substantially so for infants.[5]

The task faced by the Board was, therefore, daunting. 455,000 elementary places were needed in 1872 and approaching 800,000 by 1902. But the Board had cracked the accommodation problem by the end of the 1880s, as indicated in Table 2.2.

TABLE 2.2

Year	Accommodation Required	Church Provided	Board Provided	%	Total Provided	% of that Required
1872	454,783	249,705	28,227	10.1	277,932	61.1
1878	517,846	274,451	198,470	41.9	472,921	91.3
1884	627,236	262,075	334,309	56.0	596,384	95.0
1890	688,057	260,449	419,974	61.7	680,423	98.9
1896	728,845	256,863	497,751	65.9	754,863	100+
1902	787,678	218,376	565,325	72.1	783,701	99.5

Source: LSB Final Report, 1904.

Thus from providing only 10 per cent of London's public elementary places in 1872, and many of these in old buildings taken over from the churches, the Board was offering well over 50 per cent by 1884 and over 70 per cent by 1902. By the 1890s the accommodation by and large matched the demand. But this overall match hid disparities between the School Board divisions. In the 1890s the City, Westminster and Marylebone divisions had significant surpluses, and Tower Hamlets and Southwark small ones. The others remained in deficit, as much as 9.1 per cent in Hackney. By the late 1880s board school accommodation exceeded that of the voluntary agencies in all areas except the City, Westminster and Marylebone.[6] As we shall find, even within divisions in surplus there were pockets of deficit. This could be worsened where there were unplanned changes in provision as between the board and the voluntary sector. Thus a local deficit for Nonconformist children could not be met by offering them places in a Church of England or a Catholic school which had vacancies.

The cost of filling the gaps was colossal. In 1875 the London School Board precept amounted to £149,866, representing a 1¾d rate in the £. In 1903 the precept was £2,437,772, a 14.66d rate, amounting to an 838 per cent increase on 1875.[7] It is not surprising therefore that the London School Board was accused of extravagance. Yet on its demise in 1903 some of its sternest critics, including the *Daily Telegraph, The Times, St. James's Gazette* and *Pall Mall Gazette* were among the many who paid tributes to its extraordinary achievement.

London owes much to the London School Board. It has not had quite thirty-four years of life, and in that time elementary education in the Metropolis has been entirely transformed. Before the School Board came into being, only one-third of the children of London received any elementary education at all; now practically all the eight hundred thousand children of school age come within the educational net. This is a great result, and the Board deserves the highest credit for so vast an accomplishment. For the education imparted steadily improved and widened in scope until it was found that the frontiers laid down by the Act of 1870 were being left far behind.[8]

QUALITY OF PROVISION

The accommodation provided not merely met the numerical targets, but was also of a quality not previously contemplated in the sphere of elementary schooling. The Boards realized that innovation was required in the nature of the accommodation they provided.

An important ... consequence of the institution of school boards was a salutary revolution as to what was desirable in the planning and building of schools ... schools hitherto were simply big rooms usually ill-adapted to their special purpose and not seldom defective in points of ventilation, lighting and warming. In the vast majority of cases board schools were entirely new buildings erected under rules formed by the Education Department which were particularly directed to securing the health and convenience of children and of teachers. Thus a standard was created and lodged in the public mind.[9]

While later critics might dismiss urban board schools as constructions of 'utilitarian ugliness' and excessive permanency,[10] the London School Board and its supporters were inordinately proud of their buildings, which also attracted favourable comment from more disinterested observers. Particularly admired were those designed by the Board's best-known architect, E.R. Robson.

A 'Robson School' with its great windows, high Flemish gables, and dainty brickwork is still a familiarly repetitive London landmark. It was a new and exciting accent in the London sky-line of the seventies.[11]

The leap in architectural aspiration can be seen by comparing Plate 5, which shows the first purpose-built London board school in Old Castle Street, completed in 1873, and one of Robson's most famous schools, Mansfield Place (later Holmes Road) in Kentish Town (Plate 6), opened in the late 1870s. Robson aimed to match the degree of elaboration of the buildings to the social character of the area in which they were located. Thus Robson considered Mansfield Place at fault 'in being somewhat beyond the mark of an Elementary, and suggesting in

5. Old Castle Street, the first School erected by the
London School Board, 1873

appearance rather the uses of a Secondary or Grammar school'.
But for a Clerkenwell slum 'the plainest of plain structure could
alone be suitable'.[12]

Internally, there were also significant advances over the
traditional voluntary school. The inside of an archetypal London
board school was described thus:

Its most conspicuous feature is the hall, with its wood-blocked floor, its
distempered walls, ornamented by pictures of many kinds ... At one end of the
hall is a slightly raised platform, upon which stands the head master's desk ...
Some of the classrooms open out of the hall, while others open into a wide tiled
corridor, on one side of which is the cloakroom with its multitude of enamelled
iron pegs.[13]

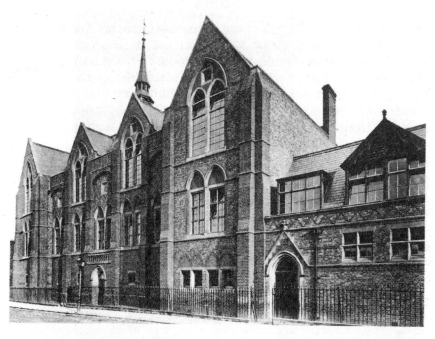

6. Mansfield Place (later Holmes Road) School, Kentish Town, a Robson
Board School

Not for the only time, the London School Board's thinking was
in advance of that of the Education Department, which was
reluctant to offer grants for providing school halls. The Fleet
Road case demonstrates the significance such halls were to have,
both in their flexibility of use and in the facility they created for
bringing parents and other interested parties into the school.
They promoted a more expansive image both of the particular
school, and of what schooling had to offer in general. The board
schools developed 'a municipal air, an official precision'[14] and,
notwithstanding complaints about their cost, ultimately became
objects of civic pride. Yet in carrying high 'the flag of education'
these 'tall sentinels'[15] manifestly epitomized a new and in some
ways more rigorous approach, in compelling children to attend,
for they were backed up by an elaborate and intrusive bureaucratic infrastructure, and in raising the expectations of what
might be required of them once in school.

THE SOCIAL GRADING OF SCHOOLS

The post-1870 expectation of the voluntary agencies that the new rate-supported board sector would confine its responsibility to bringing in the street urchins was not to be fulfilled. Any narrow definition of their role was speedily rejected by the major urban boards, so long as not dominated by voluntaryist members. The boards were helped by the critical fact that they could charge anything from 1d to 9d in fees. Indeed, the Education Department gave instructions to boards to charge what the local market would bear. This required an assessment of the socio-economic status of particular neighbourhoods.[16] It was not a new policy. The Wesleyan and British schools in particular had pioneered the use of the high fee to keep their provision select.[17] The die was cast for socially respectable but educationally inferior private adventure schools well before the 1870 Act. The activities of progressive urban boards made such institutions much less attractive.

The exclusiveness of the higher fee has tempted parents to withdraw their children from the inferior teaching of private adventure schools ... Without sympathising with the innumerable class distinctions which abound in every grade of English life, great allowance should be made for the mother's dislike of the society of children whose home circumstances interpose difficulties to modesty or even decency. I dislike the term gutter children, as attaching some odium of the child's circumstances to the child itself; but the eagerness of some voluntary schools to raise themselves above the level of the lowest class proves the existence, in considerable number, of children who are not likely to reflect credit on their schools ... Besides children who are proper inmates for reformatories and industrial schools, there are many degrees of dirty habits and filthy language, whose mere presence would deter the mothers of the nicest children.[18]

The dual system therefore generated not just arenas for the confrontation of opposing religious forces, but a contest of the market place. In a situation where parents were presented with a range of choice of schools, there was intense competition for the respectable clientèle. The inevitable consequence was a hierarchical grading of elementary schools.

One was offered in Booth's first London survey. His assistant Mary Tabor's detailed descriptions of the different rankings of the classification provide valuable documentation. Of the best board schools she wrote:

A more inspirating [sic] and satisfactory sight can hardly be desired than that presented ... The great bulk of the children are wholesome, bright-looking, well-fed, well-clad, eager for notice, 'smart', and full of life. 'Smartness' is much cultivated in schools of this class.[19]

The middle grade of schools was more variable, the 'tone and aspect' depending very much on the quality of the teachers. A good headteacher brought up the standard of such schools to those of the higher grade.

A middle-grade school will show as many open intelligent faces among the boys, as much refinement and decision among the girls, as one of quite the upper grade that has been managed by a mere mechanical driver for 'results'.[20]

Tabor valued those schools which brought in and won the confidence of parents. She viewed with favour the trend towards penny banks, libraries, Swedish drill, Bands of Hope and cricket and football clubs. The penny banks were in particular singled out as the 'best corrective' to spending money at the sweet-shop, 'the child's public house', which offered 'an excellent training in those habits of heedless self-indulgence which are the root of half the misery of the slums'.[21]

The lower grade schools provoked more detailed comment. These included the 'schools of special difficulty', the schools with 1d fees and marked by few children over school exemption age, a rapid turnover, and children of such a character as to impose special difficulties on the teachers. In such schools headteachers and staff received salary increments of £20 and £10 per annum respectively. There were 22 such schools at the time of Booth's survey, taking about 21,000 children. The typical locale was

usually on the skirts, or standing in the midst of a crowded, low, insanitary neighbourhood. The main streets, narrow at best, branch off into others narrower still; and these again into a labyrinth of blind alleys, courts and lanes; all dirty, foul-smelling, and littered with garbage and refuse of every kind. The houses are old, damp and dilapidated.[22]

The classrooms of the 'schools of special difficulty' were often depressing to experience:

The slum look is everywhere. It penetrates like a slimy fog into the school itself. 'Slum-born' seems written on the faces of the children, hardly one of whom impresses us as well up to the average ... We see numbers of half-imbecile children throughout the school; big boys in low standards who cannot learn, try as they may; children of drinking parents chiefly ...[23]

35

It was such children the Nonconformists and Anglicans in particular wished the board schools to accommodate. The Catholics were in the least favourable position for they had neither the resources of the board schools nor the level of respectability of Church of England, Wesleyan and British Schools. Their historic role was to supply the needs of the children of the poor Irish population. Indeed their Society was called the 'Catholic Poor Schools Society'. It was said that respectable Catholic parents were less than enthusiastic when their children received attendance medals labelled with the name of the Society.

Meanwhile, the urban boards were inexorably attracting more and more respectable children away from voluntary schools, as HMI Morell outlined in his report on the Greenwich district in 1875:

The idea which at first prevailed when the new board schools were started was that they would be filled by scholars of a lower class ... and that the voluntary school would approach somewhat to the middle-class type adapted to the requirements of those who object to the indiscriminate mixture of their own children with those of rougher description. This idea, I find, has not by any means been realised. So far from that the tendency is rather the contrary, the board school, where circumstances favour it, showing a much more decided tendency to assume a middle-class form than the others.[24]

By the 1880s the erosion of their lower-middle-class clientele had raised the fury of the voluntary agencies to a fever pitch. Cardinal Manning expounded the views of the Catholic sector:

the Board schools were avowedly intended to receive the children of the poor. But the character of the Board Schools has been gradually so raised that the poor children are thrown upon the voluntary schools, and the Board Schools are largely frequented by the children of the middle class.[25]

The Nonconformist interpreted the competition in Darwinist terms, lacking sympathy for what it judged to be the cheese-paring of the churches:

in this competition the weaker schools – that is the denominational schools – must necessarily suffer ... anyone who studies the subject has only to pass from a Board school to a denominational school to understand very clearly how the former has the advantage in the struggle for life.[26]

The Nonconformists in general supported the undenominational policy of the school board system and no longer saw the need to provide new schools for their children. The comment of their journal was indeed not disinterested. The higher quality of the educational provision of the large urban board schools was, however, plain for all to see, including Her Majesty's Inspectorate:

it will be noted that the percentage of passes in board schools is higher by seven or eight than in voluntary schools. I am bound to add that this superiority is not confined to standard work, but is equally marked in infant work and in class subjects. This is not to be wondered at. The premises of board schools are, as a rule, lighter, loftier, better ventilated, more spacious, and more convenient in every way. The apparatus is more complete. The teaching staff is far stronger. The voluntary school is often half-starved; the board school has the rates at its back.[27]

It must be stressed, however, that the voluntary sector retained a strong residual hold on large numbers of parents. This could reflect no more than the chance of location. Clearly in an area of 'schools of special difficulty' the more reputable parents shunned the board schools. Thus the Vicar of St. Clement's Church in the notorious Notting Dale district informed Booth that the children attending his school were not of the lowest class, his parents not intending their offspring to mix with those attending the nearby penny board school.[28] One of the characters in George Gissing's novel, *The Nether World*, set in slum areas of Clerkenwell and South Islington, was quite clear his daughter should go to a church school, though the expense was 'greater than the new system rendered necessary ... But a prejudice then (and still) common among work-people of decent habits made him hesitate about sending his girl to sit side by side with the children of the street.' His reluctance was confirmed by his daughter, who spoke with contempt for board schools. 'Clara also precociously perceived that a regard for religion gave her a certain distinction at home, and elsewhere placed her apart from the "common girls".'[29]

Another milieu in which the churches retained a high level of parental loyalty was that in which voluntary provision had kept up with demand, where their schools were well-established, leaving at most only a peripheral need for board schools, because there were fewer gaps to fill. Such situations were most frequent in the City, Westminster and Marylebone divisions of the London School Board. Hampstead was, of course, in the Marylebone area and an archetypal example of one in which the established church continued to hold sway.

It was manifestly not the case that the board sector had cornered the market of respectable children, therefore. Booth's survey provides a useful check on the claims and counter-claims that were being made during the 1880s (Table 2.3).[30]

TABLE 2.3

Booth Classification	Numbers in Board Schools	%	Numbers in Voluntary Schools	%
Lower grade	181,338	41	42,023	20
Middle grade	194,005	44	122,839	59
Upper grade	66,266	15	43,080	21

The position for the Protestant schools was indeed more favourable than these figures suggest. Catholic schools provided for a larger percentage of poor children than even the board schools. Seventy per cent of the children attending Catholic schools were in Booth's poverty categories as against 60 per cent in board schools. By contrast, non-Catholic voluntary schools had the advantage of 75 per cent of their intake from homes in Booth's 'in comfort' category. So far as fees were concerned, 5,000 non-Catholic and 5,500 Catholic children were being schooled free, and 6,700 and 2,800 were paying 1d per week, out of totals of 175,000 and 32,500 respectively. At the other end of the scale over 40,000 children in Anglican schools were being charged 6d and over, as against fewer than 500 in Catholic. The statistics showed therefore that the board schools were indeed bearing the vast brunt of the provision for poorer children: over three-quarters. At the same time, there was support for the voluntary sector complaint that they were attracting large numbers of children from the respectable categories. For while only 15 per cent of board school children were in upper grade schools as against the 21 per cent in the voluntary sector, the numerical figures were 66,266 against 43,080.

In the strongest voluntary divisions, the City, and Marylebone, the balance was different, with the advantage very heavily on the side of the church schools. In a place like Hampstead the expectation would have been for almost all the upper-grade children to be in the voluntary sector and lower-grade in the board system, with some overlap of middle-grade. Yet, as Fleet Road will illustrate only too clearly, such a pattern did not apply in any deterministic way at the grassroots level.

SCHOOL ATTENDANCE

In registering the view that the Fleet Road pupil would not 'know the meaning of the word TRUANT'[31] Charles Morley implied that this was not a usual circumstance. In the broader metropolitan context poor attendance was endemic in some areas and seen as perhaps the most subversive factor obstructing the Board in achieving its objectives. One of the main problems facing the attendance officers was the transitory nature of the population in the inner city, as Booth confirmed:

In many districts the people are always on the move; they shift from one part of it to another like 'fish in a river'. The School Board visitors follow them as best they may, and the transfers from one visitor's book to another are very numerous.[32]

It has been more recently suggested that the educational system had to adjust itself to about one quarter of the nation's children moving at least once a year from one residence to another. The migration had a variety of incentives, including seeking employment, often casual, escaping debt collectors and finding new creditors, and avoiding authority, such as the attentions of school attendance officers.[33]

As in other respects, the London School Board was quick to attend to its responsibilities. It had appointed 74 attendance officers by 1872 and over 300 by the 1890s. It was restrictive in allowing early exemption from school and in supporting the half-time system,[34] two escape routes too easily accepted, it was felt, in other places. Even London judged realistically that all that could be achieved was to stamp out bad cases of non-attendance, of the order of seven or more half-day absences per week. Those attending seven or more times a week were usually ignored, a fact some parents came to take advantage of and school managers to deplore. As time went on, however, the noose was tightened. The procedures followed by the London School Board were considered harsh.

The first stage was to issue an 'A' Notice, a caution to send children to school. The second stage was to send a 'B' Notice, demanding the attendance of the parent at a Committee 'B' meeting, which brought charges upon the Board of harassment of parents whose life condition made it difficult to get their children to school regularly. The final stage was to issue a summons.[35]

The Board faced difficulties with the magistrates at Stage 3. It identified the judiciary as a key factor in undermining its efforts. The magistrates in turn viewed the system as interfering with the liberty of parents. In this they were supported by elements of the press. Thus *The London Figaro* castigated the Board in its columns, headed by titles such as 'School Board Nuisance' or 'School Board Impertinence'. It accused the Board's officers of 'impudent obtrusiveness' and of 'meddling' in the domestic arrangements of parents.[36] The particular thrust of this campaign was against the Board pursuing parents who claimed they were sending their children to private schools to avoid them mixing 'with the ragged children of the fever slums and courts'.[37]

Apart from the frequency of parental movement, the School Board visitors faced fearful day-to-day problems on the ground. These included the labyrinthine geography of the back streets, courts and warrens they had to patrol, and the hostile responses of mothers obviously stressed to breaking point by poverty and brutalized personal relationships, often depending on the earnings of their errand-boy sons, or on their older daughters to look after younger siblings while the parents went out to work. There were also a multitude of sweated occupations which required the efforts of the whole family to sustain the budget at a minimal level of subsistence.

In addition there were the predictable problems of infectious disease, attendance being decimated in outbreaks of scarlet fever, measles, whooping cough, diphtheria, infantile diarrhoea, and even typhoid and smallpox. This 'constant tyranny of infectious diseases' as Rubinstein described it,[38] affected all elementary schools, but particularly those in poorer districts. Indeed the promiscuous mixing of children in crowded and ill-ventilated classrooms spread the diseases more rapidly. Hunger was another problem. The London School Board coordinated charitable effort and in 1895 over 50,000 children received cheap or free meals in schools, which proved to be a useful incentive in improving attendance.

The most serious disincentive was the need to pay school fees, even though remission was possible in some cases, and the average London fee of only just over 2d per week was on the low side. But in the six months to the end of March 1887, for example,

5,666 children were refused admission for non-payment of fees.[39] In 1891 nearly 100,000 children had fees remitted. The Board pressed for the abolition of fees. As a pronounced disincentive and also time-consuming to collect, they were increasingly seen as more bother than they were worth. The 1891 Act was a major step forward, for the first time making elementary education free. It was regarded less favourably by the voluntary schools, who were more heavily dependent on school pence.

Average attendance in London had remained obstinately below 80 per cent in the 1870s and 1880s, and did not top 80 per cent until the mid-1890s, reaching 82 per cent by 1902 and 88 per cent by 1904.[40] The overall figures concealed huge variations between districts. On Booth's calculations, the average was round about 65 per cent in inner city areas as late as 1900.[41] On the whole, the problem had been solved, in part because of the natural evolution of second-generation parents after the 1870 Act, having been to school themselves and become acclimatized to the idea that the school was the work-place of children. The fact that in spite of a consistently high level of interventionism by the London School Board, figures by the end of the century remained at about 80 per cent suggested some success, but not universal enthusiasm, within the parent cohort.[42]

WIDENING THE CURRICULUM

The Codes which followed the infamous Revised Code of 1862 gradually ameliorated the worst excesses of the payment by results system. To an extent the concept of 'standards' was useful to the school boards in offering a publicly recognizable measure of achievement. In the case of the London School Board, for example, passes in reading rose from 88 per cent in 1873 to 98 per cent in 1891; in writing from 83 per cent to 93 per cent and in arithmetic from 77 per cent to 91 per cent. After slow early progress there was rapid improvement.[43] Another important index of success was the increasing number achieving the higher standards,[44] bearing in mind that children above Standard V would today be attending secondary schools (Table 2.4).

While on all indices there was evidence of a major achievement, it was one with limitations. By 1902 there were still only just over 100,000 children in London in Standard V and above, and in the meritocratic vanguard in VII and ex-VII only 23,000.

TABLE 2.4

Standard	% in 1886	% in 1902
Below I (Infants)	26.6	30.1
I	20.0	15.5
II	15.1	12.8
III	13.7	12.1
IV	11.7	10.6
V	7.8	8.8
VI	3.9	6.0
VII	1.2	3.3
ex-VII	–	0.8

Source: LSB Final Report, 1904.

More significant than the quantitative improvement was perhaps the London School Board's influence in changing definitions of the scope of elementary education. In its early work the Board was inevitably constrained by the restrictions of the Codes. Grant-earning had to come first. But it appointed a Committee presided over by Thomas Huxley to look at the nature of the curriculum provided. To a storm of protest, it proposed that above the subjects laid down by the Code, the teaching of morality and religion, physical sciences and elementary social economy should be regarded as essential, and algebra and geometry, and Latin or a modern language as discretionary, for all children above infant level. It also recommended that grants should be offered to allow elementary school children to gain access to endowed secondary schools. This led to a pioneering scholarship system, which was to become a critical performance indicator for schools like Fleet Road; and it will be examined in detail in Chapter 10. Following accusations of extravagance and unfair competition with the voluntary sector, the Board prevaricated over the Committee's report, and suggested that the scheme set forward was what was ultimately desirable, rather than what was immediately attainable.[45]

Despite the curricular advances which the London School Board sponsored it was regarded, even by supporters and members such as Lyulph Stanley, as lagging behind in its provision of true 'higher-grade' schools. Such schools had been mooted from 1879, designed for the needs of lower-middle-class and upper-working-class children. In 1881, the London Board appointed a sub-committee which urged the provision of high-status schools with fees of 6d in the lower and 9d in the upper departments,[46] to meet this need. But nothing was done. There was also debate about the relative merits of the Bradford system, which provided higher-grade schools for the more affluent districts, and the Sheffield system, which offered a centrally located school for the city as a whole. Lyulph Stanley, who favoured extending higher elementary provision but was suspicious of socially motivated higher-grade schools, preferred the Sheffield approach.

The London School Board had determined that none of its schools shall be class schools. Other Boards may establish 'Higher Grade' schools and continue to charge a 9d fee; the [London] School Board only establishes 'schools for the upper standards' and makes them all free.[47]

Higher elementary provision was difficult to offer cost effectively, as generally relatively few children in a particular area were potential candidates. Thus at one stage in the mid-1880s only one of London's board schools had more than 40 scholars above Standard VI. The 9.2 per cent of the school population in Standard V and above was scattered round 581 departments.[48] In 1888 the Board decided to concentrate higher elementary provision in certain schools. But the success of the scheme was inhibited by headteachers resisting the transfer of their best pupils at Standard V.[49]

The long-standing ambivalence of the London School Board over the provision of higher elementary education brought it under the scrutiny of the *School Board Chronicle*, which asserted that London's contribution was 'far in arrears of the large provincial boards'.[50] A further complication was the equation of higher-grade schools with science schools. While in the late 1890s London was to define 44 of its higher elementary schools as 'higher-grade',[51] of which Fleet Road was one, the more stringent definition restricted the title to the science schools following the strict requirements of the Science and Art Department. Only five of London's board schools were thus described.

Criticism was countered by the argument that it was not in London's best interests to promote science schools. The orientation of higher elementary education in the capital city should be rather towards commercial than industrial education, as a report to the Technical Education Board of the London County Council stressed.

Enough has been said to show that the question of commercial education is one of national importance. But we are of the opinion that it is a question which concerns the citizens of London more than any other British subjects. For London stands alone as the greatest commercial centre in the world and as the heart of the British empire. London has not only a larger proportion of 'clerks' than any other city in the world; it has probably a larger proportion of clerks to the whole population than most other cities. Everything which affects British trade must affect London in a special degree; and it is only fitting that any measures which are to be taken for the defence of our commercial supremacy should be put forward in the first instance by the merchants and citizens of London.[52]

It was of course the rival London County Council (LCC) through its Technical Education Board (TEB) and not the London School Board which counted itself responsible for such provision. London board schools were in the unenviable position of having to respond to the far from complementary demands of their own School Board, the Education Department in White-hall, the Science and Art Department in South Kensington, and the Technical Education Board of the London County Council. All provided resources of one kind or another. The Technical Education Board was reluctant to recommend commercial education being provided in the elementary schools controlled by the London School Board, and indeed deprecated 'specialisation on commercial subjects in primary schools'.[53] In the event, it offered, on request from the School Board, advice on the type of practical commercial teaching which might profitably be undertaken in higher elementary schools. It conceded that in the higher departments, building on the general education given in the lower standards, a more specialized training might be offered to those intending to enter business at about the age of 14, by giving instruction in 'handwriting, précis writing, French, shorthand, typewriting, and the elements of book-keeping'.[54] Schools such as Fleet Road had already anticipated the huge demand brewing for commercial training. But as we shall find (Chapter 8), it was a type of provision which significantly excited the disapproval of the Board of Education.

NEW ATTITUDES TO POPULAR EDUCATION

Of all the criteria for judging the success of the 1870 Act and the work of the school boards, that of changing the attitudes of the bulk of the population, generally appraised as negative in the period before the 1870 Act, could be regarded as the most important. Compulsion, coming 'slowly and in easy stages' had been accepted, as Smith put it, 'with surprisingly good grace'.[55] It was influentially argued that the most significant fact in progress after the 1870 Act had been 'the increased importance which has been attached by the nation at large to the efficiency of its schools', and 'the growth of a new public sentiment in favour of education'.

This change in public opinion has made possible much which the zeal of educational reformers, the goodwill of local authorities, the liberality of subscribers, and the experience and devotion of the teachers would otherwise have been powerless to effect. It has permitted great expenditure in order that, within the lifetime of a single generation, dangerous deficiencies might be removed ... It has created in a great number of places the atmosphere of sympathy and encouragement which is necessary to the welfare of schools. And the change may be traced to a growing belief in the value and necessity of education, which cannot fail to increase the number of persons competent to take part in the local administration of educational affairs, and thus form the best guarantee for wise advance, intelligence criticism and prudent expenditure in the future.[56]

Booth and his team were interested in the actual grassroots impact of this perceived change. The general consensus arising from their interviews with officials and school representatives was that there had been a decided improvement in the 'manners and morals' of children in school over the school board period. The headmaster of Nichol Street Board School, in one of the most notorious slum areas in London, described his school as 'the great civilizing power' in the district.[57] Similarly the head of Summerford Street Board School claimed that despite his catchment area becoming more crowded and poorer through the 1880s, the children were 'less savage and lawless' than their parents had been, 'now perfectly amenable to discipline'. In the early days the 'slightest rebuke brought filthy language', while the 'closets were a mass of obscene writing from top to bottom'.[58] Such problems had disappeared, but what remained was the abject poverty and intellectual dullness of many of the children, described by Booth's team as 'poor, thin, anaemic little mites, many of them very ragged'.[59]

Members of staff reinforced the view of the headteacher. One was particularly forthright.

I have emphatically to record that a great and pronounced change has in my time taken place in the whole demeanour of the native born child. The old ruffian child is fast disappearing. Where are the rebels and outlaws and young villains of a dozen years ago? The school has not existed for nothing.[60]

Another teacher stressed the significance of the fact that the parents of the current generation had themselves been perhaps the first generation to have had an elementary school training. As a result they sent their children to school more tidy and were more anxious about their progress.[61] But the story of the board schools in the poorer districts continued to be one of catering for grinding deprivation, with frequent comment from Booth's interviewees on the irregularity of employment, domestic poverty and discomfort, drunkenness and debauchery, and brutalized relationships, which made the adjustment to the culture of the school so difficult for the children.

In the end, Booth and his colleagues gave strong if guarded approval to the influence of education in improving the social condition, and certainly were more enthusiastic about the efforts of the schools than the churches.

Like the rest, the educationalist clings to a belief in the efficacy of his gospel: he still has faith in the infusion of knowledge for raising the character of the people.

In each case, though not exactly according to their hopes, something has been won. The ragged rascal may never reach the Sunday school; the Sunday school children never join the church; the accomplishments of the fourth standard may be all forgotten ... but something still remains. Habits of cleanliness and order have been formed; a higher standard of dress and of decency have been maintained, and this reacts upon the homes; and when children who have themselves been to school become parents, they accept and are ready to uphold the system, and support the authority of the teachers ... Schoolmasters need no longer fear the tongue of the mother or the horse-whip of the indignant father.[62]

Booth's team was less convinced by the purely educational results of schooling:

A whole generation has been through the schools, but in scholarship there is not much to show for it. Almost all can, indeed, read, but with some effort; and write, after a fashion; but those who can do either the one or the other with the facility that comes of constant practice are comparatively few.

On the other hand, in particular cases, there were children eagerly grasping every opportunity and, 'even if by units', were justifying 'the perfecting of the ladder of learning now reaching from elementary school to university'.[63]

If the conclusions of Booth and his team were mediated and even flawed by moralistic and paternalistic overtones, they were based on more solid evidence than hitherto collected, and ended up as cautious, qualified and credible. They confirmed that a comprehensive and effective socializing process was in place, based on a meritocratic ideology. Access to the higher reaches of elementary provision, let alone secondary and tertiary, was still a prospect for the few, but it was an advance on there being no prospect at all. And access to the lower reaches was demanded of all, and offered free, as elsewhere. In London, indeed, board school accommodation was generally of a quality, and the teaching of a proficiency, which could hardly have been conceived of in the 1860s. As implemented by schools such as Fleet Road, the concepts of the London School Board were in advance of their time and led to claims that the elementary provision on offer was ahead of any in Europe. It represented a blueprint for a relatively democratic and balanced secondary provision for the twentieth century, for it had strayed well beyond the bounds of normal elementary phase definitions. As we know, the option was rejected by the higher circles which had for some time viewed the aspirations and interpretations of the London School Board with suspicion.

REFERENCES AND NOTES

1. M. Tabor, 'Elementary Education', in C. Booth (ed.), *Labour and Life of the People: London, vol. II* (London, 1891), p.486.
2. *SBC*, 29 July 1871, p.326.
3. Booth (ed.), *op. cit.* (1891), vol. I, p.5.
4. This table is based on LSB, *Finance Committee Minutes*, 21 Feb. 1884; and Booth (ed.), *op. cit.* (1891), vol. II, Appendix, Table II.
5. A map illustrating these disparities can be found in W.E. Marsden, 'Education and the Social Geography of Nineteenth-century Towns and Cities', in D.A. Reeder (ed.), *Urban Education in the Nineteenth Century* (London, 1977), p.52.
6. *Ibid.*, p.54.
7. LSB, *Final Report, 1870–1904* (London, 1904), p.343.
8. *Daily Telegraph*, 29 April 1904, quoted in T. Gautrey, *'Lux Mihi Laus': School Board Memories* (London, 1937), p.173.
9. J.W. Adamson, *English Education: 1789–1902* (Cambridge, 1930), pp.359–60.
10. G.A.N. Lowndes, *The Silent Social Revolution* (Oxford, 1955 edition), p.7.
11. J. Summerson, 'London, the Artifact', in H.J. Dyos and M. Wolff (eds.), *The Victorian City: Images and Realities, Vol. I* (London, 1973), p.322.
12. E.R. Robson, *School Architecture* (London, 1874; Leicester reprint, 1972), pp.315–16 and p.344.

13. S.E. Bray, 'The Ordinary Day School' in T.A. Spalding and T.S.A. Canney, *The Work of the London School Board* (London, 1900), p.184.
14. *Ibid.*, p.177.
15. Booth (ed.), *op. cit.* (1891), vol. I, p.129.
16. See W.E. Marsden, *Unequal Educational Provision in England and Wales: The Nineteenth-Century Roots* (London, Woburn Press, 1987), p.104.
17. *Ibid.*, pp.94–7.
18. *Reports of the Committee of Council on Education (hereafter RCCE) 1873–4* (London, 1874), p.190.
19. Booth (ed.), *op. cit.,* (1891), vol. II, pp.507–8.
20. *Ibid.*, p.504.
21. *Ibid.*, p.506.
22. *Ibid.*, pp.491–2.
23. *Ibid.*, pp.500–1.
24. *RCCE 1875–6* (London, 1876), pp.369–70.
25. H.E. Manning, 'Is the Education Act of 1870 a Just Law?' (1882) in *National Education* (London, 1889), p.7.
26. 'Reaction at the London School Board', *The Nonconformist*, vol. 7, 4 Feb. 1886, p.104.
27. *RCCE 1878–9* (London, 1879), pp.592–3.
28. C. Booth, *Parish Notes* (Booth Collection, London School of Economics), Group A, vol. 43, p.26.
29. G. Gissing, *The Nether World* (London, 1889; Brighton, Harvester Press edition, 1982), p.80.
30. For a fuller account, see W.E. Marsden, 'Residential Segregation and the Hierarchy of Elementary Schooling from Charles Booth's London Surveys', *The London Journal*, vol. 11 (1985), pp.127–46.
31. C. Morley, *Studies in Board Schools* (London, 1897), p.85.
32. Booth (ed.), *op. cit.* (1891), vol. I, pp.26–7.
33. T.R. Phillips, 'The Elementary Schools and the Migratory Habits of the People', *British Journal of Educational Studies*, vol. 26 (1978), pp.177–8.
34. D. Rubinstein, *School Attendance in London 1870–1904* (Hull, 1969), p.37.
35. *Ibid.*, pp.47–8.
36. *The London Figaro*, 11 March 1874.
37. *Ibid.*, 22 April 1874.
38. Rubinstein, *op. cit.* (1969), p.76.
39. LSB, *Report of the Byelaw Committee and School Management Committee*, 28 July 1887, p.446.
40. D. Rubinstein, 'Socialization and the London School Board 1870–1904', in P. McCann (ed.), *Popular Education and Socialization in the Nineteenth Century* (London, 1977), p.258.
41. C. Booth (ed.), *Life and Labour of the People in London: Third Series: Religious Influence: Notes on Social Influences* (London, 1902), pp.222–3.
42. Rubinstein, *op. cit.* (1977), pp.254–8.
43. Spalding and Canney, *op. cit.* (1900), p.171.
44. LSB, *Final Report, op. cit.* (1904), p.158.
45. Spalding and Canney, *op. cit.* (1900), pp.92–5.
46. J.D. Mellor, 'The Policy of the School Board for London in Relation to Education in and above Standard V' (London University, unpublished M.A. thesis, 1954), p.80.
47. L. Stanley, 'The Work before the London School Board', *Educational Review*, vol. 3 (1891), p.77.
48. Mellor, *op. cit.* (1954), p.92.
49. *Ibid.*, p.143.
50. *SBC*, 25 Feb. 1893, p.222.
51. Spalding and Canney, *op. cit.* (1900), pp.197–9.
52. *The London Technical Education Gazette*, April 1899, p.65.

53. *Ibid.*, p.69 and p.78.
54. London County Council Technical Education Board, *Extract from Report of Finance and General Services Committee*, 20 June 1900 (Public Record Office, Ed 14/102), p.4.
55. F. Smith, *A History of English Elementary Education, 1760–1902* (London, 1931), p.314.
56. M.E. Sadler and J.W. Edwards, 'Public Elementary Education in England and Wales 1870–1895', in Board of Education, *Special Reports on Educational Subjects, 1896–7, Vol. I* (London, 1897), p.8.
57. C. Booth, *Miscellaneous Notes* (Booth Collection, London School of Economics), Group A, vol. 39, p.11.
58. C. Booth, *Notebooks* (Booth Collection, London School of Economics), Group B, vol. 225, p.55.
59. *Ibid.*, pp.61–3.
60. *Ibid.*, p.67.
61. *Ibid.*, p.271.
62. Booth, *op. cit.* (1902), vol. II, p.53.
63. Booth, *op. cit.* (1902), *Notes on Social Influences*, p.202.

CHAPTER THREE

Hampstead and Popular Education

There are few places in the world more 'behind-hand' in
everything than Hampstead ... It is impossible to conceive
a more painful position for any parish than to contrast
unfavourably 'even with St. Pancras'.[1]
(*Pall Mall Gazette*, 1874)

In his Report for 1873, HMI C.H. Alderson, inspecting the
schools of the Marylebone District, aroused widespread metropolitan interest by a highly critical review of inspected voluntary
schools, deficient in quality if not in quantity, in the parish of
Hampstead:

In certain parts of my district a much higher standard of efficiency is attained
than in others ... A Paddington boy reads and spells more than twice as
correctly than a St. Pancras boy; his arithmetic is nearly 17 per cent more
accurate than that of a Hampstead boy ... It is not so easy to understand why
Hampstead, as a whole, falls far behind the rest of the district in efficiency of
instruction; it is not for want of schools, for it is better supplied with schools
than any other part ... However it is to be explained, the fact remains that in
writing, spelling and arithmetic, Hampstead contrasts very unfavourably with
the rest of the district, even with St. Pancras ... It is not, as I have said for want
of schools, is it *because* of its many schools? Where schools of different
denominations are plentiful, a mischievous canvass for scholars is apt to arise.
Parents too, who have many schools within reach are apt to think they confer a
benefit on the one they select; they show an independence which often leads
them to withdraw their children upon very trivial offence ... At all events,
Hampstead seems to illustrate the truth of the observation ... that you may
multiply schools without creating efficient instruction.[2]

The editor of the *Hampstead and Highgate Express* affected no
surprise at these revelations, pointing out they were symptomatic of the borough, which had also failed to provide public
baths, washhouses, a vestry hall, and a literary and scientific

50

institute. He looked to clergy, teachers and parents to 'lift the parish out of this degraded condition'.[3] A more favourable situation relative to surrounding areas was, however, recorded by Alderson in his 1877 Report on the Marylebone District. Hampstead children's percentage failures in reading, writing and arithmetic were respectively 4.8 per cent, 11.5 per cent and 16.3 per cent, as against 11.0 per cent, 16.8 per cent, and 22.8 per cent for St. Pancras.[4] The Vestry also became more active, building a Vestry Hall in 1878, orchestrating the public protests against the Fever Hospital, and providing washhouses and baths in the 1880s, and a library and electric lighting in the 1890s.[5]

THE GROWTH OF ELEMENTARY EDUCATION IN HAMPSTEAD

A relatively large proportion of Hampstead's children of course belonged to social groups which eschewed publicly provided elementary education. Many attended selective private schools and increasingly the quality day secondary schools which developed after the Taunton Report of 1868. A London Technical Education Board Survey of the mid-1890s showed Hampstead second only to Lewisham in numbers per 100,000 attending endowed and proprietary secondary schools. The range was from 1,355 per 100,000 in Lewisham to 95 in Newington. Hampstead's figure was 1,044, and the average for London as a whole, 453.[6] An accompanying table indicated numbers of children in private and semi-private schools on the lists of the London Matriculation and Oxford and Cambridge Local Examinations and College of Preceptors examination bodies. The figures were less reliable in that only 126 out of 360 schools furnished returns. But for what they were worth, they suggested Hampstead was fifth among London parliamentary boroughs in ranking, with 324 scholars per 100,000, as against a maximum of 716 in Wandsworth and a London average of 86.7. Of Hampstead's 324, 282 were girls.[7]

The 'Hampstead of the villas' seems even to have been suspicious of allowing private schools in its midst until the 1890s, when difficulty in letting some of the huge residences in Belsize Park and adjacent areas allowed 'a rash of discreet girls' schools' to break out. By contrast, Mrs. Coghlan's school, opened in Thurlow Road in 1877, was only permitted as a favour because it had religious connections, having been previously run in the vicarage of Christ Church, and because it catered purely for the upper classes of Hampstead.[8]

Totally excluded from respectable Hampstead were the cheaper 'Dames' schools' which, however, remained popular for a variety of reasons well into the 1870s, not least in Marylebone, where HMI Alderson expressed his distaste for the social motivation which enabled 'the Dame' to survive:

She flourishes upon a deeply seated foible of the national character, the passion for the genteel or the supposed genteel, which beats as strongly in the bosom of the petty tradesman and the well-to-do artisan, as in that of any class of the community. A cracked piano and a couple of mouldy globes, with a brass plate on the doors inscribed with the words 'Juvenile Academy' outweigh with too many parents all the merits of correct spelling and sound arithmetic.

The dames were upset by Alderson's presence 'not from any personal disinclination to inspection, but as tending to dissipate the halo of gentility by which their establishments had hitherto been environed'.[9]

At the time of the 1851 census, Hampstead had already 51 day schools, of which 12 were categorized as public and 39 as private. Of the former, nine were provided by religious bodies, of which eight were Anglican and one Roman Catholic, one was a ragged school, one an orphan school, and one a school for the blind. The Church of England schools catered for 705 children, the Roman Catholic for 49, while there were 26, 15 and 62 in the three 'special' schools respectively. In all, the Census recorded 1,577 children enrolled in Hampstead's schools and 1,415 in attendance on Census Day. While there were 39 private schools, they provided for only 36 per cent of the children enrolled.[10]

It has already been noted (Chapter 2) that Marylebone was one of the few divisions of the London School Board to come near to possessing a sufficiency of school accommodation in 1870. Hampstead was an area in which there was a reasonable quantity of voluntary provision. It had the advantage of an early start. Hampstead Parochial School, at first a Sunday School, accepted day school pupils as early as 1788. The schools were run by 'The Hampstead National Sunday and Day School Committee', their object to afford 'moral and religious instruction for the children of the poor in this place and neighbourhood' by means of voluntary contributions. The education was according to the principles of the established church. By the time of the 1870 Act, separate boys', girls' and infants' schools had been merged on one site in the centre of Hampstead,[11] behind Bradley's Buildings, near the High Street, by no means a salubrious part of the village.[12]

By the mid-1840s the three schools together were accommodating 370 pupils, easily Hampstead's largest venture at this time. By the 1851 Census, there were also schools connected with St. John's Church, Downshire Hill (established 1840), with Emmanuel Church, at the west end of Hampstead (1845), and at North End (1849), while the Roman Catholics used a small schoolroom in Holly Place (1849). During the 1850s and 1860s the most important new schools were established by Christ Church, on the other edge of Hampstead Village from the Parochial Schools, and opened in 1855, and by the British Society in Heath Street (1862). By 1871, Christ Church had become the largest school, with 342 pupils, fees of 2d to 4d per week, and 71.6 per cent average attendance. The Parochial School had similar fees, 295 children on the books, and 84.1 per cent average attendance. Heath Street, in common with other British Schools, had higher fees for 40 of its more advanced pupils, who paid 6d per week. This was one-sixth of its enrolment. Average attendance was 71.2 per cent.

The other, smaller, schools included St. John's (Downshire Hill), described as private and Church of England, with 137 pupils; St. Stephen's C. of E., with 105; Emmanuel, C. of E., with 76; Rosslyn Hill Unitarian, run on British School lines, with 56; North End C. of E., with 30; St. Saviour's C. of E., opened for only a week, with 17; and Holly Place Roman Catholic, with a mere 15 boys.

Apart from great differences in size, the school provision was very variable in quality. The Roman Catholic school's building was described as 'quite inadmissible' while, for a time, All Souls' in South Hampstead was accommodated in a hay loft over and surrounded by stables. This and the lack of ventilation made the inspector's job 'a distressing one'. The master was 73 years old and the instruction was seen as very inefficient.[13] On the other hand, Heath Street was regarded as 'a school of very considerable pretensions', its success attested by a growth in numbers from less than 100 in the 1860s to over 300 by 1887, and due to the local reputation of its headteacher, W.H. Davies.[14]

From its nadir in 1871, the Roman Catholic provision

improved, with a new school opened by St. Mary's Chapel in Holly Place in 1874, its room being described as 'plain but lofty and well-ventilated'. The average attendance rose to 50.[15] The school was enlarged to take 60 children in 1876. By 1896 numbers were about the same, but the Inspector was criticizing the school as being too small, leading to an appeal for funds.[16]

Christ Church was clearly a major voluntary school but appears to have sought little publicity. Its affairs rarely excited the interest of the local newspapers, though when its headteacher, David Taylor, died in 1877, at the early age of 31, it was said that under him the school had 'attained to a degree of efficiency and prosperity unparalleled in its history'[17] (in fact amounting to 22 years).

Voluntary activity in Hampstead during the School Board period, as in comparable places, was largely geared to keeping at bay the threat of board schools appearing in the area. Thus on Downshire Hill new schools were built in 1877, behind the site of the existing girls' school, for St. Stephen's and St. John's. At one time the transfer of the old school to the London School Board had been contemplated, but it had subsequently been determined to keep it denominational. The old schoolroom continued to be used for the girls. Altogether, the Downshire Hill site was designed for 400 children.[18] The new schools cost £1,300 and repair of the old £400.

The tension between living with the costs of subscribing to voluntary schools, or with the increased rate burdens of supporting board schools and, worse, as was the case where the dual system operated, the chagrin of doing both, was quintessentially expressed in Hampstead.[19] In 1880, the Parochial Schools were in debt, but determined not to encourage more board school encroachment into Hampstead. An illustrated lecture and concert was held to help to reduce the debt.[20] Most Hampstead voluntary schools struggled to survive the School Board period. The only remaining voluntary schools in 1903 were the Parochial Schools, accommodating 462 children, Christ Church (381), St. Mary's, Kilburn (365), Emmanuel (256), Trinity, Finchley Road (243), and All Souls' (166) and St. Paul's (205) in South Hampstead. St. Mary's Roman Catholic School took 85 children. North End was still open, accommodating 39 infants.

The contrast in the relative scales of voluntary and board schools is shown dramatically on Map 5. The small size of three of the board schools, Heath Street, Rosslyn Hill and Worsley Road, is deceptive in that these were voluntary schools recently transferred to the Board. The disparities are further evidenced by the amounts at which the schools were assessed – in the case of board schools in Hampstead, by a professional valuer. The assessments ranged from £840 for Fleet Road to £5 for North End. The cumulative valuation of all the voluntary schools listed in a table in the Cross Commission came to £576. The highest assessment for a church school was the £76 for St. Stephen's, Worsley Road.[21]

The map reveals three clear-cut territorial divisions, reflecting pronounced social divides. Thus in the Belsize Park area, no public elementary provision was sought or made. In Hampstead Village and South Hampstead, there was sufficient admixture of the less well-off to require a modest development of elementary schools, and here voluntary provision held its own. But where the railways emerged from the tunnels under Hampstead, packed but often respectable working-class quarters, and a heavy concentration of board schools, were generated, especially in Kentish Town.

BOARD SCHOOLS IN WEST KENTISH TOWN

As we have seen (Map 1), by 1870 West Kentish Town was fully built up. It was also sorely lacking in school provision. Its particular social mix plus the fact that its growth was recent and predominantly working-class, meant there were not the resources for adequate voluntary initiatives, as were present in older-established and more affluent areas such as Hampstead. Indeed, there were only two voluntary schools, St. Andrew's (C. of E.) and St. Dominic's (R.C.), both large by voluntary school standards.

An interesting private venture in the area was Wilkin Street 'Elementary and Middle Class Training School for Children' which, as the brochure indicated, was near the North London railway line, evangelical but undenominational, offering a varied secular training for children from respectable families, with 'propriety of manners and deportment' given special attention. It was intended for girls and infants, though boys were accepted on a restricted entry. The fees for infants were 6d per week, for juniors 8d, and for seniors 9d all, interestingly, within the range

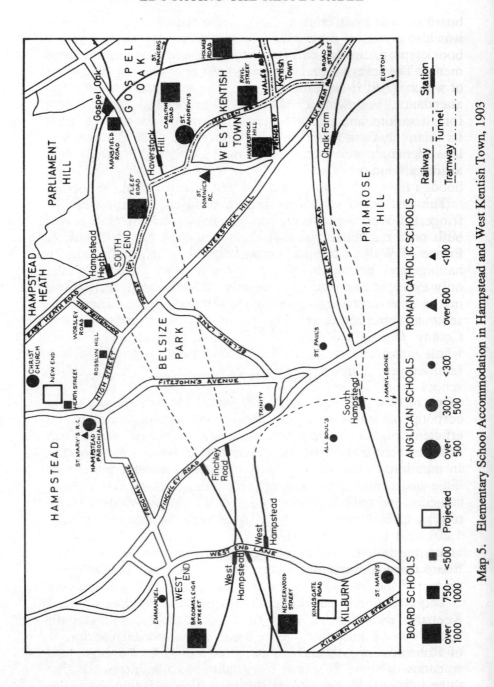

Map 5.   Elementary School Accommodation in Hampstead and West Kentish Town, 1903

board schools could charge, though most of course did not. There was also a 'select' department for girls at 1/- per week, offering bookkeeping, dressmaking and principles of household management.[22] The school lasted out the School Board period, at the end of which it had 192 children on the registers, with 140 in average attendance. Following demands from the Board of Education for alterations and improvements, the school closed in 1906.[23] Its relatively long lease of life would suggest it was meeting a local demand, presumably for parents of girls and infants glad to find an outpost of gentility in a largely proletarian neighbourhood.

The first board school to be opened in the area was on the fringes of West Kentish Town: Haverstock Hill School. It was built on a restricted triangle of land between Haverstock Hill, Prince of Wales Road and Crogsland Road. It was unusual in having three entrances and being the London School Board's only example of a one-storey school.[24] It was also a prototype mixed elementary school, the boys and girls having, however, separate entrances and schoolrooms. As a much later London County Council inspector's report indicated, throughout its whole existence 'its pupils were almost exclusively drawn from families very comfortably placed'.[25] In 1881 fees in the mixed school were 3d or 4d, and for infants 2d. The inspector's report of 1881 praised the school's very good discipline, with little corporal punishment, its very good tone and organization, its efficient, regular and punctual teachers, its well-kept registers and premises, and satisfactory provision of books and apparatus. In addition to the 'three R's', there were drawing, music and bible instruction. Geography and grammar were taken as class subjects, and animal physiology, domestic economy and literature as specific subjects. In 1881 there was accommodation for 1,201 and the average attendance of 84.1 per cent was well above the London average for the time. As the London School Board inspector concluded, it was a 'satisfactory school in every respect'.[26]

The next board school was Mansfield Place (Plate 6), near Kentish Town Station (Map 5), to be later renamed Holmes Road. As we have seen, this was widely recognized as one of Robson's most distinguished board schools, 'the most conspicuous of those designed and contracted for during the first three years of the Board's existence'.[27] The infants' school was here on the ground floor and the boys' and girls' lifted on piers and arches to obtain for all three departments ample and protected playgrounds. Despite this auspicious start, the school was in a less favoured area than, for example, Haverstock Hill. Reports suggested that as other schools opened in the area, children left Holmes Road. Thus in February 1884

nearly the whole of the scholars attending this school, upon the opening of the Carlton Road Board School, migrated thither. The great bulk of the children who now form the school are of a poor and comparatively destitute class.[28]

The school's fees were 2d for the boys and girls and 1d for the infants. As Fleet Road was at this time rising quickly to the top of the local hierarchy of elementary schools, so Holmes Road was in rapid descent towards the bottom.

The managers' reports at the turn of the century paint a depressing picture. The opening of Rhyl Street Board School (Map 5) led to a new exodus of pupils.[29] There was a further decrease of numbers reported in 1901 as a result of the replacement of small houses with business premises.[30] By 1903 the situation would seem to have deteriorated even more.

Many of the children who attend the school are drawn from a very poor and thriftless class; the effect of this is seen in the ragged clothes, bad boots and pinched faces of the scholars, and it is a cause also of a low moral tone among some of the boys, several cases of which have given trouble to the teachers.[31]

The government report for that year suggested the teachers were doing their best with 'a very difficult type of scholar', but the London School Board inspector pointedly remarked on the over-frequent absences of the headteacher, who lived a long distance away in Plumstead, and urged he should reside nearer the school.[32]

Overcrowding at this school in the early 1880s had led to the London School Board opening temporary schools in Wilkin Street and Lismore Road, the latter having previously served as a temporary school prior to Fleet Road's opening. Carlton Road at this time was a relatively well-to-do area with three-storeyed houses occupied by single families. But its long-term social future was not secure in the presence of nearby railway sidings, locomotive sheds, brickworks, timber yards, a coal depot, and piano and other factories. On its opening in February 1884, Carlton Road Board School's social niche, on a fee basis, was between Haverstock Hill and Holmes Road, with fees of 3d in the junior school and 2d in the infants. The influence of good headteachers, Mr. Groome for the boys and Mrs. Groome for the girls, was seen as a reason for the success of the school. When Mrs. Groome retired in 1901 she had completed more than 50 years as a teacher. 'For the last 28 years she has laboured in Kentish Town, and her influence for good among the girls of the neighbourhood is well known.'[33]

As we shall find, the Groomes were not the only significant husband–wife headteacher pairing in the northern parts of the Marylebone Division.

Throughout the School Board period there was endemic pressure on school accommodation in West Kentish Town. The popularity of Carlton Road, second only to that of Fleet Road, and presumably the unpopularity of Holmes Road, resulted in its enrolling more children than it strictly had places for. There was some relief when Rhyl Street was completed in 1898. It was filled almost immediately.[34] The construction of the school had involved the demolition of existing houses in the street. Its siting was objected to by Wilkin Street Training School on the grounds that it was opposite their Infant School entrance. This meant that the delicate children the school specialized in attracting would meet with the 'rougher companionship' of board school children, a situation objected to by careful parents. The Wilkin Street managers had also appealed to the Board not to demolish houses in Rhyl Street, 'one of the best streets in the locality', but rather in Litcham Street, which contained some 'wretched houses'.[35] Charles Booth's survey did in fact confirm it as the poorest street in West Kentish Town (Map 1). The district was at this time probably in the first stages of social decline, for a much later LCC inspector's report of 1926 referred to the Rhyl Street area unfavourably as suffering from overcrowding, multi-occupation of property, and acute poverty linked with unemployment. Most were casual workers, with just a few in more secure jobs on the railway or in the piano factories.[36]

Pressure on Carlton Road and Fleet Road led to the building of the final London board school in the area (New End, not opening until the LCC period), Mansfield Road, hard by Gospel Oak Station (Map 5).[37] It began with 372 children in temporary accommodation in 1898, and rose to an intake of 772 when its permanent buildings were available, in 1901, still the smallest of all the board schools in the district.

Thirty years of almost continuous activity by the London School Board in West Kentish Town, with no fewer than seven major initiatives, including Fleet Road, was in stark contrast to its absence in Hampstead, with its many church schools. Within a socially subtly heterogeneous area, which Booth and his team had found hard to code unequivocally, the London School Board pursued a government-approved policy of grading schools by fees, measured by what the local market was perceived to be able to bear. In this case the market graded from solid comfort at its northern end, where most of the pink streets of which Fleet Road School took advantage were located, to evident poverty to the south-east where the lowest feed school, Holmes Road, was found. By the end of the School Board period, whatever the fee, the schools had a clear hierarchical ranking in parental esteem. Rhyl Street and Mansfield Road had been in existence too short a time to be properly assessed. Of the rest, Carlton Road and Haverstock Hill were rated as good, and Fleet Road as outstanding, with Holmes Road not appropriate for the respectable.

HAMPSTEAD: ATTITUDES TOWARDS BOARD SCHOOLS

The presence of good board schools on its fringes, however, aroused little interest in Hampstead proper. As part of the Marylebone Division of the London School Board, the area had provided a majority of unsectarian progressives in the low-key early elections to the Board. In 1876 the *Hampstead and Highgate Express* made known its surprise at the lack of impact in the elections to that date of 'denominationalists and impugners of the Board's policy', and expressed regret that the public interest in school board matters was 'at a very low ebb'.[38] The apathy continued into the early 1880s, when only 1,343 of the 6,475 entitled to do so voted at the 1882 election.

By 1885 the situation had changed. It was in fact concern over the spiralling rate burden rather than religious issues as such which raised the tempo. In that year the first six candidates elected were advocates of 'economy and efficiency'. The progressive Lyulph Stanley lost his seat. Edward Barnes, who topped the poll, had pledged to do everything in his power

I. To reduce the unnecessary Expenditure and check the gross Extravagance.

II.   To prevent the crushing out of Denominational Schools, which are carried on efficiently without any assistance from the Rates, and to preserve Bible Teaching in all Day Schools.

III. To oppose Free Schools ...

IV.   To counteract all Educational fads, and to carry out the Act of 1870 in its original spirit.[40]

This election was the turning point in the Marylebone Division. While Lyulph Stanley was to regain his place, the liberal progressives never achieved their earlier support. The so-called 'moderates', who advocated economy in expenditure, maintained their power on the London School Board until 1894.

If at the aggregate level board schools were objected to as an expense on the rates and as unfair competitors to voluntary schools, at the individual, as we have seen, they were rejected on social grounds. Professor H.C. Barnard recounts how in his middle-class north London suburb it would have been considered 'an unspeakable disgrace' to be transferred to a board school.[41] Such reminiscences are reinforced by contemporary views that, for the tradesman classes, board school attendance stigmatised the children:

To intelligent ratepayers, especially of the tradesman and professional class, it is, we believe, a great hardship to be compelled, through necessity, to use Board School schools [sic]; and few who value the future of their children and know the advantages of the superior associations to be found in the best private schools would dream of sacrificing their class distinctions – omitting the moral tone – by sending their children to mix up with ... the 'waifs and strays'.[42]

The affluence of the residents of Hampstead proper meant that this was not for them a burning issue. The rates burden increasingly aroused their wrath, but apart from slight flurries of anxiety that the financial state of certain voluntary schools might lead to take-over by the London School Board, and occasional newspaper correspondence from the Nonconformist minority in the place about the lack of efficient board school accommodation in Hampstead Village, and the lack of opportunities offered by the voluntary sector in the scholarship stakes,[43] the public provision of elementary education was not in the forefront of local debate. Not until the last years of the London School Board was Hampstead 'aroused to an unusual interest',[44] over the question of finding a site for a new board school in Hampstead itself.

THE BOARD SCHOOL SITE CONTROVERSY

As already noted, three of the voluntary schools in Hampstead proper (Map 5) were in the late 1890s transferred to the London School Board. Its acceptance of these schools was a kind of 'Trojan horse', for the Board only agreed to use them temporarily, pending the erection of a new board school in the borough. The Education Department had in 1893 queried the condition of St. Stephen's Infant School. The St. Stephen's girls and infants used buildings on Downshire Hill and the boys one on Worsley Road (Map 6). The managers appealed to the Department on a number of occasions for time to raise funds to repair the deficiencies. It then applied to the London School Board to transfer the girls and infants from the unfit Downshire Hill buildings. In the event, the girls joined the boys in the temporary Worsley Road Board School.[45] But there were still more than 50 infants in the Downshire Hill accommodation in 1902.[46]

The transfer of the two Nonconformist schools, Heath Street and Rosslyn Hill, was less problematic. The latter had ostensibly accommodation for 345, but only 64 on the rolls.[47] On its transfer, the accommodation figure was reduced to 228.[48] Numbers enrolled had increased to 103 by 1903.[49] Heath Street was transferred with 420 on its rolls, but accommodation for only 338.[50] All the transferred schools were closed on the opening of New End by the LCC in 1906.

It was clear that the London School Board was intent on filling the Hampstead gap. The major need was in the relatively 'poor' areas of Hampstead Village, round about New End and Flask Walk. But there was also the matter of overcrowding at Fleet Road, which had taken on some of the children from St. Stephen's. Part of the thinking of the London School Board was to find a site which would meet both these needs. The area in the vicinity of the old St. Stephen's schools was an obvious choice (Map 6).

The first site to be chosen was in John Street, to which children from New End could walk down Willow Road, and from the Fleet Road area up South End Road. The proposal predictably aroused the protests of the residents of this well-to-do area. They forwarded a petition to the Education Department. Their first argument was that Keats had resided in one of the houses in the

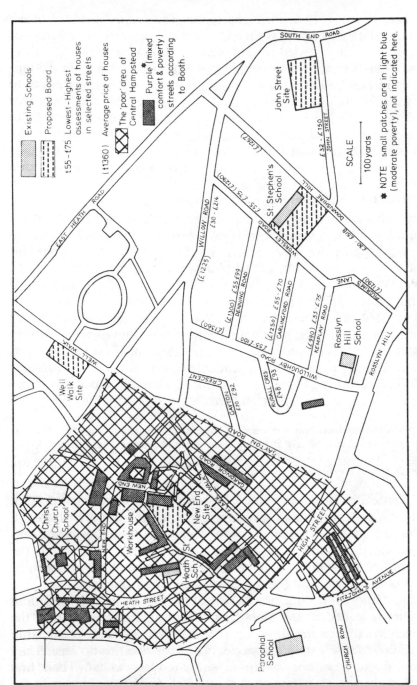

Map 6. Hampstead: Board School Sites Controversey, 1900–03

Legend:

- ▦ Existing Schools
- ⬚ Proposed Board
- £55–£75 Lowest–Highest assessments of houses in selected streets
- (£1360) Average price of houses
- ⊠ The 'poor' area of Central Hampstead
- ✴ Purple (mixed comfort & poverty) streets according to Booth.

SCALE
100 yards

✴ NOTE small patches are in light blue (moderate poverty), not indicated here.

Labels on map: SOUTH END ROAD, John Street Site, £32–£150, JOHN STREET, DOWNSHIRE HILL, (£1267), St. Stephen's School, (£1290), £55–£75 (£1250), WORSLEY ROAD, £30–£518, WILLOW ROAD, £30–£214, (£1225), (£1300), £55–£99, DENNING ROAD, (£1250) £55–£70, CARLINGFORD ROAD, PILGRIM'S LANE, (£1790), (£1360), £55–£100, WILLOUGHBY ROAD, £75, (£990) £55–£75, KEMPLAY ROAD, Rosslyn Hill School, ROSSLYN HILL, RUDALL CRES, £93, £48–£70, £92, CRESCENT, GAYTON ROAD, EAST HEATH ROAD, WELL WALK, Well Walk Site, Christ Church School, NEW END, Workhouse, New End Site, GARDNOR ROAD, WORSLEY ROAD, Heath St Sch, ELM ROW, HEATH STREET, HIGH STREET, FITZJOHN'S AVENUE, Parochial School, CHURCH ROW street, giving it an historic character. The second was the grave financial consequences for the owners of houses in John Street of having a board school in their midst. A complementary reason was that the rating assessments of the street proved it did not contain children of a class wanting public elementary schooling. It was also judged that the site was too inaccessible for the former scholars of Heath Street and Rosslyn Hill, who came largely from the upper part of the town. It was finally suggested that the enlargement of Fleet Road school and the exclusion of the part of its intake coming from outside the area would relieve the problem of the Fleet Road area itself.[51]

The John Street proposal was withdrawn and the attention of the School Board turned to two other possibilities, in Well Walk, on the north-eastern edge of Hampstead Village, and in Worsley Road (Map 6). An even greater flood of protest letters landed on the desk of the editor of the *Hampstead and Highgate Express*. Well Walk was the site of Weatherall House and the great historic Long Room of Hampstead, attesting its great days as a spa, when it was associated with well-known society figures of the time. Worsley Road was equally well regarded as a residential thoroughfare. The proposed 'despoilation' of 'two of the finest roads in the parish' was denounced as 'a sheer act of vandalism'. Another correspondent, who lived in Denning Road, near the Worsley Road site, put it more mildly:

It will certainly better suit the views of my neighbours not to have the school in the Worsley Road. Should it come there we may look forward, at no distant date, to the music of the bell and the gambolling to and fro of the scholars and the attendant horrors of noise and clatter ...[52]

Depreciation of the value of property was again anticipated, and much energy was expended in publicizing the value of housing in the immediate area (Map 6). One correspondent speculated that his property would lose half its value, with the school converting his own street into 'a noisy thoroughfare'.[53]

There was general feeling that Fleet Road school should take more children from the south-eastern part of Hampstead, and could do so if 'the intruders from other districts be expelled', a perennial complaint of the church interest, objecting to its wide and favourable catchment zone. The real deficiency was in the old village area, and for this a site round about New End was required. The residents of the Downshire Hill district raised a petition and forwarded it to the Mayor of Hampstead, deploying very similar arguments to those used earlier against the John Street site.

Nonconformist parents generally exercised less influence, but stressed that lack of a good board school was a deprivation for the children of Hampstead. One correspondent noted the scholarships that 'have gone year after year to the children at the foot of the hill' (i.e. Fleet Road), while the children in Hampstead itself were handicapped by the limitations of the voluntary schools:

The 'three R's' are all very well, but to get on in the world nowadays, something more in the way of intellectual equipment is needed, and so far the Board Schools have proved themselves the only means of providing this for the working classes.[54]

The bitter dispute culminated in a public enquiry, held at St. Stephen's School, and led by HMI R.J. Alexander. At the inquiry the so-called Site J, at New End (Map 6), came to the forefront of the debate. A number of local residents, perhaps not wishing to seem implacably opposed to the board school principle, and finding a site whose use would not directly affect them, suggested that the New End site was worthy of consideration. But the London School Board was strongly opposed, claiming that the New End site was insufficient to meet Board of Education requirements in space terms.

Alexander concluded that damage would indeed be caused to the interests of the residents of Worsley Road if a board school was erected on that site. He argued also that it was half a mile down a steep hill from the centre of Hampstead, and was therefore inconvenient for the large potential intake from that area. Considering the deficiency in the Gospel Oak area, down the hill, he noted there was unlikely to be a problem there on the completion of Mansfield Road Board School. It followed, therefore, that it was in central Hampstead that the difficulty needed resolving. He urged that either an offer from the Vicar of Hampstead to extend the Parochial Schools should be taken up, or houses acquired on the New End site to provide a large enough space on which to build a new board school.[55]

Alexander's first suggestion followed a compromise solution suggested by the correspondent of the Parochial Schools. He argued that the deficiency of places in central Hampstead was for less than 300 children, and that as all the sites considered had aroused strong local opposition, a speedy conclusion of the affair could be achieved by enlarging the Parochial Schools by 300 places. A small board school would be a costly alternative. He omitted to mention that only Anglican parents would support this solution.

Within the new Board of Education, it was insisted that property depreciation was not a matter within its 'province of enquiry'. But the selection of an accessible location was identified as crucial. There was no dispute about the fact that accommodation was required for the 'poor area' at the top of Hampstead High Street (Map 6).

A barrage of Board of Education memoranda suggests increasing impatience over the issue, particularly about the tactics of the London School Board. At first there was the suggestion that the Vicar of Hampstead's offer would provide the best solution, supported by Alexander. There was obvious sympathy for the hawkish line that it would be a good idea to 'terminate the comet-like career' of the London School Board in Hampstead and indeed a possible letter to the Board was couched, stating

that in as much as the statistical deficiency will at once be supplied by voluntary effort they need no longer continue their hitherto ineffectual research for a suitable site in Hampstead.

More temperate counsels advised a less abrasive approach, on the lines that the London School Board would relieve themselves of a very difficult task of acquiring a site in Hampstead compulsorily if the Parochial Schools' offer were to be accepted. Reference was made to the strength of the local opposition, and the problem of finding a large enough site in a suitable location. It was agreed that a letter should be sent to the Vicar of Hampstead stating that his proposal would be accepted if the London School Board concurred. Provocatively, at this stage, the London School Board reopened the possibility of building a school 'lower down the hill', notwithstanding Alexander's view that Mansfield Road would solve the problem of accommodation in the Gospel Oak area. But it kept the pot stirring.

The London School Board appeared to be encouraged by the inconsistencies in the Board of Education's stance. The latter had rejected the Worsley Road site, lower down the hill, on the grounds that accommodation was needed near the top of the hill, and also that local opposition was so strong. The School Board expressed the hope that it could now confidently rely on the Board of Education to support a top of the hill site.

The School Board for London submit that where so great and important an object as the education of the children is to be secured, middle class occupiers shall not be entitled, in the interests of the amenities of their own homes, to throw the whole burden of provision of a site upon the working class, who must suffer far more by the removal from the neighbourhood and from the vicinity of their work and other causes ... than a very few middle class families would do.

This was a prelude to the logical but provocative proposal to reopen the issue of the Well Walk site (Map 6), or one close to it.

The Board of Education replied impatiently. The London School Board had allowed a year to pass without acquiring the New End site which, athough the School Board claimed it to be too small, was 25,000 square feet as against the 26,465 of Well Walk. It had clearly rejected the Parochial School's proposal in that it affirmed that the New End location was the best site, in the midst of poor population and likely to be less opposed than other suggestions. But another enquiry was held by Alexander, on 27 February 1902. He supported views that the Well Walk site was 'undoubtedly picturesque' and that a board school there would 'certainly be incongruous'. The location was suitable in terms of access, but the New End site was obviously better. There was no support for yet more proposals: the Grove site, adjoining the Heath, and one in Gayton Road (Map 6).

While the rejection of the London School Board's second proposal for Well Walk by the Board of Education had been supported by a local petition with 840 signatories, conflict was renewed as a counter-lobby supportive of the Well Walk site emerged. Presumably a group with Nonconformist sympathies, it emphasized that the children still attending Heath Street school were doing so in sub-standard conditions. It was generally accepted that the Worsley Road site was too far away from the area of most need. At the same time, the New End site was unsuitable, shut in by lofty tenements, and requiring the eviction of 26 families if it was chosen. The Well Walk site met the needs. To suggest its 'sanctity' on historical grounds was dismissed as 'ridiculous'. It was said that the two houses thought of as in need of conservation had in the great days of Hampstead spa been used for illicit purposes by ladies of easy virtue. It was further made clear that if the Parochial Schools' solution was proceeded with, the Treasurer of Heath Street would consider reopening as a British School. A meeting of working men in the Town Ward strongly supported this stance, and urged the construction of a board school in the Ward. There was further reinforcement from the Hampstead Free Church Council.[56]

The opponents of Fleet Road reentered the fray, and once more complained about the scope of the school's catchment area. Even though it was further from Town Ward than the Worsley Road site, it was still thought that the eviction of Fleet Road's non-Hampstead children would resolve the problem. It was also asserted, in a slighting reference to the nature of the schooling offered at Fleet Road, that the enlargement of the Parochial Schools was the best solution, for in such 'the children are taught manners and decent speech, though possibly their acquaintance with botany and the piano may not be as great as many advocates of public education would desire'.[57] But by early 1903 the managers of the Parochial Schools had withdrawn their offer. A further London School Board aberration, to acquire premises in Flask Walk (Map 6), also a locally sensitive milieu, was counter-productive. The Board of Education had completely lost patience, reminding the School Board that it was the fourth year of unsuccessful search for a suitable site. It threatened to withdraw altogether permission to build a new board school in Hampstead if the New End site was not acquired. At the same time, it asked Hampstead Borough Council to take in hand the rehousing question consequential upon the use of New End for a board school. The School Board succumbed to the pressure and confirmed in October 1903 that it had obtained compulsory powers to take over the New End site. On this they would erect a three-storey school for 612 pupils. It was opened as an LCC school in 1906.

The Hampstead board school sites controversy offers detailed insight into the whirlpool of competing and overlapping interests, religious, residential, educational and bureaucratic, that conspired to delay a solution. The skirmishing of the conflicting lobbies of local parents, local voluntaryists and board school supporters, and officials in Whitehall and at the School Board, epitomizes the political consequences of the establishment of a kind of double duality: church versus state (or local authority) and state versus local authority. While there existed significant differences in the opinions of the middle-class groups mostly involved, there was never any doubt that the underlying residential interest would, in one way or another, win the essential social battle. The prospect of hundreds of working-class (or even lower-middle-class) children descending on a well-to-do residential area was too much for Hampstead-type residents to contemplate. It was hardly surprising that this group would assail the 'injurious absurdity' of the School Board, and were equally suspicious of the London County Council:

Within a few months each of these bodies has put forward a proposal, the one for tramways and the other for a Board School site, which would, carried out, have gone very far towards vulgarizing Hampstead beyond recognition.[58]

REFERENCES AND NOTES

1. *Pall Mall Gazette*, 28 July 1874.
2. *RCCE* (1873–4), pp.31–2.
3. *HHE*, 1 Aug. 1874.
4. *RCCE* (1877–8), p.404.
5. F.M.L. Thompson, *Hampstead: Building a Borough, 1650–1964* (London, 1974), pp.407–17.
6. In *Bryce Commission*, vol. 9 (1895), pp.430–3.
7. *Ibid.*, pp.434–7.
8. Thompson, *op. cit.* (1974), p.345.
9. *RCCE* (1873–4), p.25.
10. *BPP* (1852–3), XC (1851 Education Census), pp.8–9 and p.54.
11. *HHE*, 21 Sept. 1901.
12. Thompson, *op. cit.* (1974), p.316.
13. *PRO*, Ed. 3/19.
14. *HHE*, 15 April 1899.
15. *HHE*, 22 Aug. 1874.
16. *Hampstead Record*, 4 July 1896.
17. *HHE*, 24 Nov. 1877.
18. *HHE*, 19 May 1877.
19. See, for example, *HHE*, 9 Dec. 1876.
20. *HHE*, 10 April 1880.
21. *Cross Commission*, 2nd Report (1887), p.1070.
22. *PRO*, Ed. 14/1.
23. *PRO*, Ed. 21/11951.
24. E.R. Robson, *School Architecture* (London, 1874; Reprint, Leicester, 1972), pp.346–7.
25. *LCC*, Inspector's Report on Haverstock Hill School, 20 Nov. 1935.
26. *LSB*, Inspector's Report on Haverstock Hill School, April 1881.
27. Robson, *op. cit.* (1974), pp.342–6.
28. *LSB*, Government Inspector's Report on Mansfield Place School, 1885.
29. *LSB*, Manager's Yearly Report, Holmes Road School, Dec. 1899.
30. *Ibid.*, 1901 Report.
31. *Ibid.*, 1903 Report.
32. *LSB*, Government Inspector's Report on Holmes Road School, 1903.
33. *LSB*, Government Inspector's Report on Carlton Road School, 1901.

34. *LSB*, Manager's Report, Rhyl Street School, for the four weeks ending December 1898.
35. *PRO*, Ed. 14/12.
36. *LCC*, Inspector's Report on Rhyl Street School, 1925.
37. *HHE*, 30 Nov. 1901.
38. *HHE*, 18 Nov. 1876.
39. *HHE*, 2 Dec. 1881.
40. *HHE*, 24 Oct. 1885.
41. H.C. Barnard, *Were those the Days? a Victorian Education* (Oxford, 1970), p.57.
42. *Camden and Kentish Towns, Hampstead, Highgate, Holloway and St. Pancras Gazette*, 7 June 1879.
43. *HHE*, 10 Feb. 1894.
44. *HHE*, 1 Dec. 1900.
45. *PRO*, Ed. 21/11579.
46. *School Board for London Gazette*, vol. 6 (1901–2), p.80 and p.82.
47. *School Board for London Gazette*, vol. 4 (1899–1900), p.66.
48. *Ibid.*, p.126.
49. *PRO*, Ed. 21/11587.
50. *PRO*, Ed. 21/11581.
51. *HHE*, 13 Jan. 1900.
52. *HHE*, 10 Nov. 1900.
53. *HHE*, 17 Nov. 1900.
54. *Hampstead Record*, 31 Aug. 1901.
55. The following discussion is largely taken from the official documentation of the controversy in the Public Record Office. Covering the period March 1901 to October 1903, it can be found under *PRO*, Ed. 14/13.
56. *HHE*, 30 Nov. 1901.
57. *HHE*, 7 Dec. 1901.
58. *HHE*, 24 Nov. 1901.

CHAPTER FOUR

Fleet Road School and its Catchment

We ought to say something of the position of the Fleet Road School ... It is situated in a pleasant and healthy suburb, within a few minutes' walk of Hampstead Heath, and not far from the foot of the fine open fields of Parliament Hill.[1]
The Practical Teacher, 1894

You cannot fail to note at once how well-placed the Board School is. I had come up from Broad-street, over the railway arches that bestride the great Sahara of streets between that station and Dalston Junction. Out of it all, at varying points, big Board schools rise, bleak and void of beauty. They grow out of the mass like monuments marking the rise of progress, foretelling a time, let us hope, when men and women who gathered round them as children, will have learnt to despise the great grey streets and shabby dwelling houses, and claim the right to more air and sky and open space, and to cities of greater beauty. But our school at Hampstead has most of these advantages already. Fleet-road itself carries you almost on to the Heath.[2]
London, 1898

I now leave the depths of the dismal Borough and wild Walworth, and beg you to accompany me to the heights of Happy Hampstead ... Would there were more Hampsteads! But you might as well cry for the moon. Merit is so very much a matter of environment ...[3]
Morley, 1897

These three perceptions of the local setting of Fleet Road School, written in the 1890s by invited journalists travelling up from central London, tacitly connect it with the social prestige accruing to Hampstead proper. They were the views of outsiders. The image of Fleet Road from Hampstead itself was, as we have seen, very different. The social fringe location of Fleet Road was

71

strikingly evident from whatever the vantage point. Two are shown on Plates 7 and 8. Though a relatively recent photograph, Plate 7 offers a reasonably representative picture of the urban fabric on the southern edge of Hampstead Heath in the late nineteenth century. It does not, however, convey an accurate representation of what was a sea of terraced housing and small factory development in West Kentish Town, in the right background of the photograph. Most of this has been cleared in late twentieth-century urban renewal schemes. But the Fleet Road area, in the centre of the photograph, has altered less, apart from the monolithic intrusion of the Royal Free Hospital block on the right.

7. The Fleet Road area from Hampstead

Plate 8, which predates Plate 7, looks up the hill towards Hampstead, and was taken before the buildings of the old fever hospital were cleared to provide part of the site of the Royal Free Hospital. In the bottom left a patch of the working-class housing extending from West Kentish Town (between Dunboyne Street and Fleet Road on Map 8) remains. The rest of the foreground comprises the late-nineteenth-century lower-middle-class residences of the Agincourt Road area. The school buildings are shown in their entirety, just prior to the demolition of two of them in the 1960s. Industrial development also remains, including the old tram sheds, the last vestige of high intensity urban land-use

8. Hampstead and the Fleet Road area

before the more spacious layout of Hampstead proper, in the background of the photograph.

THE OPENING OF FLEET ROAD SCHOOL

In November 1877 the London School Board decided to purchase a site in the Fleet Road area for the purpose of erecting a public elementary school, described thus:

A piece or parcel of land situate at the rear of the houses on the north side of Fleet Road in the parish of Hampstead, at its junction with Mansfield Road, together with a portion of the bakery premises and gateway connecting the same with Fleet Road aforesaid, and containing 45,250 square feet or thereabouts.[4]

Apart from the bakery, the property was made up of grassland, a warehouse and stable, and gateway and yard.[5]

The Board at the same time moved that a tender from Messrs Wall Brothers of Kentish Town of £10,114 for the erection of a school for 800 children be accepted.[6] It was quickly resolved to widen the classrooms proposed to allow an increase in the accommodation from 800 to 896.[7] But the rapid growth of population in the neighbourhood so alarmed the Statistical Committee that it urged the Works Committee to plan for 1,200 rather than 800 intake.[8] The Education Department supported this proposal. The extra cost was £3,000.[9] An additional £615/16/10d was asked for furniture, representing 14/10d per capita.[10] Books, maps and apparatus cost £131/8/9d.[11] Continuing pressure on places meant that extra desks had to be acquired for use in the hall as a temporary measure until a projected enlargement could be completed. These cost another £229/15/0d.[12] It was further agreed that as the classrooms had been built 22 rather than the normal 20 feet wide, the eight classrooms of the mixed school should count for 576 instead of 480 children, meaning 72 pupils per classroom.[13] The ultimate cost of buildings, furniture and fittings at this first stage amounted to £16,972/0/8d.[14]

The voracious local appetite for school accommodation was still not satisfied, however. In February 1881 it was proposed to place an additional row of desks in the four remaining classrooms and to use the hall, accommodating an extra 120 children, pending the completion of Carlton Road Board School.[15] In

November 1882, the Statistical Committee of the London School Board urged that an extra 400 places now required in the sub-division should be added to Fleet Road School. An adjoining plot of land on Agincourt Road was duly purchased, and a tender from the builders of the main school, for £4,946, accepted. A Junior Mixed School was erected which ultimately cost £5,661/1/7d, and opened in January 1884.[18] In 1890 an additional 120 places were provided in the infants' department.[19] Fleet Road's departments ended the board school era with accommodation for 1,779 children, of whom 603 were in the infants' section.[20] Over the period as a whole, crowding was endemic, and normal use of the hall frequently restricted owing to the need for additional classroom accommodation.[21]

The original eight classrooms of the mixed school were 29½ feet by 22 feet and 14 feet high. The central hall measured 70 by 40 feet. The Infants' Department originally had two classrooms. Light, drainage and ventilation were described by the Education Department as good.[22] The Junior Mixed Department was built with a rather smaller hall and seven classrooms.[23] A later plan of the schools (Map 7) shows little was changed, apart from the modernization of the infants' school, by the 1930s. Bearing in mind the inconsistent orientation of the departments on Map 7, the detail of the plan can be matched with the photograph (Plate 9). The continuing pressure on space in the area, as great in the early 1960s as it was when the school was opened, is also evident.

Map 8, surveyed in the early 1890s, shows that at that time the school grounds were entered from Agincourt Road, though at their opening could be approached by a gateway on Fleet Road, opposite Park Road. Presumably the school was called Fleet Road rather than Agincourt Road because at the time it was planned Agincourt Road had not been named. The separate entrances for the three departments can be seen on Plate 9.

Noting that Hampstead itself was well served by voluntary schools, the local newspaper described Fleet Road's situation on its opening as at

one of the extreme edges of the parish ... intended partly, if not principally, for the accommodation of the northern portion of St. Pancras parish, as well as for the Gospel Oak district.[24]

Like Haverstock Hill school nearby, Fleet Road was one of the London Board's 'bungalow' school developments, intended for

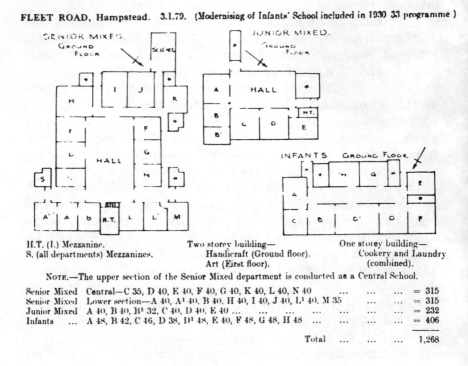

FLEET ROAD, Hampstead. 3.1.79. (Modernising of Infants' School included in 1930 33 programme)

H.T. (I.) Mezzanine.
S. (all departments) Mezzanines.

Two storey building—
Handicraft (Ground floor).
Art (First floor).

One storey building—
Cookery and Laundry
(combined).

Note.—The upper section of the Senior Mixed department is conducted as a Central School.

Senior Mixed	Central—C 35, D 40, E 40, F 40, G 40, K 40, L 40, N 40	= 315
Senior Mixed	Lower section—A 40, A¹ 40, B 40, H 40, I 40, J 40, L¹ 40, M 35	= 315
Junior Mixed	A 40, B 40, B¹ 32, C 40, D 40, E 40	= 232
Infants ...	A 48, B 42, C 46, D 38, D¹ 48, E 40, F 48, G 48, H 48	= 406
	Total	1,268

Map 7.   Plan of Fleet Road School, Hampstead

urban fringe areas where the costs of land were cheaper. At its
opening Sir Charles Reed, Chairman of the London School
Board, made reference to the 'noble' hall, in the centre of the
largest of the school buildings on Plate 9. It was one of the first to
be erected by the Board, and was capable of accommodating 500
people.[25] As we have seen, London School Board resisted the
Education Department's antipathy towards providing grants for
halls, regarding them as both convenient and inspirational. They
allowed more than one use as accommodation, improved the
circulation of children within the school, reduced the need
for corridors, made possible the surveillance of classrooms
through internal windows round the hall, and provided space for
assemblies, examinations, prize-givings and drill displays.[26] As
we shall find, Fleet Road made optimum use of the facility. The

9. Fleet Road School (1960s)

quality of the accommodation must have seemed heaven-sent to the newly appointed headteachers, Walter Bateman Adams and Louisa Walker, who on their appointments to Fleet Road had had to make use of inadequate temporary accommodation in schoolrooms in the Lismore Road area (Map 8), pending the completion of the permanent buildings.[27]

THE CATCHMENT AREA

At the time Fleet Road opened in 1879, most of the area shown on Map 8 between the school and the Hampstead Junction (North London) Railway was open space. In building up the reputation of the school with parents, a critical problem for the head-teachers was overcoming the poor image of the immediate environs of the school itself. As already noted, Fleet Road had

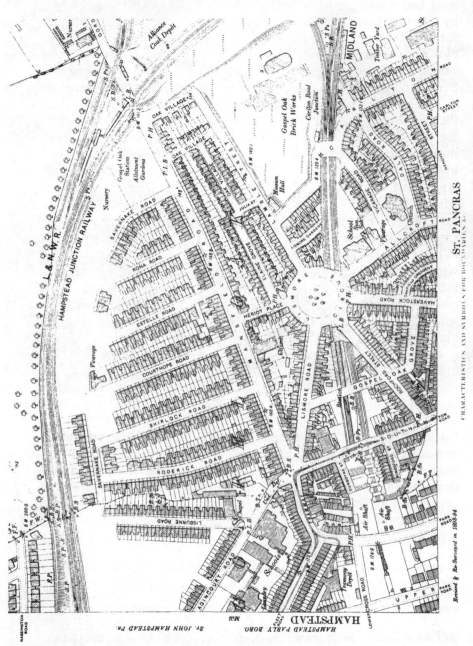

Map 8.   Ordnance Survey Map of Fleet Road area, 1890s (25" scale)

long had a bad press in Hampstead, and was indeed judged later by Charles Booth to be in social decline.[28] It provided the route for a tramway, the site for a notorious fever hospital, and was in close proximity to a brickfield, a laundry, and two sets of tram sheds. Yet within a decade the school was so famous that parents from far afield were clamouring to send their children there.

The social reason for the success is not hard to find, and lay in the developing nature of the catchment area. As already noted, the school faced north, away from Fleet Road, a fact of symbolic importance. The school's good fortune was the timely erection of lower-middle-class housing to the north of Mansfield Road and Agincourt Road during the 1880s and 1890s. The area west of Lisburne Road (Map 8) was belatedly built up because it took so long for it to recover from the anxieties associated with the smallpox outbreak in the Fleet Road area in the early 1880s (Chapter 1). As Booth confirmed, these were the streets from which the school's scholarship children chiefly came.[29] So that as this area was built up, the opportunity was taken to pivot the catchment away from West Kentish Town, for which intake the school had been chiefly built, and towards the lower-middle-class community developing to the north of the school.

It is useful to place Fleet Road school in Charles Booth's classification of London schools, covered in Chapter 2. In recognizing the close ecological relationship between residential segregation and school grading, Booth and his team classified the elementary sector into upper, middle and lower grade schools. In the upper grade of schools, there was a minority of parents living in poverty, ranging from 33 per cent in Class IV to just under 7 per cent in Class VI schools.[30] Mary Tabor's previously cited description of the climate of an upper-grade school would certainly have applied to Fleet Road. She went on to conclude that, despite the inhibiting effect of the education codes, the schooling offered was still

in quality, scope and teaching power, distinctly in advance of what even middle class parents, a few years ago, could secure for their children in the ordinary private school. In some, with a head teacher of a superior type, not the work alone, but the whole spirit and tone of the school are admirable.[31]

Tabor had accurately assessed the importance of a favourable social context and the inspirational effect of an energetic and capable headteacher. This potent mix applied to Fleet Road and attracted a small number of children even from the servant-keeping middle class proper. Just a few came from prestigious homes in Parliament Hill and South-hill Park (Plate 13), red streets in Booth's classification (Map 3). Yet it was clearly not anticipated that such would be the case. The Board set the fees for the mixed school at 3d and the infants' at 2d,[32] inferring that they would draw on a reasonable but not particularly aspiring lower-middle-class catchment, which would have justified a fee of 4d. Even when the junior mixed department was opened in 1884, the Board proposed a 2d fee, as in the infants'. This was turned down by the Education Department on the grounds that a 3d fee would be 'more proportional to the parent's ability to pay in this neighbourhood',[33] the Department not for the first time displaying either a keener social insight or a stronger commercial instinct than the Board. In 1888, to combat an influx of children to the school from outside the Board's jurisdiction, or at least to allay local feelings about this possibility, it was agreed that a 6d fee be charged for all children residing outside the metropolitan area which would include, for example, Willesden children.[34] Otherwise, Fleet Road was not a high-fee school by London standards, even after its catchment area was well known and its reputation established. When fees were abolished in 1891, the London School Board had only two schools at which the maximum fee of 9d was charged, Bloomfield Road in Greenwich and Oxford Gardens in Chelsea. In the Marylebone division only Medburn Street extracted as much as 6d: Fleet Road not even 4d.[35]

ALLEGATIONS OF EXCLUDING POOR CHILDREN

Fleet Road's spectacular rise to fame at metropolitan level won plaudits not always echoed locally. Pointed attacks were made during the disputes accompanying the 1885 School Board election. A correspondent to the *Hampstead and Highgate Express*, James Hewetson of Hampstead High Street, revived the voluntaryist argument that the board schools were designed by the 1870 Act for 'the waifs and strays, the poor neglected children of our great cities'. Yet the London School Board was abusing the law in allowing 'many thousands of well-to-do people' to enjoy 'an elaborate education for their children at 2d per week'.[36] Such was commonplace criticism of the London

School Board, but on this occasion the local debate was kept running by a response from W.B. Adams, headmaster of Fleet Road Senior Mixed School, which brought his school into the forefront of the argument.

Under the transparent pseudonym W.B.A., he described Hewetson's letter as 'full of fallacies'. He dismissed the 'waifs and strays' argument and suggested that as a result of the work of the London School Board 'waifs and strays at no distant period' would become 'an extinct race'. He invited Hewetson to explain what he meant by 'well-to-do people'. He provocatively quoted a local HMI's report as confirming that the elementary education given in the board schools of the district was better than that of any of the denominational schools. While he acknowledged that the Board had made mistakes, 'it would be wrong in every way, and unwise in every sense, to deal with this great work in a narrow, niggardly, and parsimonious spirit'.[37]

Hewetson replied promptly, tartly observing that the 'anonymous correspondent W.B.A.' argued 'like a Board schoolmaster'. His accusations now became more specific. He had not suggested that poor children attending board schools had been deprived of true elementary provision, but more seriously had been deprived by not being admitted at all to some board schools.

It is obvious that highly trained teachers [the expense of which was another bone of contention] decidedly prefer the more congenial duty of instructing their pupils in the higher branches of knowledge.

The second charge brought by Hewetson was more pointed and more contentious still:

There is a Board school not far from here where a highly trained talented master administers most efficiently the higher branches of the Code. It is well known that children of prosperous parents attend that school in large numbers ... A Board 'inspector' of the surrounding district assured me that, in his rounds of inquiry after absent pupils, he had frequently hesitated at knocking at the doors of handsome villas, the occupiers of which had been placed on his list. And it is well known in Hampstead that this Board school sends applicants, who are poor and ill-clothed, to adjoining voluntary schools, while children of a higher class are frequently admitted.[38]

Adams responded with equal alacrity, demanding that Hewetson should quote chapter and verse to support his accusation that poor children had been excluded from Fleet Road. He observed that in the six months from May to October 1885, no fewer than

107 children had been admitted unable to pay the 3d or 2d fee. He pointed out that 'the poor people of the district are found in large numbers in the unlovely neighbourhood of Fleet Road'.

At the same time, a divisional member of the London School Board, Rosamond Davenport Hill, wrote to say that the accusations were serious and it was the duty of the Board to investigate. She had demanded from Hewetson specific evidence to support his 'grave imputations' but apart from a preliminary reply saying he would endeavour to supply such information, she had received no further comment.[39]

Hewetson was at the same time very visible at the public meetings associated with the 1885 School Board election, clearly using the Fleet Road case as symptomatic of the extravagance of the Board, and as showing the need for local tradesmen to support the party which would promote 'strict economy in all departments of the Board'.

At one of the many School Board election meetings, comparison was made between the costs of Heath Street British Schools and those of Fleet Road. Those at the voluntary school amounted to £1/3/0d per child, as against £2/14/0d at the board school, provoking cries of 'shame'. The speaker told that Heath Street schools had always received good inspector's reports, and this was proof that 'the School Board had been guilty of reckless extravagance − (Hear, hear) − thoughtless expenditure, and gigantic jobbery (Applause).'

On the specific local issue the correspondence in the *Hampstead and Highgate Express* became more bitter. Hewetson accused the Editor of giving too much prominence to the attacks on him 'of your thinly veiled anonymous correspondent W.B.A.' He dismissed Fleet Road School's claim to be taking in poor children as far from the normal. The school had prepared no fewer than 364 pupils for passes in algebra, French and domestic economy, and he denounced such provision as a 'monstrous absurdity and incongruity' for poor children, 'whose brains are tortured and permanently injured by this unnatural treatment'. But of course most of the children were not drawn from the poorer districts.

It is notorious that a very large proportion of the children attending there are drawn from residents in South-hill Park, Her Majesty's Inspectors of Schools, and other wealthy people.

Upset by Rosamond Davenport Hill's letter which, he claimed, had given him too little time to reply, Hewetson now appended a series of communications from interested parties in the voluntary sector, purporting to demonstrate that Fleet Road had been refusing admittance to poorer pupils. Most of them, however, offered no hard evidence, rather suspicions and affirmations of support for Hewetson's cause, not difficult to harness in Hampstead. The only corroboration of any substance was from the Vicar of St. Andrew's School in Malden Road, Kentish Town, who indicated that the headmaster of his school had recorded cases of poor children being refused entry at Fleet Road on the grounds that the school was full, at times when other children were being enrolled. He indicated, however, that proof could not be found to substantiate that the refusal was solely for reason of poor appearance. At the same time, he knew that working people in the area complained they were unable to enrol their children at the school.

While there is no doubt that Hewetson overstated his case, it was well known at the time that the dual system was being manipulated by headteachers and parents as part of the process of evolving a hierarchically graded system of elementary schools. Aspiring schools, given the right context, enhanced their status by making themselves select, which involved ensuring a balance in favour of respectable children. The unusual aspect of the Fleet Road case was that the school allegedly excluding poor children was the local board school. It was usually the other way round. In a situation of continuing overcrowding, it was difficult to monitor decisions on intake. Adams interviewed all parents prior to admitting their children, and in a context of demand overwhelming supply was in a controlling position, as well as being sophisticated enough to ensure that his school achieved a favourable balance without becoming a fully lower-middle-class school. There are scraps of evidence which suggest the London School Board was not entirely happy with the enrolment policies of the school. Thus in 1894 Adams was reported for refusing entry to a pupil, but had to submit to the Board overturning his decision,[40] while in 1897 Mrs. Adams was criticized for 'excessive enrolment'.[41]

In the mid-1880s Adams was called on by the Cross Commission to offer opinions on social intake. He confirmed his support for the current practice of grading schools in accordance with the social nature of the catchment area. He expressed sympathy for schools in poor areas which found it difficult to obtain the 'excellent' merit grant.

I have said that I object to the same code for all schools because an inspector has to judge the work of a school in a good district by the same standard that he uses in judging the work of a school in a poor district ... To rectify this state of things, I should suggest three grades of schools ... First of all, I would have a code for very poor scholars in poor districts, where reading, writing, and arithmetic, singing, drawing and drill should form the subjects of instruction. I should not reduce the grants to those schools; I should give them larger grants for doing good work under special difficulties ... I may say that the London School Board have really, to some extent, graded the schools now. They have schools which are called 'Special difficulty schools', and I believe that the teachers are paid higher for teaching in them.

For the next grade, the curriculum would be that 'of the ordinary, average elementary schools' without specific subjects. For his upper grade, Adams defined a school whose children were beyond Standard IV, in Standards V, VI and VII.[42]

Adams was also questioned about the nature of the Fleet Road intake, and he stressed that while he did have some privileged children, his was a diverse enrolment, which included a minority from the lowest ranks of society. He described the character of the neighbourhood round Fleet Road School.

The population is a very mixed one; we have the children of bricklayers and labourers; a considerable sprinkling of the parents of the children are employed on the Midland and North-western Railways. The great industry of the neighbourhood is pianoforte making, Cramer's, Chappell's and Brins-mead's, and a great number of the parents of the children are employed there. Then we have a new neighbourhood springing up of small villas, which are occupied by people engaged in City warehouses, and so on. That is the new part of the district.[43]

It is clear that Adams was very sensitive to the charges made in Hampstead that he was running a middle-class school. It may be that he was so sensitive because he was genuinely keen to attract working-class children, so long as they were clean and capable. It can be inferred there were enough of them to sustain the negative social stereotype of the board school in the eyes of Hampstead parents who valued the respectable aura of a church school more highly than the educational aspirations of Fleet Road. The locational ambivalence of the school also clouded decision-making. But for parents of meritocratic disposition, the offering was ideal: a stimulating infants' department (Chapter 6); a junior mixed department which attended to the elementary school basics; and a senior mixed which was in essence a middle school, preparing pupils single-mindedly for upward occupational mobility, particularly through the scholarship system (Chapter 10).

MAPPING THE CATCHMENT AREA

While there is not, unfortunately, a particularly rich source of school records for Fleet Road, enough remains to be able to build up a reasonably accurate picture of the character and extent of the catchment area. It is not possible to match the 1881 enumerators' returns[44] (the latest available) with school admission register detail, for none remains for that time. But the senior school catchment for 1916 can be mapped from admissions register detail (Map 9), and compared with the catchment of 1894–1903 scholarship winners (Map 10). The two maps are similar enough to suggest no great change over time. Both reveal that, far from Fleet Road being swamped by distant children, the majority lived within half a mile of the school. The major differences were that few of the scholarship holders resided in Fleet Road itself, though many of the intake came from that street, and more of them than would be expected came from beyond the map area. Interestingly, none of them lived in the Parliament Hill district, which Hewetson asserted supplied Fleet Road with many of its most well-to-do pupils.

Of the children living within a quarter of a mile of the school, a high proportion resided in Fleet Road itself, the lowest-status street in the vicinity. Thus Adams' insistence that he did not run a middle-class school is corroborated. A large minority of the children was drawn from the socially mixed streets of West Kentish Town. In this densely-populated area, there were major overlaps of catchment zone between the local board schools and the two main voluntary schools, St. Andrew's and St. Dominic's (Map 5). Map 9 shows an unexpected outlier of Fleet Road's catchment in Belsize Park. It can be explained by the presence in a mews area of the homes of high-grade servants of rich carriage folk. The number crossing the railway from Parliament Hill and South-hill Park again is quite small, and from Hampstead Village negligible. If this 1916 pattern was present in Adams' day, as seems likely, then again the exaggerations of the anti-Fleet Road lobby are revealed.

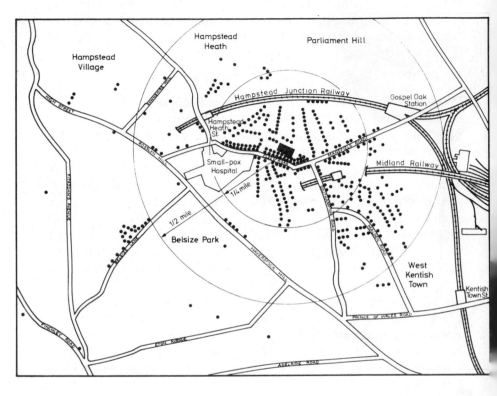

• -Pupil   ■-Fleet Road School   HH -Haverstock Hill Station   Scale = 6" to 1 mile
N. B. Dots placed approximately. About 25 not in map area.

Map 9.   Fleet Road Catchment Area, 1916

Map 10 confirms Booth's contention that it was the 'best pink' streets in the vicinity of Mansfield Road which brought Fleet Road School its scholarship reputation. A significant minority of winners lived in Kentish Town, but virtually none north of the Hampstead Junction Railway. The complaint of residents in Hampstead Village was of course that children from this area were not winning scholarships from the voluntary schools either (Chapter 10).

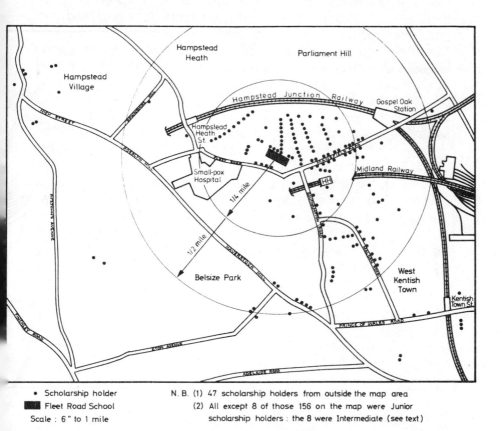

• Scholarship holder
▒ Fleet Road School
Scale : 6" to 1 mile

N. B. (1) 47 scholarship holders from outside the map area
(2) All except 8 of those 156 on the map were Junior
scholarship holders : the 8 were Intermediate (see text)

Map 10.   Fleet Road School Scholarship Holders, 1894–1903:
Location of Homes

THE SOCIAL SPECTRUM OF FLEET ROAD SCHOOL'S
CATCHMENT AREA

Detailed studies of streets within Fleet Road School's catchment
zone reveal the intricacies and nuances of differential socio-
economic status embedded within the broad middling groups in
urban society with which we are mainly concerned. From the
extreme vantage points of, say, Belsize Park and Spitalfields, this
would have appeared a socially homogeneous district. But not
from within. Leaving aside the largely irrelevant extremes as
represented by Booth's yellow, dark blue and black categories,

four streets are selected as representative of the school's catchment area. They are Fleet Road itself (part light blue and part purple); Grafton Terrace, in West Kentish Town (purple); Mansfield Road (pink) and South-hill Park (red). The discussion assumes that there was no major social change between the time of the 1881 census returns and Booth's surveys of the following decade. Booth appropriately hedged his bets in placing many of the streets of West Kentish Town in his catch-all purple category, as well as refining the pink category by describing streets as of the 'best pink' or pink streets with red edging. But this would appear to have been a more credible adjustment to complexities discovered in the field than a confidently clear-cut classification.

One factor common to three of the streets, as Table 4.1 indicates, was the very high proportion of married heads of households, over 80 per cent in each case. The exception was South-hill Park, with more spinster heads of households among its inhabitants.

TABLE 4.1

Status of Head of Household	Percentages			
	Fleet Road	Grafton Terrace	Mansfield Road	South-hill Park
Married	87.9	82.7	81.3	73.5
Widowed	8.7	12.7	13.5	13.6
Unmarried	3.4	4.6	5.2	11.9

The inference that Fleet Road, the lowest-status street, and South-hill Park, the highest, had respectively the most youthful and the most elderly population, is supported by Table 4.2, which demonstrates the truism that areas with most young couples generated the largest demand for elementary schooling.

TABLE 4.2

Age of Head of Household	Percentages			
	Fleet Road	Grafton Terrace	Mansfield Road	South-hill Park
Old (over 60)	9.7	11.8	12.5	17.0
Middle-aged (40–59)	37.9	44.6	38.5	50.5
Young (under 40)	52.4	43.6	49.0	32.5

There was again a range of sizes of households (Table 4.3) from 3.86 persons in Fleet Road to 6.7 in South-hill Park. While the high figure of the latter could in part be explained by the presence of servants, families were also larger, averaging 2.64 as against 1.98 in Fleet Road. Clearly the more youthful nature of the population in Fleet Road meant that families were in an early stage of producing children. While the proportion of servants was higher in South-hill Park than in the other streets, the figure for Mansfield Road indicates some presence there also. Here one in four households had one general servant. The scholar–non-scholar ratios suggest that by 1881 there was no longer a major problem in getting children enrolled at school, with over 90 per cent figures in each case. This did not of course necessarily imply regular attendance.

TABLE 4.3

	Fleet Road	Grafton Terrace	Mansfield Road	South-hill Park
Average Size of Household	3.86	4.54	4.68	6.70
Av. No. of Children per Household	1.98	2.20	1.97	2.64
Av. No. of Servants per Household	0.05	0.004	0.230	1.29
Scholar/Non Scholar Ratio	94.4%	95.8%	91.8%	97.5%

Moving on to poverty/comfort indicators, an important measure is crowding, here expressed in terms of multi-occupation (Table 4.4).

TABLE 4.4

Houses with	Fleet Road	Grafton Terrace	Mansfield Road	South-hill Park
More than 1 Household	90%	69.4%	50.4%	6.2%
3 and more Households	61.4%	36.7%	14.2%	–
4 and more Households	34.2%	6.1%	0.8%	–
5 Households	8.6%	–	–	–

89

Having taken into account varying sizes of houses, it remains clear that Fleet Road suffered from the most serious over-crowding, while South-hill Park benefited from the least, confirming Booth's assessment of Fleet Road's problems. A similar picture emerges from Table 4.5 which attempts to analyse socio-economic groupings, based on an adaptation of Anderson's scheme, in which SEG I covers higher professional groups; SEG II lower professional; SEG IIIa skilled white-collar workers; SEG IIIb skilled blue-collar; SEG IV semi-skilled manual; and SEG V unskilled, often casual labouring groups.[45] While cautious interpretation is needed, not least because descriptors of occupation in the returns were the layman's definition, not a sophisticated academic category, a definitive aggregate picture emerges, and one confirming the general accuracy of Booth's survey. Table 4.5 indicates that the Fleet Road catchment, in which three of the streets shown were significant contributors to the intake, did not draw on zones of SEG I population. At the other extreme, Fleet Road itself was one of the few streets with significant numbers in SEG V.

TABLE 4.5

	Percentages			
SEG	Fleet Road	Grafton Terrace	Mansfield Road	South-hill Park
I	–	–	–	12.8
II	12.9	14.4	49.7	71.8
IIIa	9.0	17.0	22.6	12.8
IIIb	27.9	47.9	23.7	1.0
IV	24.0	9.3	3.0	0.6
V	26.2	11.4	0.3	1.0

Hence a definite social hierarchy emerges, from Fleet Road at the lower end through Grafton Terrace and Mansfield Road to South-hill Park. But there was heterogeneity within each street. Thus over 95 per cent of Mansfield Road's population was in the range of SEGs II, III and IIIb, but this inevitably meant within individual households, let alone within the street, the emergence of subtle status differences. At the street level, Fleet Road was largely manual working-class, Grafton Terrace shaded tangibly into a more respectable working-class/lower-middle-class bracket. Mansfield Road was lower-middle class, while the inhabitants of South-hill Park were genuinely within the servant-keeping middle-class stratum, though well short of the social heights of Belsize Park.

A final piece of evidence from the census enumerators' returns was the presence or absence of working wives. A very large majority of wives did not work, but there were variations between the four streets, as shown on Table 4.6, the larger percentage in Fleet Road reflecting the wives of poorer families working as charwomen, taking in washing and the like.

TABLE 4.6

		Percentages		
	Fleet Road	Grafton Terrace	Mansfield Road	South-hill Park
Working wives	5.76	1.03	1.09	1.53

A more detailed sense of place can be achieved by comparing social material from the census enumerators' returns with a visual recording of matched houses or groups of houses, in this case of recent photographs of houses still standing. While large areas of Gospel Oak and the south side of Fleet Road and Mansfield Road have been demolished, the original dwellings survive on the north sides of these streets, as Plate 9 shows.

Plate 10 is a recent photograph of numbers 22 and 24 and part of 26 Fleet Road. In 1881, prior to renumbering, these were 55 to 57. This group of houses was recorded by Booth as in mixed poverty and comfort. The 1881 census returns show 55 and 56 as occupied respectively by five and four households, and collectively accommodating 32 people. Of these, only eight were of school age. Of those in employment, ten out of twelve were in SEGs IV and V, including a railway porter, two brick-makers (suggesting the local nuisance of the brick-field was still in operation), two labourers, a sweep and a domestic servant. The 1916 admissions registers show children from numbers 20 and 24 enrolled at Fleet Road School. This was very much the poorer end of Fleet Road. Higher up the street, the SEGs included almost as many in III as in IV/V, with occupations including clerks and transport workers, as well as gardeners and workers in the building trade.

The picture of numbers 31 to 37 Grafton Terrace (Plate 11) is of houses which were, with one exception, in single occupation in 1881. The heads of households were in SEGs II, IIIa and IIIb

10. 22/26 Fleet Road   11. 31/37 Grafton Terrace,
                                        West Kentish Town

and included carpenters, a decorator, a railway clerk and a rent collector. From No. 29, just off the photograph, the Merrian children, their father a railway clerk, attended Fleet Road School, and in 1901 and 1903 respectively won junior scholarships of the London Technical Instruction Board. Children from No. 31 attended the school in the 1916–18 period. Apart from the other evidence, the setting back of the houses from the road, and the bay windows, testify to a higher status social setting than Fleet Road, albeit not one in absolutely secure comfort.

The photograph of Mansfield Road (Plate 12) suggests a further rise in the social spectrum, with more elaborately moulded bay windows and canopies over the doors. Of these six houses in 1881, three were singly occupied and three by two families. The average number per house was eight, and all the heads of households were in SEGs II, IIIa and IIIb. One was a boarding-house keeper, one a clerk and one a teacher, for example. The teacher was none other than James Walker, husband of Louisa Walker, headmistress of Fleet Road infants' school (Chapter 6).

This group of houses produced three scholarship winners for the school in the 1900–3 period, sons of a cook and two journeyman carpet-workers.

Plate 13 covers ten houses, all under single occupation in 1881, in South-hill Park. Two of the heads of households were in SEG I and the rest in SEG II. These included a broker, an engineer, an engraver, a managing clerk, a solicitor, two civil servants and a retired farmer. Two of the households kept three servants, two kept two, and the rest had one. Fifty-six people lived in these ten large, four-storey houses, of whom only four were children of

12. 28/38 Mansfield Road, Gospel Oak

13. 57/75 South-hill Park, Hampstead

school age. One produced one of the nine scholars who attended Fleet Road School from South-hill Park and South-hill Park Gardens in the 1916–18 period.

By 1916, the admissions registers of Fleet Road give a more detailed picture of the social nature of the school's catchment at that time. The situation in Fleet Road itself appears to have changed little, the children coming from families of small shop-keepers, men in building trades, with a sprinkling of skilled and semi-skilled workers. There is a hint that Mansfield Road had possibly sunk a little on the social scale by this stage, with the large majority of children in SEGs IIIa and IIIb, and not in II. By this stage the Walkers had left for a more up-market area (Chapter 6) and it may well be that the upwardly aspiring families who settled on the street in the 1870s and 1880s had moved up the social ladder.

Apart from this, there is little tangible evidence that the social intake of the school during the First World War was different from that in Adams' period. The vast majority of the children came from white-collar and skilled artisan families, with a minority only of children of unskilled workers. There is oral testimony offered by two brothers who attended the school prior to the First World War, giving detail on the Fleet Road neighbourhood itself. Their grandfather was a signalman who lived in Gospel Oak Grove (Map 8) and worked at Gospel Oak Station. Their father, one of six children who attended Fleet Road School, was a liftman at Euston Station. One of the brothers recalls living on Fleet Road, and attending school with the children of postmen, railway men, boot and shoe repairers, policemen and shop assistants. The other remembers school-mates who were the sons of a butcher, a baker, a boot repairer, a provisions merchant, a gymnasium caretaker, a postman, a civil servant, and two railway personnel.[46] Of course living on Fleet Road would give a slight skew to the sample. It seems to reflect very closely what might have been expected from this locality.

TRAVELLING TO SCHOOL

As already indicated, a frequent complaint of the guardians of the ratepayer interest in Hampstead was that Fleet Road School was overcrowded because of its policy of recruiting middle-class children who lived a long distance away from the school. It has been shown that the charge was exaggerated. At the same time, there is no doubt that Fleet Road did attract a larger proportion of train children than was normal for a non-secondary school. Of a sample of nearly 50 of its scholarship winners, ten were children of teachers, and all of these travelled in from afar. It could be inferred that they benefited from knowledgeable parents playing the system. It is worth speculating on how easy it was for such pupils to travel to and from school daily. One obvious mode was the railway, with nearby stations at Haverstock Hill (Map 8) and Hampstead Heath (Map 3).

Bradshaw railway timetables for the period[47] illustrate the time element involved. For children living in Upper Holloway and Tufnell Park, and some of these certainly attended the school, a journey of over a mile each way meant public transport was a necessary means of travel. Such children could have caught the 8.32 from Upper Holloway (also the 8.36 from Highgate Road), changed at Kentish Town, and arrived at Haverstock Hill at 8.45, in time for a 9.00 a.m. start. Those living in the West Hampstead and Finchley Road districts could have met the 8.37 from West Hampstead (also the 8.40 from Finchley Road), and reached Haverstock Hill at 8.44.

Trains similarly arrived at Hampstead Heath Station from points east at 8.44 and 8.48. Children from Canonbury could catch trains at 8.12 and 8.27, and those getting on at Highbury, Barnsbury and Camden Town a little later than this. From the other direction a train passing through Willesden at 8.37 and Brondesbury at 8.43 arrived at Hampstead Heath at 8.49. For the odd child in west London, there was a service running round from Mansion House via Victoria, Earl's Court, Uxbridge Road and Willesden Junction, the train arriving at Hampstead Heath at 8.34.

While it is highly conjectural as to how many Fleet Road children used these services, the possibilities of journeying to school were present, and there are several references in the records to train children. The proximity of the school to two suburban stations was therefore of dual benefit. On the one hand, the Fleet Road immediate catchment area attracted clerks and shopworkers who travelled into the City and the West End, because the nearby railways made commuting so convenient. The railways equally facilitated a counter-movement of youthful commuters, train schoolboys and girls. In this way Fleet Road, a higher-grade school but technically in the elementary sector, matched the success of prestigious secondary schools in persuading parents that the wear and tear, and indeed hazards, of daily travel to school from a distance were worthwhile.

REFERENCES AND NOTES

1. *The Practical Teacher*, vol. 15 (1894), p.2.
2. *London*, vol. 7 (1898), p.153.
3. C. Morley, *Studies in Board Schools* (London, 1897), pp.85–7.
4. PRO Ed. 5/64.
5. PRO Ed. 5/65.
6. LSB, *Report of Works Committee*, 3 April 1878.
7. LSB, *Report of Works Committee*, 5 June 1878.
8. LSB, *Report of Statistical Committee*, 17 July 1878.
9. LSB, *Report of Works Committee*, 11 Dec. 1878.
10. LSB, *Report of Works Committee*, 18 Dec. 1878.
11. LSB, *Report of School Management Committee*, 22 Jan. 1879.
12. LSB, *Report of Statistical Committee*, 12 Feb. 1879, and *Report of Works Committee*, 23 April 1879.
13. LSB, *Report of Statistical Committee*, 3 March 1880. Also PRO Ed. 14/12, letter from London School Board dated 4 March 1880.
14. LSB, *Report of Finance Committee*, 12 May 1880.
15. LSB, *Report of Statistical Committee*, 24 Feb. 1881. Also PRO Ed. 21/11580, letter from London School Board dated 28 Feb. 1881.
16. LSB, *Report of Statistical Committee*, 16 Nov. 1882.
17. LSB, *Report of Works Committee*, 12 April 1883.
18. LSB, *Report of Works Committee*, 31 Jan. 1884.
19. LSB, *Report of Works Committee*, 31 July 1890.
20. LSB, 29 Oct. 1903, pp.902–3.
21. PRO Ed. 21/11580, letter from London School Board dated 10 July 1896.
22. PRO Ed. 7/75, dated 12 Feb. 1879.
23. PRO Ed. 21/11580, dated 12 May 1883.
24. *HHE*, 11 Jan. 1879.
25. LSB *Final Report* (London, 1904), p.35.
26. R. Ringshall, M. Miles, F. Kelsall, *The Urban School: Buildings for Education in London 1870–1980* (London, 1983), p.18.
27. *HHE*, 11 Jan. 1879.
28. C. Booth, *Police Notes* (Booth Collection, London School of Economics), District 20, A.38, pp.21–2.
29. *Ibid.*, p.22.
30. For a fuller account, see W.E. Marsden, 'Residential Segregation and the Hierarchy of Elementary Schooling from Charles Booth's London Surveys', *The London Journal*, vol. 11 (1985), pp.131–4.
31. M. Tabor, 'Elementary Education', in C. Booth (ed.), *Labour and Life of the People: London, Vol. II* (London, 1891), p.508. See also note 19 in Chapter 2.
32. LSB, *Report of School Management Committee*, 4 Dec. 1878.
33. LSB, *Report of School Management Committee*, 28 Feb. 1884.
34. LSB, *Reports of School Management Committee*, 28 June 1888 and 19 July 1888.
35. LSB, *Report of School Management Committee*, 23 July 1891.
36. *HHE*, 26 Sept. 1885.
37. *HHE*, 3 Oct. 1885.

38. *HHE*, 17 Oct. 1885.
39. *HHE*, 24 Oct. 1885. The account which follows is largely based on this issue.
40. SBL 669, *School Management Committee*, 28 Sept. and 12 Oct. 1894.
41. *Ibid.*, 2 April and 7 May 1897.
42. *Cross Commission*, 2nd Report (1887), p.48.
43. *Ibid.*, p.45.
44. For a fuller methodological account see W.E. Marsden, 'Census Enumerators' Returns, Schooling and Social Areas in the Late Victorian Town: a Case Study of Bootle', in R. Lowe (ed.), *New Approaches to the Study of Popular Education, 1851–1902* (Leicester, 1979), pp.16–33; and W.E. Marsden, 'Social Environment, School Attendance and Educational Achievement in a Merseyside Town 1870–1900' in P. McCann (ed.), *Popular Education and Socialization in the Nineteenth Century* (London, 1977), pp.214–24.
45. *Ibid.*, pp.196–7. See also W.A. Armstrong, 'The Use of Information about Occupation', in E.A. Wrigley (ed.), *Nineteenth Century Society: Essays in the Use of Quantitative Methods for the Study of Social Data* (Cambridge, 1972), pp.191–223.
46. I am grateful for this information to Messrs. A. and H.J. Newcombe, who attended Fleet Road School prior to the First World War.
47. *Bradshaw's Railway Guide*, Aug. 1887 (Newton Abbot, 1968 reprint), pp.181–3 and 246–7.

CHAPTER FIVE

The Headteachers:
The Adams Family

The Fleet-road, Hampstead, School of the School Board for London has for years past stood as an object-lesson in the practical possibilities of School Board management, where the conditions are, not by any means extravagantly, but reasonably favourable. The children of that school have had the happiness to fall into the hands of a headmaster and mistress, in the persons of Mr. and Mrs. W.B. Adams, who perceived opportunities of service and success in their position under the Board, which others might have overlooked. They were not satisfied with working in a groove, nor with the mere fulfilment of the specific duties of their position. They sought and found occasion for such liberal enlargements of the conception of their office, as have made the Fleet-road School the distinctive corporate entity which every school some day will become ... amongst the elementary schools of London, Fleet-road has led the way towards that healthy individualism, those human relationships between teachers and scholars which are the invaluable characteristics of the life of the English public schools. They had the good fortune, at a fairly early stage, to enlist the personal interest of several influential members of the Board in their plans and endeavours. But that interest was gained and retained because their work was good and their ideas were practical as well as lofty. What Fleet-road is, every Board School, according to its own sphere and circumstance, some day may be.[1]
School Board Chronicle, 1898

THE ADAMS FAMILY

William Bateman and Mary Adams, like the Groomes at Carlton Road (Chapter 3) and James and Louisa Walker (Chapter 6) formed a London School Board headteacher pairing. Reconstructing their daily journey to school from their residence at

10, Willow Road (Plate 14), it may be inferred that they walked down the hill, with an open view of Hampstead Heath on their left, leaving the breakfast things for their two servants to clear away. Past Hampstead Heath station and the tram terminus at South End (Map 3) they would presumably have turned left into Constantine Road, thence into Agincourt Road as far as the school entrance.

14. 10 Willow Road, home of the Adams family

In this journey they daily traversed a social divide between the red streets of Booth's classification to the north of the railway, and the pink streets and, in the case of Fleet Road, purple, to the south. The Adams family embodied meritocratic advance. Earlier residential moves in London were consistent with upward mobility. On leaving Finchley in 1870 (p. 103), the Adams had first lived at 254, Caledonian Road, a 'pink' thoroughfare near King's Cross station, not an entirely salubrious neighbourhood. In 1877 they moved to a more desirable residential area in St. John's Wood. Their new home was in Lorne Gardens, in a block of property 'occupied mainly by well-to-do people keeping servants'[2] facing Regent's Park. The detached houses of this 'red' street were surrounded by even more prestigious 'yellow' avenues. Though Adams became the head of Fleet Road school in 1878, the family, including his son and sister-in-law, were still resident in Lorne Gardens at the time of the 1881 census. Soon afterwards they moved to a not dissimilar location, Heath Rise, later to be renamed Willow Road. Here the houses, on the basis of prices at the end of the nineteenth century, averaging in fact £1,225, suggest that by their late thirties the Adams had achieved an affluent status for the time. Their income was sufficient to maintain two servants,[3] a criterion of genuine middle-class status.

William Bateman Adams (Plate 15) was born at Orielton, near Pembroke, on 20 September 1841. His father, John Adams, taught at Stackpole National School, about three miles away from Orielton. In February 1848 he informed Borough Road teacher training institution that he wished to spend two or three months there to gain a thorough knowledge of the British School system, prior to becoming headmaster of Pembroke

15. William Bateman Adams

Dock British School, opening in July 1848. He asked for cheap accommodation to be found for his family, including four young children.[4] The Pembroke Dock British School Committee had already appealed to the British and Foreign School Society for funds to equip their new school, and asked that Mr. and Mrs. Adams should spend time at the College, as their previous teaching experience of five or six years had been in a National School.[5] It would seem therefore that they had both been appointed to the school, for a combined salary of £70 for the first year was mentioned. A 'commodious house' was provided.[6] HMI Joseph Fletcher was later to appraise Pembroke Dock British School as near to being a model of its type.

John Adams subsequently became headmaster of Swansea British School, and here his son William Bateman served as pupil teacher, prior to entering Bangor Training College as a Queen's Scholar.[8] In his evidence to the Cross Commission, Adams revealed that he would have preferred to attend Carmarthen College, only 30 miles from Swansea, but was debarred because he was not a member of the Church of England.[9]

For a time the waters of family history become muddied. In his responses to the Cross Commission and in an interview for a feature in *The Practical Teacher* (1894), Adams claims that his first appointment at Pembroke British School,[10] where he became master in charge on completion of his training in 1863, lasted until 1868.[11] The records of the British and Foreign School Society tell a fuller story of a period of storm and stress.

In 1865 Mary Jannaway was appointed as an assistant teacher at Swansea British School. Daughter of a shoemaker, she was born in Brentford, Middlesex, on 9 November 1844. She was a pupil teacher at Brentford British School prior to entering the British and Foreign School Society's Stockwell College in 1863. Here she qualified, in the First Division, after two years' training. Following her application to Swansea, John Adams wrote to the Society to say that she would be given every encouragement but hoped she would give the school 'her undivided attention' and would be 'willing to take a kind hint or two'.[12]

Here she presumably entered into the relationship with John Adams' son, and as early as November 1865 it was clear the couple were determined to be married. This caused some consternation because she needed to complete a year at Swansea before gaining her parchment. The local agent and schools inspector of the British and Foreign School Society, David Williams, expressed concern that her intended partner 'would not hear of it'.[13] John Adams shared this anxiety.

I am sure the two young people would be very unhappy if they knew the Society suffered anything by them. They are both very conscientious and beloved and respected by all who know them, and as a parent I should be very sorry to mar their happiness especially as the match is approved by all the parties concerned.[14]

A further letter informed the Society that the marriage would take place at Christmas,[15] but was quickly followed by the news that William Bateman had acceded to his bride-to-be remaining at Swansea until the June inspection, so ensuring that the grant the College would receive once Mary had gained her parchment was not jeopardized. The inspection over, her parchment secured, the couple were free to join each other in the summer of 1866. But she was not to move to Pembroke.

A letter from William Bateman Adams to the Society in August 1866, addressed from Cyfarthfa Schools, Cefn, Merthyr Tydfil, recorded that he and his wife had been engaged together at the local school. But they had to present their testimonials personally to the manager. In asking the Society for a testimonial, Adams mentioned that they would both have preferred an appointment in England, 'as we do not understand the Welsh language'.[17] A later communication confessed that their ignorance of Welsh was 'a great drawback to our complete success as teachers ... We are quite excluded from any converse with parents, and have two miles from an English place of worship.' He had resolved to move to England, and sought the Society's support to gain an appointment for one or both of them, preferably in the London area.[18]

Asked to provide more details about himself, Adams informed the Society that he was 26 years old and was connected with the Calvinistic Methodist denomination. He was looking for a post with a minimum salary of £100 and a house, or a joint salary of £140–150 for them both, preferably in London, following the spring or midsummer vacation of 1867.[19] Apparently these demands elicited a starchy response, for in a hasty follow-up letter Adams stressed that he was not 'in the remotest degree [doubly underlined] activated by pecuniary motives [also doubly underlined]'. But his reasons for leaving Merthyr were so urgent that he had already handed in notice of resignation as from 25 March 1867. He was prepared to accept as a starting salary what the Society considered 'a fair and reasonable remuneration for beginners in a new district.'[20]

The Merthyr experience was evidently a traumatic one for Adams and his wife, and was suppressed in later public accounts he gave of their professional careers. But from this point their fortunes improved. The British and Foreign School Society was in the process of finding staff for a new British School in Finchley, and had been informed by Thomas Hill, spokesman of the Committee setting up the school, that they favoured the idea of appointing Mr. and Mrs. Adams. The Society was requested to undertake the negotiations on salary, to ensure they were 'presentable people', and supply further details about them. Hill indicated his Committee was not short of funds and intended to make the Finchley schools second to none in the district.[21]

Adams accepted the salary offered and agreed that any future increase would depend on results.[22] He expressed his pleasure at the new appointment. 'I am certain that the present place does not agree with my health.'[23] His salary was to be £120, plus one-tenth of government grant. He was also to be offered fuel at a nominal rate.[24] Another letter from Cefn evinced surprise that prior to formal appointment they had received a visit from a member of the Finchley Committee: 'rather an unusual course of procedure ... but I don't think I have any reason to regret the ordeal.'[25] The visitor from Finchley had evidently been impressed, and returned with 'a very favourable report'.[26]

On moving to Finchley Adams and his wife took up residence in Homan's Cottages in nearby Whetstone. A letter to the Society conveyed his satisfaction that the Committee had agreed to accept government grant.[27] It was thus an inspected school. It would seem Adams had some success. The grant for the 74 pupils in average attendance in 1868 was £15/18/3d,[28] which had risen, for the same number of pupils, to £24/10/8d in 1870.[29] But he left in 1870. A letter from Hill confirmed that the Adamses had 'done good service'.[30] The main family event in Finchley was the birth of their only son, John William Bateman, on 11 June 1868.

The next move represented a considerable step up the professional ladder. It was an appointment as Headmaster of Portland Street, off Langham Place, the largest elementary school in the West End. The surroundings of the school were later described by Booth as 'very mixed'.[31] Portland Street British School appears on the official records as receiving grant in 1861. In 1870, on Adams' arrival, its average attendance was 424 and grant £184/19/0d.[32] The fees for most of the pupils were from 2d to 4d, but a handful paid between 4d and 9d,[33] suggesting a favourable social location.

Portland Street School had been founded by Dr. James Martineau. The Unitarians had raised £8,000 for the new buildings, and had not called on government support. Adams later remarked that his appointment was on the recommendation of Matthew Arnold. Arnold had written to Martineau thus:

I seldom interfere in the appointment of teachers, but Mr. Adams is so efficient a teacher, that I cannot help writing to say that I think him so. You need have no anxiety, as he is a certain success.[34]

Apparently Arnold had known John Adams for in a letter to W.B. Adams he acknowledged:

I shall always be interested in your success, especially as the son of a teacher who at one time conducted one of the most remarkable elementary schools in the country.[35]

Adams was soon to be disenchanted with his new school, however, as religious differences of opinion arose. In an anxious letter to the British and Foreign School Society in 1874 he complained that the 'Church Party' there was 'very strong' and 'would move heaven and earth to injure us'.[36] The situation worsened in 1875, prompting John Adams to intercede on his son's behalf. He wrote to the Society to suggest that the problems had arisen on Martineau's retirement as 'chief manager'. The new manager

wishes all the teachers to be Unitarians and my son says he cannot submit to this ... The whole thing is plain. Mr. Alderson [the Marylebone HMI] and Mr. Matthew Arnold know all about my son, and report on his school as being the best in Marylebone. He says he should like a 'Board School' and if possible in Marylebone ... You see the case is very peculiar. My son's connections are evidently not Unitarian. He has been brought up with orthodox views. Can you possibly aid him in this matter? I am so sorry for him. He has worked very hard ... He is very intelligent, and has splendid practice and good experience.[37]

The Society duly approached the London School Board, as a letter of thanks from W.B. Adams verifies. He assured the Secretary of the Society that anything suggested would be treated as 'strictly confidential'.[38] A letter of February 1876 tells that the situation had not altered and that he was 'resolved to adhere to what my conscience tells me is the right course to pursue'.[39] The possibility of a post at Buckhurst Hill was suggested, but as the school was small and there was no opening for Mrs. Adams the offer was declined.[40] Another proposal was refused on the grounds that his wife 'would not care to accept any appointment except as Headmistress of a girls' school'.[41] Again in 1877 he declined to move because the post was outside London. He wished for an appointment in a good board school within the metropolis. This he found in Gospel Oak, though in the first place in temporary accommodation in Rochford Street in the former buildings of Gospel Oak Schools, later to become the William Ellis School.[42] The Board had identified a deficiency of 760 school places in this district in 1877. It was agreed the old schoolhouse should be used for one year only, prior to the erection of a new school, in Fleet Road.[43]

Adams left Portland British School in February 1878. Despite the religious difficulties, the work there had brought him favourable publicity. He had written a history text-book (see Chapter 8). Some of his pupils had won early scholarships from the London School Board, and this and the favourable reports of HMI C.H. Alderson had drawn him to the attention of Lyulph Stanley and James Watson of the School Board.[44] He received a good testimonial from James Martineau, notwithstanding the religious wrangles in which he had been entangled.

Mr. Adams' conspicuous success here during the last eight years has been due to his rare skill as an organiser, his untiring zeal and enthusiasm, and the stimulating power of his own quick intelligence among the scholars. His honourable ambition to equip his scholars for the front rank in the competitions of their life is sufficient alone to stamp him as a teacher of the first order. The anxiety with which the managers receive his resignation is the sincerest tribute they can render to the value of his services.[45]

While sufficiently convinced of Adams' qualities to appoint him to the headship of Fleet Road in 1878, the London School Board were not entirely satisfied with his qualifications. Adams had not fulfilled all the Board's criteria for appointment and had to undergo the indignity of obtaining a complete full Drawing Certificate and at least one advanced Science Certificate in the course of his first year.[46] His starting salary was £145 per annum. It rose to £155 in March 1880 on receipt of a good report.[47] To this was added a share of grant based on the last examination. In each of his first five years Adams received a £10 increment for a good report. By 1884 his fixed salary had reached £185 but a £223 share of grant gave a total of £408.[48] His financial position was helped by increasing numbers as well as good reports. By the time of the Cross Commission there were 901 children in the Senior Mixed School, of which 258 were in Standard III, 206 in IV, 182 in V, 142 in VI, and 113 in VII and Ex-VII,[49] a remarkable total in the higher standards for that time.

During W. B. Adams's incumbency of Portland Street British school, his wife became an employee of the London School Board. She was first appointed to Campbell Street, Paddington,[50] and from 1877–81 to Nightingale Street, Lisson Grove.[51] Nightingale Street was not far from the Adams' home in Lorne Gardens, albeit across a major divide in terms of social distance. The proximity of Lorne Gardens to her school was presumably the reason for the family delaying a move to Hampstead. This came when she was appointed Headmistress of Netherwood Street, a new board school in Kilburn, in November 1881. Kilburn was at the western end of Hampstead, in an almost mirror image situation to Fleet Road. The area round the school had been 'transformed during the last few years into a neighbourhood closely resembling the thickly populated portions of Kentish Town which bound the parish of Hampstead on its eastern side'.

Netherwood Street was Hampstead's second board school, Fleet Road being the first. The local newspaper highlighted the fact that the new Headmistress was the wife of W. B. Adams, Headmaster of Fleet Road school. Both schools, it was stressed, were located on the extreme edges of the parish: 'Hampstead was on a hill, very difficult to be got at by cabs or School Boards, or anything else which tried to reach it.' The opening celebrations at Netherwood Street were concluded by a concert in which the Fleet Road staff took part. The Adamses were moving closer together professionally. The *Hampstead and Highgate Express* hoped that Mr. and Mrs. Adams 'would be able so to work as to join hands in a third school at Hampstead'.[52] This somewhat opaque comment was to prove, in a way, prophetic.

Inspectors' reports on Netherwood Street were good. The London School Board inspector described the school in 1883 as 'in excellent order' having passed a 'very creditable examination'.[53] Similarly the government report of that year indicated that despite teething troubles caused by two abnormally large lower standards, the work showed 'thoroughness and good quality'.[54]

After two years at Netherwood Street, Mary Adams successfully applied for the headship of the new Junior Mixed Department at Fleet Road.[55] The Department, 420 children strong, took Standards I and II. Like her husband, she consistently achieved annual increments for good reports, though at the rate of £4 as against £10 for a male headteacher. By 1894 her salary had reached £260 per annum,[56] giving a combined income for the family of over £650.

To an extent, the Junior Mixed Department basked in the glory of the Senior Mixed, making secondary contributions to concerts and prize-givings. For ten years or so after her appointment, all seemed well with Mary Adams' department, but from 1895 she suffered frequent bouts of ill-health. In the summer of 1895 she was absent for sixty days with 'nervous debility', for example, and in November 1897 for twelve days as a result of insomnia. She also had time off for colds, headaches and indigestion. In 1897 she was warned that her salary would in future be stopped if she failed to supply a medical certificate when absent. She retired early, aged 53, in June 1898. Then until 1903 she filled in as a supply teacher when staff were away.

Her retirement occasion was described in the local press as 'an unique presentation', the account being headed 'The Apotheosis of the School Mistress'. She was given a silver entrée dish, a silver tray with monogram, an escritoire, chairs and tapestry screen in dark mahogany, and an elaborate autograph album headed 'Floreat Fleetonia', and signed by managers, staff and 'other friends of education'. The album included an ode written by 'no less a poet' than Sir Lewis Morris.

> Thrice happy lot, content to bear
> The load of Duty to the end
> The Teacher's crown of Work to wear
> Which in each Learner gains a friend.
>
> Besides life's silent liturgies
> What profits rank, or gold, or name
> A brighter radiance shines on these
> Than lights the pinnacles of fame.

Contributors to the testimonial numbered an impressive range of well-known names including, from the educational establishment, Sir George Kekewich, Lyulph Stanley, members of the inspectorate, principals of training colleges, university representatives, and also bishops, nobles and members of parliament.

The Chairman of the occasion noted that Mary Adams had been 'sandwiched' in the Junior Mixed Department 'between two noble schools, the famous Senior School and the equally famous Infants' Department' but had 'done good work' in her own right. The school was sorry to lose her, but was glad in a way, 'for of all men in the world who needed a peaceful home those connected with education should have it'. W.B. Adams responded to the effect that his wife 'had helped him in many times of difficulty'. Following the vote of thanks to his own wife for presenting the testimonial, Kekewich regretted Mrs. Adams' retirement but returned jocularly to the domesticity theme opining, to laughter, that

lady teachers had harder work than men, for they had to look after children at home as well as at school, and besides disciplining their scholars had to discipline their husbands. All the world of education knew how much Mrs. Adams had helped to make Fleet-road a great school. She had aided in bringing about that *esprit de corps* which had made all the scholars proud of it. She had aided her husband in the best work that could possibly be done.

Having accepted the presentation, Mary Adams modestly claimed to be undeserving of the good things said.[57] The British and Foreign School Society's *Educational Record* joined 'heartily in the all-round congratulations and good wishes' offered to their former Stockwell College student, and noted that W.B. Adams was now head of both the Senior and Junior departments at the school.[58] The occasion was also recorded by the *School Board Chronicle*, describing Mary Adams as the wife of the 'popular Headmaster of Fleet Road Board Schools, Hampstead'.[59]

Five years later W.B. Adams fell mortally ill after a heart attack at the school. The local newspaper recorded that in the week before his death his wife and trained nurses had cared for him night and day. But she was not mentioned as present at the funeral, where the son was the chief mourner.[60] Neither did she attend the unveiling of the W.B. Adams' memorial tablet at a ceremony at the school in October 1903, though she wrote to say that she was 'with them in spirit'.[61] It must be presumed that her nervous state or some physical ailment made it impossible for her to attend. She herself died from heart failure at 10, Willow Road on 18 February 1918, aged 73. John William Bateman Adams was again the chief mourner. The local newspaper seemed to have forgotten her own significance as a headteacher, recording her merely as the wife of W.B. Adams, formerly headteacher of Fleet Road School.[62] For a woman teacher she had attained relatively high status. But caught between the dominating personalities of her husband in the Senior Mixed Department, and Louisa Walker in the Infant, she was inevitably consigned to a secondary role. Following W.B. Adams' death, apart from the brief mention of her own death, she fades from the records.[63]

As already noted, the Adamses had one son, born in 1868 during the time they were at Finchley. John William Bateman was also to become a teacher, his progress as proudly and concernedly followed as W.B's had been by John Adams. As W.B. Adams declared to the interviewer from *The Practical Teacher* in 1894:

There is something in heredity; I think I inherited my love of school work, and I trust my son ... may also carry on the tradition and be successful in some branch of educational work.[64]

Adams might have added that his brother, F.J. Adams, had also been a pupil teacher at his father's school and gone on to Bangor Training College. After a short teaching career in Wales he followed his brother as Headmaster at Finchley British Schools, before moving on to Whitefield Tabernacle Schools, City Road, a career line astonishingly similar at that stage to that of W.B. Adams. Thereafter he pursued a different course, in 1879 being appointed Clerk to the first Tottenham School Board. He was called to the Bar in 1888. He was frequently invited to social events at Fleet Road. He died in 1901.[65]

The help of heredity and family patronage was to reproduce itself in the case of J.W.B. Adams. He was a pupil teacher at Fleet Road from 1883 to 1886. Here he made regular contributions to the musical events, both as singer and accompanist. He came 25th out of a national total of 128 in the entry examinations to Borough Road College. John William Bateman was a pupil at Fleet Road just prior to its surge of successes in the scholarship stakes. At Borough Road he was 13th on the lists at the end of his first year and 23rd out of 29 in the First Division at the end of his second.[66]

Credentials as well as family support were, of course, required.

Credentials J. W. B. Adams acquired with some avidity. He was awarded an M.A. by Pembroke College, Oxford, in 1894, and a B.A. at London in 1900.[67] In 1894 he accepted a temporary appointment at Borough Road College, with which the Adams family, as we have seen, had had long connections. Here he tutored in classics and literature. The situation did not develop to his father's liking, however, on the evidence of a confidential letter to the Secretary of the British and Foreign School Society, in which W. B. Adams referred to 'the shabby treatment of the Principal' towards his son. But he was pleased that in the event this had proved to be a 'blessing in disguise'. Adams was at this time an influential member of the Pembroke County Club. Nostalgia for this English part of Wales was strong. During the 1890s the Adamses holidayed at Tenby. At the London branch of the County Club, W. B. Adams met the M.P. for Pembroke and informed him of his son's problems at Borough Road. The M.P. mentioned that a headteacher was required for a new school in Tenby. The result of this conversation proved 'most gratifying to us all'. The post was the Principalship of Tenby Intermediate and Technical School. W. B. Adams described the appointment as 'most desirable in every way'.[68] The Principal was to be responsible for the appointment of new staff, and was offered a house. In addition to personal lobbying, J. W. B. Adams was able to provide powerful testimonials, from Lyulph Stanley and no fewer than five members of Oxford colleges, including the Master and Dean of Pembroke College.[69] The new school was officially opened by the Mayor of Tenby in September 1896, with an intake of 40 boys and girls.[70]

The following year J. W. B. Adams returned to Hampstead to marry Pauline Alberta Laura Frank. The bride was the daughter of a local naturalist, resident in Haverstock Hill, a generally prestigious 'red' and 'yellow' thoroughfare, according to Booth. The wedding was described in the local newspaper as of 'considerable local interest', attended by a 'fashionable company'.[71] It marked socially for J. W. B. Adams what his degrees signified professionally: upward mobility.

J. W. B. Adams' career at Tenby is well recorded in Wilfred Harrison's history of the school.[72] His approach faithfully reflected values imbibed in his educational experience, not least at Fleet Road. Great stress was laid on success in competitive examinations. Entertainments were prominently featured and achieved great local popularity. As had his mother, so Mrs. J.W.B. Adams helped with the concerts and provided tea for visitors. She was apparently not as popular with the pupils as her husband, who was described as 'tall, slim, clean-shaven, light brown hair – impressive – quite definitely elegant – without being obtrusive'. He introduced the practice of boys wearing mortar boards, and of pupils responding 'adsum' when their names were called at registration. He had a maxim there would 'always be hewers of wood and drawers of water'. Like his father he taught history, in a fashion 'most scholarly'.[73]

As early as 1903, however, there were signs of a wish to return to London, though the motivation might have been related to the death at the time of his father. He was one of over 500 applicants for a sub-inspector's job with the London School Board, but failed to gain a place on the 'long short list' of 45.[74] Finally, in January 1911, he was for the second time appointed as Head of a brand new school, Ashford County Secondary School, Middlesex. He took up residence at 7, Hyde Park Mansions, near Baker Street Station, not too far from his parents' earlier residence in Lorne Gardens.

J.W.B. Adams was to remain little over two years at Ashford. Here he was again described as 'tall, slim, silver haired and blue suited with a pleasant voice and pleasant personality'.[75] In October 1913 the governors received the following letter from their Headmaster:

I deeply regret to inform you that in view of a nervous breakdown I am unable to continue my school duties and in consequence am compelled to ask you to accept my resignation. I need hardly say that it is a great grief to me to have to relinquish my work here, and sever my connection with the school which I began and to which I am devoted.[76]

It would seem very likely that the breakdown was associated with estrangement from his wife, who returned to Tenby to marry the Town Clerk there.[77] The professional history of J.W.B. Adams then becomes unclear until 1925, when he was appointed as Head of Christchurch Congregational School, an elementary school which was transferred to the local authority. Named Christchurch Council School, it became a Senior School in 1927. It acquired new buildings in 1931 as Christchurch Senior Central School. This upward translation of a former elementary school enabled Adams to introduce the features he had absorbed so well at Fleet Road and practised at Tenby. Competitive examinations, school concerts and a school magazine were given high priority. As at Tenby, much was made of the Headmaster being an Oxford M.A. It was never pointed out he was once also a pupil teacher. Like his father before him, J.W.B. Adams caused problems locally by concentrating on more able pupils, an extended furore surfacing in 1926–7 as priority given to the senior intake of the school caused a shortage of places at the lower end.[78]

Adams was awarded the M.B.E. in the New Year Honours list of 1933,[79] and retired in March 1934.[80] The *Christchurch Times*[81] noted he had gone to share control of a private preparatory and grammar school at Horsmonden in Kent.[82] He finally returned to Hampstead, finding accommodation in lodgings at 7, Denning Road, just at the back of Willow Road, where he had lived in his youth. He died on 12 January 1946 in New End hospital. The informant at his death was J. Jannaway, no doubt a relative on his mother's side.

W.B. ADAMS AS HEADMASTER OF FLEET ROAD SCHOOL

W.B. Adams built up Fleet Road's reputation above all on its scholarship and choral competition successes, to be considered later. There were other features that made Fleet Road unusual among London schools. Apart from its atypical bungalow form, it was also coeducational and divided into senior and junior mixed departments. Taking his public statements at face value, Adams was committed to both these arrangements, though it needs to be said that when his wife retired his commitment to separately headed departments waned.

Coeducation remained a controversial form of school organization through the board school period. While, as *The School Guardian* debated, some teachers felt the presence of girls created a wholesome rivalry in a school, others argued that the dominant 'moral tendency' was to make the girls 'rough, if not coarse'. The journal concluded that to be successful a mixed school needed extra care from the headteacher, who had to be 'keenly alive to any appearance of over-familiarity between the boys and girls'.[83]

On his appearance before the Cross Commission, Adams was faced with some tough questioning on coeducation. He stuck forcefully to his view that the ideal state of a school should be that of 'a well-ordered family'. He argued that not only were mixed schools more efficient organizationally, but also they created an atmosphere in which the boys became more civilized without hardening the girls.

It is assumed that the school room is the only place where a common atmosphere is pernicious. If so, I think nature erred in sending boys and girls into the same family. Boys and girls are allowed to go everywhere even with the most prudish aunts; they are allowed to go to parties together, to church together, to entertainments together; the school is the only place where they are to be separated. I cannot, for the life of me, understand the logic of that argument.

Adams also proposed that more female teachers were needed in junior mixed departments, covering seven- to nine-year old children. He considered women in many respects equal to men in the upper standards, and found them decidedly superior for classes of younger boys and girls.[84] He believed that manners were improved by the presence of girls, who in turn benefited from the higher academic expectations of girls in mixed than in girls' schools.

They undoubtedly gain in courage and in candour, while their presence has a good influence on the behaviour of the boys, who never like to be punished or disgraced before girls.[85]

While current opinion might, with some justification, judge Adams' arguments for coeducation as flawed, it is equally the case that, so far as many contemporaries were concerned, his views were in advance of their time and over-zealously championed. There is no doubt that girls were important in his curricular and extra-curricular scheme of things, an essential contribution to a school climate that stressed good manners, tidiness, temperance and committed effort. As we shall find (Chapter 8), visitors to a man were impressed by what they perceived as the unusual poise and confidence of the girls of Fleet Road School.

When the population imperatives of the Gospel Oak area made clear that Fleet Road's accommodation needed extension, the London School Board elected to provide an additional building for a Junior Mixed Department. This was staffed by women and pupil teachers. It was here, rather than in the specialist Senior Mixed Department, that pupil teachers followed their apprenticeship. The Senior Mixed Department, technically a higher elementary and then a higher-grade school, took children from Standard III to Ex-VII. An increasing number of teachers were graduates (Chapter 7), a necessary upgrading for the more specialist work demanded in what was in effect a middle school on current definitions.

On his wife's retirement, the arrangement of the school continued as before, but the headship of the Junior Mixed Department lapsed, the two departments being brought under the control of W.B. Adams, though without benefit of additional salary. The day-to-day running of the Junior Mixed Department became the responsibility of a new appointment, of senior teacher status. The appointee was Charlotte Cockram, a former assistant at two prestigious London board schools, Medburn Street and Burghley Road, 32 years old, at a salary of £158. For three years, Adams listed the staff in his log book as belonging to one department, Miss Cockram being described as 'Senior Mistress'.

From 1901, he perhaps felt safe enough to designate the Junior and Senior departments separately, as in Mrs. Adams' time. The merging aroused great controversy. Louisa Walker, Headmistress of the Infants' Department, strongly objected, but was instructed by the School Board to carry out its wishes.[86]

The dispute raged fiercely within the London School Board. Gautrey, the teachers' representative, as a matter of principle objected to the move, interpreted as an economy measure and as limiting the career prospects of women teachers. The Metropolitan Teachers' Association had objected for some years to these amalgamations, one of the leading figures in the campaign being Louisa Walker.[87] On this occasion, Gautrey moved an amendment to preserve the *status quo* at Fleet Road. He was promptly attacked by Lyulph Stanley who made what the journal *London* described as 'one of his few indiscreet speeches', comparing the teachers to the Bricklayers' Union. He accused Gautrey of not liking Fleet Road because its headmaster did not belong to the union of which he was secretary. In turn, another eminent figure on the London School Board, T.J. Macnamara, sprang to Gautrey's defence. He too was criticized by *London* for intemperate remarks.[88]

Macnamara responded to this rebuke, making public the grounds for his criticism of Stanley:

There is a Board School in Hampstead which I think *London* told us ... was 'the finest elementary school in Europe.' The head master of this school is a very estimable gentleman, whose skill as a schoolmaster is only excelled by his anxiety to impress upon School Board members, the Press, and the public generally what a most splendid school his is. Recently the head mistress of what is known as the 'Junior Mixed' department of this school resigned. Whereupon the idea is at once floated – Heaven forbid that I should suggest by whom – that it would be a good plan to let this wonderful schoolmaster take charge of his own and her departments. Yea, and he is found quite ready to do so without addition to his present salary.

So, in good time, this proposal is submitted to the Board. Whereupon Mr. Gautrey ventures to oppose. As an educationist he doubts the ability of even this rare genius properly to supervise the routine of two school departments accommodating some 1,176 children; as a trade unionist he objects to the wiping out of one of the few chances of promotion for our thousands of thoroughly efficient assistant mistresses. In this entirely justified opposition he is at once at variance with that exceedingly quick-tempered and autocratic person, the Hon. Lyulph Stanley, who gets up and denounces Mr. Gautrey for coming to the Board and emulating 'the methods of the Bricklayers' Union.'

This expression strikes me as bad form, coming from a member of the best organised trade union in the country – and I say so.[89]

This is by no means the only piece of evidence that Adams' style and privileged connections did not make him universally popular in London board school circles. The 'jewel in the crown' image disseminated by leading figures of the Education Department and London School Board was hardly calculated to endear the school to the headteachers and staff of other successful but less well publicized board schools. In 1897 a columnist of *The Board Teacher* made sarcastic comment on the boastful spirit he had found in a copy of Fleet Road's school magazine. He had discovered that Kekewich ranked Fleet Road as 'the best public elementary school in the kingdom', that its motto was 'Semper Floreat Fleetonia', and that it contained 'the very aristocracy of masters and pupils'. He noted the school had a choirmaster but no trumpeter. 'Perhaps Mr. W. B. Adams, F.R.Hist.S., does not need a trumpeter.'[90]

Responding, the Headmaster of Barrow Hill Road Board School, a former teacher at Fleet Road, denounced the comment as a 'prostitution' of the journal's columns. He was concerned that the journal of the board school sector was engaged in fouling its own nest. Should it not be uniting the profession against external foes, and concentrating on the major educational issues of the day? The Editor accepted the rebuke about the feature's 'poor fooling', and assured the Fleet Road staff that no reflection upon their excellent results was intended.[91]

In 1898 the journal *London* sounded a more serious cautionary note about the over-competitive climate it sensed at the school. Though its general appraisal of the school was extremely positive, it suggested it should 'beware of becoming too select'.

It has gone a long way in its own district towards breaking down middle class prejudice ... towards board schools; it must take care not to let grow up in its midst a feeling of prejudice of its own against other board schools ... If the children of Fleet-road carry off the largest proportion of scholarships it would be well for the proud little victors to remember that it may not be due so much to their superior ability as to their superior advantages that they are thus able to score over the less favoured lads and lasses from the poorer quarters.[92]

Adams' use of influential supporters, his manipulation of the local media and the range of honours he acquired might support a charge of careerism. His family links with the British and Foreign School Society were recognized with a seat on its Committee. He was President of the Pembroke County Club in London and, as we have seen, made use of this connection for family advancement. Through the good offices of Lord Aberdare his contributions to history teaching, which included a pair of text-books (Chapter 8), and his evidence to the Cross Commission, were recognized by his election to a Fellowship of the Royal Historical Society.[93] He was also made a Fellow of the Educational Institute of Scotland.[94] It would, however, be perverse as well as uncharitable to explain Adams' professional behaviour purely in terms of self-promotion.

He died, more or less, at the helm. On 5 March 1903 he collapsed at Fleet Road School with an 'apoplectic seizure'.[95] Too ill to be moved, the school was in consequence partially closed. He was taken home on 8 March and for a time seemed to improve, recovering consciousness. But he suffered a second and fatal heart attack on 14 March. The funeral was attended by a predictable range of prominent figures in education, politics and local society. The ceremony included Adams' favourite choral piece, 'The Pilgrim's Chorus' from Wagner's *Tannhäuser*. An old pupil, presumably wrongly though understandably, recalls the school choir in rain and cold at the graveside in Hampstead Cemetery rendering 'God the All-terrible'.[96]

It was decided to raise funds to establish a memorial to W.B. Adams, and a Committee was formed for that purpose. Its

Chairman affirmed: 'Fleet Road School was Mr. Adams and Mr. Adams was Fleet Road School.' The money was to be used to provide a bronze tablet of Adams in the school hall and an 'Adams Scholarship' for Fleet Road pupils. At the unveiling, Lyulph Stanley paid tribute to a headmaster of 'high principle, energy and great devotion to his work'. His exertions had established history as a subject for all children and a school choir of enviable reputation.[97] The British and Foreign School Society's *Educational Record* emphasized Adams' 'professional eminence' and enthusiasm for the Society's teacher-training work which had led to his election to the College Committee in 1892.[98] A Fleet Road Log Book records the tribute of the local HMI who referred to the great loss sustained by the school on the death of W.B. Adams, 'whose intense earnestness and enthusiasm for all related to the success of the school will long be remembered'.[99]

The career of W.B. Adams is of wider interest than the mere detail of his family and professional history. He was part of the early phase in the nineteenth-century rise of the meritocracy, when opportunities were being seized by aspiring families to climb the ladder provided by tertiary sector employment, in this case in the education industry. His father had already gained a place on the ladder, and the esteem in which he was held by the British and Foreign School Society, and Matthew Arnold, no doubt helped to smooth W.B.'s path. By the age of 30 he was already the headmaster of the largest voluntary school in the West End of London, and a resident of St. John's Wood. But for the introduction of the school board system he might have climbed no higher. The resources of boards such as London's introduced higher salaries and more elaborate career structures. A new plateau of social status was achievable. As George Bartle has observed, it was possible

for an industrious teacher, particularly if he obtained a headship, to secure many of the advantages of lower middle class security, such as an amply furnished house of his own in a pleasant suburb, domestic servants, a secondary education for his children, regular holidays ... and, most important of all, a respectable place in local society.[100]

In a minority of cases, such as the Adamses, where there were two salary earners in the family, more than this was possible: authentic middle-class status, with servants and a prestigious residential location.

Not the least help to the Adamses was the timing of their professional careers. They were trained and secured their professional advancement in a period of rapid educational growth, beneficiaries of hitherto undreamt of resources. The demand for teachers meant that restrictions were not placed, as they were to be in the twentieth century, on the employment of married women. In the old days of the voluntary system, it was common to employ a man and wife to run a small elementary school, at an economic rate to the managers. Prospects under large school boards were much better, considerably higher earnings being possible, albeit less for women than men. In the early 1900s between one-quarter and one-third of London School Board women staff were married.[101] The Board made arrangements for maternity leave, in part to sustain the supply of teachers, and in part as a result of the influence of strong-minded female members of the Board opposed to the domestic stereotype of women.[102]

There was also, however, widespread opposition towards the employment of married women teachers. The national press was often unsympathetic, the *Pall Mall Gazette* condemning the practice as evil, putting forward the curious argument that the high rates of pay of London School Board women teachers made them a prey to scheming men, wont to marry them for their earning capacity.[103]

W.B. Adams was quintessentially late-Victorian. Caught up in a period of rapid social and professional change, ambivalence and double standards were periodically apparent in his words and deeds. While a meritocrat, he did not hesitate to use personal connection to secure family advancement. He was ready to suppress inconvenient evidence in his professional history. But he lived in a period when self-help was a prevailing philosophy, and indeed in a transition time between an earlier phase of reliance on patronage, and the later bureaucratic processes in which formal credentials gained primacy. Adams typically deployed both routes. It would be wrong, however, to infer from his manipulative tendencies that he did not have a genuine sense of mission and public service. His professional objectives were entirely consonant with the progressive policies of the London School Board. He was concerned to offer parents in his catchment of respectable background but often modest means the opportunity for social and economic advancement, provided by the varied curricular offerings of the school and more particularly the scholarship system. He was anxious that girls as well as boys should share in these opportunities, within the social constraints that operated at the time. Visitors to the school, as will be considered more fully later (Chapter 8), were struck by the special qualities of the girls, though the opportunities being offered might be interpreted within the conventional definitions of the marriage market:

Back to the railway station, I noticed a poster near the waiting room advertising a local private school 'for the sons of gentlemen'. Who are they, and what manner of education do they seek? Is not Fleet-road fit for the daughters of gentlemen? It is certainly training daughters so that they become the mothers of gentlemen.[104]

It can be inferred that the Adams family embodied not only the aspirations and achievements of the upwardly mobile, but also nineteenth-century lower-middle-class neuroses. Striving to rise from lower-middle- to genuinely middle-class status in all likelihood heightened the stress already created by professionally demanding jobs. The correspondence of W.B. Adams with the British and Foreign School Society periodically suggests a degree of personal insecurity, a reflexive defensiveness and latent aggression. Also apparent was a suspicion of the motives of others, bordering at times on theories of conspiracy against himself and his family. He was generally intolerant of alternative views to his own. He was desperately anxious that family successes, whether professional or personal, should be publicly recorded, whether in the school log book, the local press, or in official discourse at the London School Board or in Whitehall itself. He ensured they were placed in the *Educational Record* of the British and Foreign School Society, which had been so supportive of his family over three generations.

Following W.B. Adams, the headship of Fleet Road School passed to J. Sadd, a former teacher at the school, who had quickly moved on to a more senior position at Haverstock Hill Board School. Sadd was a leader of quite different style. Log book entries suggest more preoccupation with the day-to-day running of the school and less with external relations. Perhaps his most significant early decision was to discontinue his own work with Standard VII and Ex-VII to devote himself 'to the improvement of the rank and file of the school',[105] an approach which gained the approval of the local HMI. Under the London County Council, however, the school maintained its reputation. It became a centre for Standard VI and VII work, a central school to which other institutions in the area, mostly former board schools, functioned as feeders. Successes in the scholarship stakes continued recorded, as before, in the log book. It was a long time before the Adams imprint was to be entirely erased.

The Adams family therefore take us through three generations of education in England and Wales, the first dating back to the consolidating period of elementary education for the poor; the second associated with a widening provision coincident with the rise of the meritocracy, the main subject of this book; and the third the interesting and relatively unrecorded application of ideas forged in the higher-grade board schools to newly-established secondary provision in the twentieth century,[106] notwithstanding the checking of such initiatives by the 1902 Education Act, which favoured the more traditional curricula of the old grammar schools.

REFERENCES AND NOTES

1. *SBC*, 3 Dec. 1898, p.627.
2. C. Booth (ed.), *Labour and Life of the People: London, Vol. II* (London, 1891), Appendix, p.14.
3. *HHE*, 21 March 1903.
4. *BFSS Archives*, Letter from John Adams, dated 21 Feb. 1848.
5. *Ibid.*, Letter from Pembroke Dock British School Committee, dated 12 Dec. 1847.
6. *Ibid.*, letter dated 24 Feb. 1848.
7. *MCCE* (1851–2), p.501.
8. *The Practical Teacher*, vol. 15 (1894), p.1.
9. *Cross Commission*, 2nd Report (1887), p.57.
10. *Ibid.*, p.45.
11. *The Practical Teacher*, vol. 15 (1894), p.1.
12. *BFSS Archives*, Letter from John Adams, dated 2 Jan. 1865.
13. *Ibid.*, Letter from D. Williams, dated 17 Nov. 1865.
14. *Ibid.*, Letter from John Adams, dated 20 Nov. 1865.
15. *Ibid.*, Letter from John Adams, dated 23 Nov. 1865.
16. *Ibid.*, Letter from John Adams, dated 28 Nov. 1865.
17. *Ibid.*, Letter from W.B. Adams, dated 29 Aug. 1866.
18. *Ibid.*, Letter from W.B. Adams, dated 7 Feb. 1867.
19. *Ibid.*, Letter from W.B. Adams, dated 9 Feb. 1867.
20. *Ibid.*, Letter from W.B. Adams, dated 15 Feb. 1867.
21. *Ibid.*, Letter from Thomas Hill of Finchley, dated 26 Feb. 1867.
22. *Ibid.*, Letter from W.B. Adams, dated 25 Feb. 1867.
23. *Ibid.*, Letter dated 28 Feb. 1867.
24. *Ibid.*, Letter dated 4 March 1867.
25. *Ibid.*, Letter dated 12 March 1867.

26. *Ibid.*, Letter from Thomas Hill, dated 18 March 1867.
27. *Ibid.*, Letter from W.B. Adams, dated 5 June 1867.
28. *RCCE* (1868–9), p.569.
29. *RCCE* (1870–1), p.496.
30. *BFSS Archives*, Letter from Thomas Hill, dated 18 April 1870.
31. Booth (ed.), *op. cit.* (1891), p.11.
32. *RCCE* (1870–1), p.501.
33. *PRO*, Ed. 3/19.
34. *The Practical Teacher*, vol. 15 (1894), p.1.
35. *SBC*, 7 April 1888, p.359.
36. *BFSS Archives*, Letter from W.B. Adams, dated 29 Sept. 1874.
37. *Ibid.*, Letter from John Adams, dated 30 Nov. 1875.
38. *Ibid.*, Letter from W.B. Adams, dated 9 Dec. 1875.
39. *Ibid.*, Letter dated 12 Feb. 1876.
40. *Ibid.*, Letter dated 25 Feb. 1876.
41. *Ibid.*, Letter dated 17 March 1876.
42. T. Wickenden, *William Ellis School, 1862–1962* (London, 1962), pp.27–8.
43. *LSB Minutes*, 1 Aug. 1877, Statistical Committee, p.1074.
44. Reported in *HHE*, 21 March 1903. In fact a Table in the *Cross Commission*, 2nd Report (1887), pp.1057–8, showed Portland Street British School winning two scholarships in the first year, 1875, in which a significant number of scholarships were offered, two years after the scheme first started (see Chapter 10).
45. *The Practical Teacher*, vol. 15 (1894), p.1.
46. *LSB Minutes*, 27 Nov. 1878, School Management Committee, p.731.
47. *Ibid.*, 10 March 1880, p.430.
48. *Ibid.*, 9 Oct. 1884, p.567.
49. *Cross Commission*, 2nd Report (1887), p.45.
50. *Hampstead Record*, 26 Nov. 1898
51. *PRO*, Ed. 7/75.
52. *HHE*, 19 Nov. 1881.
53. *LSB*, Inspector's Report on Netherwood Street, 1883.
54. *LSB*, Government Inspector's Report on Netherwood Street, 17 June 1883.
55. *LSB* Minutes, School Management Committee, 22 Nov. 1883, p.1003.
56. *Ibid.*, 15 Feb. 1894, p.554.
57. *Hampstead Record*, 26 Nov. 1898.
58. *Educational Record*, vol. 15, New Series (1899), p.46.
59. *SBC*, 26 Nov. 1898, p.588.
60. *Hampstead Record*, 21 March 1903.
61. *HHE*, 17 Oct. 1903.
62. *HHE*, 23 Feb. 1918.
63. Mary Adams would seem likely to have been the author of a local history text, produced in Hampstead in 1909, entitled *Some Hampstead Memories*. The British Library catalogue records the author as 'Mary Adams of Hampstead.'
64. *The Practical Teacher*, vol. 15 (1894), p.5.
65. *Educational Record*, vol. 15, New Series (1901), p.673.
66. *Educational Record*, vol. 12 (1888), pp.321–2; vol. 13 (1889), p.118; vol. 13 (1890), p.169.
67. University of London, *The Historical Record (1836–1912)* (London, 1912), p.198.
68. *BFSS Archives*, Letter from W.B. Adams, dated 26 Aug. 1896.
69. *The Pembrokeshire Times*, 20 Aug. 1896.
70. *Ibid.*, 24 Sept. 1896.
71. *HHE*, 7 Aug. 1897.
72. W. Harrison, *Greenhill School Tenby, 1896–1964: an Educational and Social History* (Cardiff, 1979), pp.83–180.
73. *Ibid.*, pp.159–60.
74. *SBL 795, Minute Book 7*, Special Sub-committee on Appointment of Sub-inspectors, 1 May 1903.

75. R.J. Clapp, *A Short History of Ashford County School, Middlesex 1911–1961* (Ashford, 1960), p.11.
76. GLC Record Office File E.Mx.4/1, *Minute Books of Ashford County Secondary School*, p.8 and p.138.
77. Harrison, *op. cit.* (1979), p.177.
78. *Christchurch Times*, 4 Sept. 1926 and 16 April 1927.
79. *London Gazette Supplement*, 2 Jan. 1933, p.10.
80. *Christchurch Times*, 24 March 1934.
81. *Ibid.*, 7 April 1934.
82. The school's existence is recorded in *Kelly's Directory of Tunbridge Wells, Tonbridge and Neighbourhood*, with W.H. Saunders, M.A., D.Litt., as Principal, up to 1938.
83. *The School Guardian*, 7 May 1887.
84. *Cross Commission*, 2nd Report (1887), p.49.
85. *The Practical Teacher*, vol. 15 (1894), p.4.
86. *LSB Minutes*, 15 July 1898, School Management Committee, p.90.
87. *The Board Teacher*, 1 Feb. 1893, p.29.
88. *London*, vol. 7 (1898), p.290.
89. *Ibid.*, p.312.
90. *The Board Teacher*, 1 Feb. 1897, pp.32–3.
91. *Ibid.*, 1 March 1897.
92. *London*, vol. 7 (1898), p.153.
93. *The Practical Teacher*, vol. 15 (1894), p.7.
94. *Fleet Road Log Book*, 9 Oct. 1900.
95. *HHE*, 21 March 1903.
96. *Hundred Years Fleet School 1879–1979* (Hampstead, 1979), p.11.
97. *HHE*, 13 June and 17 Oct. 1903.
98. *Educational Record*, vol. 15 New Series (1903), p.338.
99. *Fleet Road Log Book*, 9 Feb. 1904.
100. G. Bartle, 'George Bedloe: a London Board School Headmaster', *Journal of Educational Administration and History*, vol. 11 (1979), p.13.
101. *SBL*, EO/STA/2/12.
102. *The Schoolmistress*, 9 Feb. 1882, p.180.
103. Quoted in *The Schoolmaster*, 28 June 1879, p.724.
104. *London*, vol. 7 (1898), p.154.
105. *Fleet Road Log Book*, 18 June 1903.
106. It is my hope to undertake a study of the Adamses as a teaching family over these three major phases, encompassing one hundred years of educational development in England and Wales.

CHAPTER SIX

The Headteachers: Louisa Walker and the Infants' Department

... we are here practically at the fountainhead of the modern development of the kindergarten principle in new and practical directions, and under the guidance of the originator and chief authority on many of these varied occupations.[1]
The Practical Teacher, 1898

'A VERY FAMOUS HEADMISTRESS'

As this conclusive comment in the *Hampstead and Highgate Express* at the time of her death[2] correctly suggests, Louisa Walker was among the most eminent of the infant department headmistresses appointed by the London School Board. Fleet Road School was possibly unique in possessing two such redoubtable headteachers as Louisa Walker and William Bateman Adams. Arguably Louisa Walker made the more notable educational contribution if, for example, range of innovation and publication are considered. This chapter will show, among other things, how the Walker family, like the Adamses, took early advantage of the meritocratic developments which were opening up opportunities for professional and social advancement in the formative years of their careers; how, like her counterpart in the Senior Mixed Department, Louisa Walker skilfully exploited the media; and how she contributed to the development of infant education in the urban milieu, in a period of radical social change.

THE WALKER FAMILY

Louisa Walker, née Parker, was born at Bath on 18 March 1853, the seventh of ten children in the family of Alfred Parker, an upholsterer. At the time of the 1851 census her eldest brother, then aged 14, was an errand boy. Her two elder sisters were recorded as 'at home' even though, aged 12 and ten respectively, of normal school age. Louisa was educated in a private school until she was 13, after which she became a pupil teacher at Walcot St. Swithin's School in Bath. She later paid tribute to her headmistress, who

undoubtedly taught me to work with energy and ability ... I had charge of sixty children in Standard I, and knew that each child had to pass an individual examination for which I was responsible. Lessons were given me from seven till eight in the summer, and from twelve to one in winter, and plenty of home lessons each evening. Yet I flourished, and look back with pleasure to those days. A pupil teacher then knew the meaning of the word *responsibility*, which I doubt if the pupil teacher of 1898 has ever realized.[3]

After five years as a pupil teacher Louisa Walker was admitted to the Home and Colonial Training College in London. She completed her training in 1873 with a second class certificate.[4] While still a pupil teacher she met her future husband, James Walker. He too was born at Bath, in 1850, and was the son of a local antiquarian. After his apprenticeship at the Walcot schools, he went on to train at Battersea College. On qualifying, he was appointed Headmaster of Somercotes School in Lincolnshire.[5] While still there, he married Louisa Walker, on 24 June 1873 at St. Paul's Church, St. Pancras. At the time she was living with Robert Parker, presumably an elder brother, in respectable but modest accommodation at 48 Marquis Road, Camden Town (Plate 16). The marriage certificate notes her father not as an upholsterer, but as 'gentleman'.

Louisa Walker's obituary notice in the local newspaper[6] records her as having had eight children, of whom five had survived. The first child, Katherine Louisa, was born at The Cottage, Upper Park Road (Map 8) on 2 January 1874. About this time James Walker moved to Hampstead to become Headmaster of St. Stephen's School. During the next 15 years the Walkers, like many Victorian families, regularly switched residence, and over very short distances, moving between houses on

16. 48 Marquis Road (the house to the left of the scaffolding), Camden Town, the first residence in the area of Louisa Walker

Mansfield Road. These included number 32, one of the terrace shown on Plate 12. Their first two homes, after Upper Park Road, were on the lower status south side of Mansfield Road. At the time of the 1881 census they had three children, aged seven, six and less than a month. Three others had in fact died in infancy, two within four days of each other in April 1878 from whooping cough, and another in 1879 from pneumonia, all around the time of Louisa's move to Fleet Road. Resident also at Mansfield Road in 1881 was an artist brother of James Walker, a 17-year old servant, and a 43-year old nurse.

Approximately three months after the birth of her eldest daughter, Mrs. Walker was given charge of a voluntary school in Circus Road (later named Rochford Street, Map 8) in Gospel Oak. Here she remained until the school was transferred to the London School Board in October 1877, as a temporary measure awaiting the opening of the Fleet Road buildings, ready at the beginning of 1879. The Circus Road school was originally intended for the waifs and strays of the caravan dwellers who frequented the borders of Hampstead Heath. It was in the first place a private school, the initiative of two philanthropic ladies, but later became inspected. Prior to Louisa Walker's appointment it had received a poor Inspector's report. She vividly describes her introduction to the building:

I shall never forget my first visit to this school. We entered by a large church-door to a sepulchral passage, and then ascended by a flight of stone steps, which in spiral fashion led to the upper as well as to the infant department. About half-way up the flight two narrow half-doors opened into what was to be my first school.

It was a lofty, square room, about as large as an ordinary classroom of good size, and nearly the whole of the floor space was occupied by a huge gallery of deep steps running from floor to ceiling. In front stood three teachers abreast, trying to interest and separate a lot of crawling, dirty children. There was no idea of order or arrangement. The windows were church windows, composed of small panes, and black with dirt. Should I take it or not? I was young and full of energy, and saw immediately what I should do if I came even for three months ...

I had the windows cleaned and made to open, lines painted on the gallery for regular places, half-steps made for marching on and off, and a good show of bright, pretty pictures hung on the walls. I had two pupil teachers, and about a hundred children; the latter I classified into Standard I, and Upper and Lower Infants. We had to stand side by side or back to back on this one gallery in teaching our three divisions; *but we did it*, and produced good results ... the strain was great, and in the afternoons both teachers and children were quite overdone, and had need of rest and quiet. Then necessity became the mother of invention. On three afternoons we had needlework and writing, and finished with a gallery lesson, which I generally gave, while the pupil teachers listened and placed work. Tuesday and Friday needed some recreative work, and it was then I began to tell fairy tales, sew on buttons, fold and tear paper, make spills, have games and other enjoyments, which I soon found made these afternoons the most popular of all.

These precocious skills clearly impressed the influential local HMI, Charles Alderson, who gave Mrs. Walker a good report at her first examination and was later to describe her as 'one of the first among teachers to make the infant stage of learning bright and interesting',[7] presumably referring to the adaptation of kindergarten methods to mass urban elementary provision. She claimed it was her suggestion that led to the choice of the Fleet Road site for a new board school. There was apparently some hesitation in appointing a 26-year-old as headmistress of an important new school, but Alderson's strong recommendation, it was said, carried the day.

The starting salary was £92.10 per annum.[8] By 1880 her basic salary was £98, credit being given for receiving good reports. In addition to this there was share of grant and payment for instructing pupil teachers, which amounted to a gross salary of £202,[9] a very high sum for a woman teacher at that time. Louisa Walker's rise was therefore rapid. Her husband's was less so. Having left Lincolnshire, his first local post, at St. Stephen's School, a Church of England school in Hampstead, was as headmaster of a boys' department of 70 scholars, housed in sub-standard accommodation in a crypt under the chancel of the church. He left after three years at the school, the accommodation by this time having been condemned.[10]

James Walker was not again to become a headteacher for nearly ten years. The London School Board generally required longer experience than the voluntary sector for such promotion. His first post with the Board was as an assistant at Camden Street School, Camden Town, beginning in May 1877 at a salary of £95, of which £5 was for the possession of three science certificates. In May 1879 he became headmaster of a temporary board school in Barnsbury Street, Islington, at a salary of £125.[11] When that school closed, in 1881, he was transferred to Beethoven Street, Queen's Park.[12] In the following year he moved to Hawley Crescent, Kentish Town, at which time his salary as an assistant teacher was £105.[13] By 1885 it had increased to £136,[14] still well below the gross earnings of his wife. Not until 1886 did he achieve a permanent headteacher's position, when he was appointed to the new Broomsleigh Street Board School, in West Hampstead, at a salary of £200.[15] This was a conveniently located school in respect of journey to work, for Broomsleigh Street was close to the stations in West Hampstead on the opposite side of the tunnel to those of Gospel Oak (Map 5).

The rising combined salaries of the Walkers made it possible for them to move with their growing family in 1895 to an up-market residence at 15, Tanza Road (Map 3 and Plate 17), on the edge of Parliament Hill Fields. Here the average assessments were £82 in the area as a whole, ranging from £80 to £115 in Tanza Road itself. This compared with a range of from £30 to £214 in Willow Road, where Mr. and Mrs. Adams lived. Curiously, the first residents of Tanza Road objected to its name on the grounds of its resemblance to the German word for 'dance', not thought in keeping 'with the character of the neighbourhood'.[16] The residences of the South-hill Park, Nassington and Tanza Road

17. 15 Tanza Road, home of the Walker family, the back gate opening on to Parliament Hill Fields

estates were a serious encroachment on the Heath (Map 3) though an enviable environment for those living there. The door of the Walkers' back garden (Plate 17) opened directly on to Parliament Hill Fields. At James Walker's death in 1932, at the age of 81, it was reported that he had for long been a familiar figure at the Hampstead Heath bathing pond until compelled to stop swimming on medical advice. He was also regularly to be seen exercising his cocker spaniel dog on the expanses of the Heath in the years following the death of his wife in 1922.[17]

The Walkers' eldest daughter, Kate, also had a long and successful career with the London School Board. She began as a probationer under her mother at Fleet Road Infants' Department in 1889.[18] Having trained, like Louisa, at the Home and Colonial College, she returned to Fleet Road in 1895, first as a supply teacher but soon on permanent appointment, at an annual salary of £85.[19] By 1905 she had secured a place on the London County Council's 'Promotion List' which, on the basis of good qualifications and length of service with the authority, identified assistants deemed worthy of promotion to headships when the opportunity arose. Kate had a First-class Certificate, one advanced science and three elementary certificates, a drawing certificate, a music qualification, and London School Board physical education and kindergarten qualifications.[20] In 1907 she moved to her father's school, Broomsleigh Street, as an assistant in the infants' department.[21]

In 1909, Kate Walker married a widower, Christopher Joseph Taylor, 12 years her senior, and Under-Secretary to Lord Strathcona, Agent-General of the Canadian Government. The 'very pretty wedding' took place at St. Stephen's Church, Hampstead, followed by a reception for 60 guests at Tanza Road.[22] Soon afterwards, Mrs. Taylor was promoted as Headmistress of Star Lane Infants' Department, East Fulham. The school had been opened in 1880 and had seven staff and 482 children. Her starting salary was £150 per annum.[23] The school was reasonably close to the Taylors' home at 16, Rivercourt Road, Hammersmith, a 'red' street in Booth's classification. Here they lived until 1932. Kate Taylor retired from Star Lane in 1935, after 40 years serving with the London School Board and London County Council.[24] She had no children and, following her first husband's death and also her father's, moved back to Tanza Road, marrying again. Her second husband was Edwin Luke, a colleague of her first husband in the Canada Office.

Two of the Walker children were among the many scholarship winners of Fleet Road School. As will be shown later, Mansfield Road was the leading 'scholarship street' in the catchment. Robert Alfred Walker, born 25 June 1875, won the 6th open St. Mildred's Scholarship in 1887, at a value of £35 per annum for three years.[25] He was later to achieve a senior position on the London County Council. His younger brother Frederick was a qualified architect who worked for the London County Council and later in Shanghai. The most well-known of the Walkers' children was the younger daughter, Winifred, born 19 June 1882. In 1895 she came 18th among the junior scholarship winners of the LCC Technical Education Board.[26] She went on to Camden School of Art and became a famous flower painter. Plate 18 shows most of the Walker family at the christening of Frederick's daughter, in 1912. Only Winifred is missing. Louisa is seated second from the left, and Kate is holding her niece. James Walker

18. Members of the Walker family: Louisa Walker second from left
(seated) and James Walker on the right (seated)

is seated on the right. The men upstanding are, from left to right,
Charles, Kate's husband, Robert and Frederick.

Louisa Walker died on 19 February 1922, just short of her 69th
birthday, of influenza and ensuing peritonitis.[27] At her retirement in 1918 she had served 44 years in Hampstead. Following
her retirement she founded the National Association of Retired
Teachers, its object to improve the pensions of those who
had retired before 1919. Her fame has left us with a photographic record through the stages of her career, associated
largely with visits to the school of educational or local journalists
(Plates 19 a–c).

19 a–d. Photographs of Louisa Walker at different stages of her career

THE KINDERGARTEN MOVEMENT AND
THE LONDON SCHOOL BOARD

The London School Board was pleased with the image conveyed by its infants' schools, to which inspectors and other visitors frequently paid tribute:

It was quite a treat to go into one of these schools and observe to how great an extent it is possible to make instruction pleasant, and how easy it is to gain the affections of the children by a kind and patient manner.[28]

Philpott, an historian of the London School Board, described its infant departments as 'in great measure the history of the development of the Kindergarten idea'.[29] Louisa Walker was trained at the Home and Colonial College in Gray's Inn Road, established for the training of infant teachers on Froebelian lines. Fleet Road infants' department was quoted by Philpott as a model of good practice,[30] as it was by the correspondent of *The Practical Teacher* (reference 1).

The story of the translation of Froebelian ideas into the circumstances of mass urban elementary education has as yet been only partially told. Clearly the Fleet Road case is an important one to consider in view of the claims made by the London School Board and by Mrs. Walker herself. Later commentators have tended to be sceptical about the success of the dissemination, regarding the Froebelian vision as undermined by the pressures of the Codes on the teachers. Indeed, the Education Department itself issued warnings at the time of the dangers of debasing Froebel's ideas.[31]

Louisa Walker tells that when she emerged from the Home and Colonial College she was 'full of enthusiasm for the principles of the kindergarten system which I had heard so ably expounded by the late Mr. Robert Dunning in his lectures on "The Child" and "The Cultivation of the Faculties"'.

Louisa Walker confessed that varied occupations were introduced by her at the Circus Street School primarily as a means of keeping some children out of mischief while others were carrying on individual reading or object lessons. She claimed that at this time kindergarten occupations were unknown in the schools. They were, in fact, beginning to be introduced by the London School Board,[32] which had in 1874 appointed Miss Bishop, a

Froebelian, to lecture to its infants' teachers on the kindergarten idea.

The Robert Dunning to whom Louisa Walker referred had produced a text entitled *The Phonic System of Teaching to Read: Applied after the Methods of Pestalozzi*. This formed the basis of the teaching in the Model Infant School at the Home and Colonial College. The text laid great stress on the importance of using the best method which was, predictably, his. Children were creatures 'that receive all their first impressions through the senses' and of feeble intellectual powers. It was therefore vital to use the phonic method, reflecting the sounds on which the letters were based, rather than the alphabetical, requiring learning of the names of the letters. According to Pestalozzi, argued Dunning, each point should be taken up separately and systematically, and should embody a leading idea, which was then 'exercised'. A quite rigid structuring was offered to the would-be teacher under the progressive imprimatur of Pestalozzian thinking.[33]

The recommendations of early progressive educators were indeed child-centred purely in pedagogic terms. In the kindergarten system nature was the guide, and nature offered order as well as beauty. Play was seen as the natural activity, the work, of children. Teaching should build on the everyday experience of children. The activity moved from the familiar and the simple when the time was ripe in a gradual retreat from domicentricity. Teachers were enjoined to follow the maternal model, the 'mother made conscious'.[34] As contemporary prints reveal, the model mother was the German peasant housewife, not the lady of fashion, and still less the struggling mother of ten in an urban tenement.[35]

In the kindergarten system, the progressive pedagogy was a means to the end of inculcating at an early age, as painlessly as possible, a prescriptive moral code. Even before the advent of Froebel's kindergartens, English infant schools had promulgated the 'play way'. Thus the maxim energizing the work of Goyder's Bristol school was: 'Be thou in fear of the Lord all the day long.' But the pedagogy was geared to gaining 'cheerful obedience'. Singing was offered as part of the carrot rather than the stick approach. Each song or hymn, however, illustrated an approved principle of conduct. In Goyder's 'The Folly of Finery', for example, 'poor little ignorant children' were told they should dress cleanly and plainly, rather than in the 'fine ribbons and caps' which made them look 'foolish and vain'.[36] Froebel also stressed the importance of song. 'Do you desire that his life shall be a musical and harmonious one? If so, cultivate his love of song and the ability to sing.'[37] Like Goyder, Froebel built up the socialization into a sanctioned moral code with impressive cumulative force, in this case through a set of 'Mother's Songs'. These included verses or mottos of advice for mothers, as well as the songs for the children to hear and learn.

The emphasis was on the virtues of happy family life, where 'strife and discord never come' their 'tales of woe to tell';[38] obedience to parents, who should reward good behaviour and punish bad; the acceptance of one's lot; and an appreciation of the essential harmony of God's world. This, through the example of family unity, children were never too young to grasp.[39] The social context of the kindergarten system in its pristine form was therefore one of fixed rural orders or estates, in which a contented peasantry was gently conditioned to the unchanging constants of benevolently-stewarded, divinely-ordained rankings. It had manifestly little to do with notions of social mobility. This was a concept evolved in an urban class society, and its furtherance was precisely the purpose of the more thrusting late-Victorian elementary schools.

Froebel's brilliantly conceived gifts and occupations were part of the same overall design. The third and fourth gifts were of wooden cubes and blocks, which could be made into chairs, steps, thrones, monuments, churches, castles, columns of honour and triumphal arches. The children were told they might find monuments in a churchyard. Here a young child of their own age, who had not obeyed its mother, might be buried, like little Fanny, who had illicitly played with fire. As a result, 'her dear face was spoiled, her hands and arms and neck were all burned to a cinder, and she soon died'.[40] After the gifts, the varied occupations took over, training children in activities like cutting paper, stick-laying, sewing, rug-making, cane-weaving, and the like, all simulations of useful 'industrial' occupations.[41]

The gifts and occupations were therefore cunning inventions, again demonstrating universal harmony and unity, a love of law and social order, and a training in craft. M.E. Bailey, an English Froebelian, in 1876 made it clear that the toys were 'gifts of God' and that the objectives of the infant school included a training in the fear and love of God, duty to parents, showing kindness and goodwill to others, and ingraining the habit, through play, of regarding labour as a pleasure.[42] Another Froebelian, E.M. Mortimer, was less fundamentalist in approach, arguing in 1891 that the gifts and occupations were designed to satisfy a childish craving for investigation, to instil a sense of beauty, and gradually direct the child to an appreciation of the order, neatness and arrangement of things around.[43] G. Davidson (1901) equally stressed dual purposes, the first gift of the six soft balls, for example, conveying a notion of the softness of maternal contact, and an aesthetic training in colour.[44] There was some official suspicion in Whitehall over the way kindergarten methods were being deployed, as motivational pastimes rather than for their intellectual quality. An Education Department Circular of 1893 emphasized that 'the main object of these lessons is to stimulate intelligent individual effort'.[45]

Louisa Walker was far from an orthodox Froebelian, but was still an important pioneer of the London School Board's initiatives in the introduction of kindergarten teaching. She was an official representative of the Board at a kindergarten conference in Manchester.[46] She was called upon as a witness by the Board in an investigation of kindergarten methods following the critical Education Department Circular of 1893. She was at the same time impatient of the activities of the Froebelian movement, and was not part of it in any formal sense. Avowedly a practitioner rather than a theoretician, she claimed it had not been to her disadvantage not to have the Froebel Union Certificate. Neither did she look for teachers who had gained it, preferring the Board's own kindergarten certificate.[47]

For the practitioner, the kindergarten system posed great problems when translated from its classic rural frame of a summery open-air environment with pupil–teacher ratios of about 15 to one, into the circumstances of the urban elementary school, with 'preposterously large' classes of 60 to 70 children, and a need to follow the Code in order to earn grant.[48] More fundamentally, metropolitan society introduced social, economic and moral fluidity. The family relationships of the urban under-class bore little relationship to the social and economic structures and moral values assumed by Froebel and his disciples. Some urban groups, however, liked the message. As Steedman has observed, the 'Froebelian publicity machine' was directed towards a middle-class audience,[49] increasingly searching for lost rural values as redress against the perceived morbid descent of the city. It was in this context that the individualistic adaptations of Louisa Walker of the Froebelian gifts, occupations and, particularly, action songs, were made.

The Fleet Road Infant Department timetable (Table 6.1) was designed to cater for eight classes, Class 8 being the youngest.[53] It shows that the school assembled at 8.45 a.m. for prayers, followed by an extended period of some form of religious instruction, whether the ten commandments, the Lord's Prayer, Old or New Testament History, or hymn singing. A School Board Inspector of Scripture described the opening morning service as 'of a very pleasing and impressive character'.[54]

Following the completion of the registers at 10 a.m., the next hour was largely devoted to the basic subjects. The methods were described in *The Infants' Mistress* article.

In the 'lower infants' class the phonic method and word-building system is adopted. And in the upper classes analysis of difficult words and spelling before reading. The children are encouraged to read fluently and with distinct articulation, by pattern reading after the teacher, and then individually. Attention to pronunciation is made a special feature.[55]

As in all other things, Mrs. Walker had decisive views on how reading should be taught and, like her teacher Robert Dunning, was critical of the alphabetic method. Her pedagogic convictions here, as elsewhere, brooked no argument.

I am of the opinion that the teachers as a rule help the children too much. I will not have a spasmodic kind of reading. To a great extent I obviate that by having all the drudgery in this subject done upon the blackboard before the children arrive. The teacher then explains the words and talks about them and the children spell them. When the children get their books they recognise the words. Then the children read after their teacher. I do not like children to spell when reading – C.A.T. – D.O.G. – These letters convey no idea of sound to the child's mind.[56]

The children were encouraged to make letters in sand. Another innovation was the 'Living Letter Alphabet', described by Philpott (Plate 20).

The children form themselves into living illustrations of the letters; they are provided with boxes containing straight and curved strips of coloured card, and out of these they construct each letter for themselves, afterwards drawing it on their slates: the letters are compared with familiar objects, and a verse is said or sung about each. Thus the reading lesson becomes at once a callisthenic

TIME TABLE of FLEET ROAD BOARD SCHOOL, HAMPSTEAD.

Banners across the week:
- 8.45–9.: ASSEMBLY AND PRAYERS.
- 9.30–10.: MARKING AND CLOSING REGISTERS.
- 11.15.: RECREATION. MARCHING. SINGING.
- 12.: GRACE AND DISMISSAL.
- 2.0.: ASSEMBLY AND SPELLING. ROLL CALL.
- 2.15.: MARKING AND CLOSING REGISTERS.
- 3.30.: CHANGING CLASSES. RECREATION.
- 4.15.: PRAYERS AND DISMISSAL.

Day	Class	8.45–9.	9.15–9.30.	9.30–10.	10–10.30.	10.30–11.	11.15.	11.15–11.35.	12.	2.0.	2.15.	2.45.	3.15.	3.30.	4.0.	4.15.
MONDAY	1–8	ASSEMBLY AND PRAYERS.	Hymns and New Tunes.	MARKING AND CLOSING REGISTERS.	Reading. / Number, Writing, Reading. / Word Building. / Kindergarten Letters.	Writing. / Number, Writing. / Gift III.	RECREATION.	Singing. / Reading. / Kindergarten Number, Writing.	GRACE AND DISMISSAL.	Varied Occupat'n. Varied Occupat'n.	MARKING AND CLOSING REGISTERS.			CHANGING CLASSES. RECREATION.	Natural History.	PRAYERS AND DISMISSAL.
TUESDAY	1–8		Texts, with Explanations.		Number, Arithmetic, Reading. / Writing, Reading, Kindergarten Letters.	Number, Writing. / Reading, Writing, Sticks.	MARCHING.	Writing, Reading, Arithmetic.				Needlework. Drawing. Needlework. Drawing. Needlework. Drawing. Needlework. Needle Drill.	Tonic Sol-fa.			Geography or Grammar. Drill.	
WEDNESDAY	1–8		Old Testament History.		Reading, Number, Writing, Reading, Writing. / Letters.	Writing. / Number, Writing, Reading, Writing. / Drawing.	SINGING.	Writing. / Reading. / Singing.				Copy Books. Indiv. Reading. / Gift III.	Indiv. Reading. Recitation.			Object Lesson.	
THURSDAY	1–8		New Testament History.		Reading. / Arithmetic, Writing, Number, Writing, Letters.	Writing. / Reading, Number, Writing, Number, Drawing.		Singing. / Reading. / Games.				Needlework. Drawing. Needlework. Drawing. Needlework. Needlework. Form and Col.	Tonic Sol-fa.			Recitation. Criticism.	
FRIDAY	1–8		Ten Commandments. Lord's Prayer.		Number, Reading, Writing, Number, Reading. / Letters.	Reading, Arithmetic, Writing, Number, Writing.		Reading, Arithmetic, Reading. / Writing, Number, Stick Laying.				Drawing and Slinding. Varied Occupat'n.	Drill and Games.			Moral Lesson.	Repetition of Words of Songs and Fairy Tales.

Approved on behalf of the Education Department as fulfilling the requirements of Section 7 of the Elementary Education Act, 1870.

(Signed) GERALD FITZMAURICE, H.M. Inspector of Schools.

TABLE 6.1

(from *The Infants' Mistress*, 1893)

20. The 'Living Letters' Alphabet, Fleet Road Infants' Department

exercise, a Kindergarten game, a drawing exercise, a lesson in form, number and colour, and a conversation lesson introducing new words and ideas; and all the time the children are interested, busy and happy.[57]

The timetable makes it clear that large amounts of time were allotted to the basic subjects, with varied occupations and games confined to afternoons. A London School Board report (Table 6.2)[58] shows that even for four-year-olds kindergarten classes did not preponderate.

Other noteworthy features of the timetable were the long midday breaks, required to enable the children to travel home for a meal; and the allotment of discrete time slots for assemblies and the marking of registers. These lengthened the school day which, even for infants, extended from 8.45 a.m. to 4.15 p.m.

OBJECT LESSONS

By Louisa Walker's time object lessons were a well-established teaching strategy in the elementary school, one which perhaps

TABLE 6.2

Fleet Road Infants	Timetable Allotment		
	4 and under Hrs. Mins.	5 and under Hrs. Mins.	6 and under Hrs. Mins.
Reading	2.30	3.00	3.00
Writing	2.00	2.30	2.30
Arithmetic	2.30	2.30	2.30
Kindergarten	3.00	1.30	1.30
Object Lessons	2.00	1.30	1.30
Music	2.00	1.30	1.30
Needlework	1.00	2.00	2.00
Drill	1.30	0.30	0.30
Recitation	1.30	1.00	1.00
Other	3.00	4.00	4.00

Source: LSB, *Special Committee on Subjects and Modes of Instruction,* undated.

more than any other lent itself to mechanical implementation. In the official definition, the object lesson was designed to teach the children to observe, compare and contrast, to impart information, and to reinforce these by making the results the basis for instruction in language, drawing, number, modelling, and other handwork.

There are, however, other important uses of good Object Teaching. It makes the lives of the children more happy and interesting by opening up an easily accessible and attractive field for the exercise of brain, hand and eye. It gives the children an opportunity of learning the simplest natural facts, and directs their attention to external objects, making their education less bookish. It further develops a love of nature and an interest in living things, and corrects the tendency which exists in many children to destructiveness and thoughtless unkindness to animals, and shows the ignorance and cruelty of such conduct.[59]

To this 'important Circular' Louisa Walker's text in Cusack's *Object Lesson* series, published in 1895, was geared. The work was prepared for the Fleet Road pupil teachers for their weekly criticism lessons, to be used with older children in the infants' department. For the younger children she recommended starting with animals, prior to moving on to inanimate objects. Her introduction reveals a decisively clear view of the art of teaching object lessons. The 'DON'TS' were highlighted: pupil teachers were left in no doubt as to what they should *not* do. They were not to tell the children facts when the answers could be elicited from them; nor speak in too loud a tone of voice; nor turn their backs on the children while writing on the blackboard; nor to use language above the child's comprehension; nor to fail to recapitulate the lesson on the blackboard at the end. Woe betide the pupil teacher who gave a lesson when not thoroughly prepared; who wandered from the approved notes; or who used the excuse of nervousness when really not properly acquainted with the subject.

While the *Object Lesson* text was probably the most conventional of Louisa Walker's books, the characteristic dullness of the genre was alleviated by the introduction of 'original dialogue' in rhyme. The beginning of the section on cork provides an illustration of her style.

Teacher: This cork which I hold is part of a tree –
Which part? and where found, on mountain or sea?
From whence and for what? How, why and wherefore
Was this beautiful substance first brought to our shore?
Children: Cork is the *bark* of a little oak tree
Which grows on the shores of a very blue sea.[60]

Despite the fact that the garnish could not conceal the intrinsically mechanical approach of this interrogative, catechetical style of teaching, it was an attempt to bring the distant world into the classroom and, with the help of drawings or pictures, there was some advance on purely verbal rote learning. Government inspectors were pleased with this aspect of the work at Fleet Road. 'A great deal of information has been imparted by the object lessons' (1884); 'Object lessons have been carefully thought out, are imparted in a very intelligent manner, and fix the attention of the children' (1885); 'A marked feature of the school is the Object lesson teaching, which is extremely well illustrated' (1894).[61] More profitably, the object lessons were in some cases linked with natural history, including local nature walks. *The Infants' Mistress* reporter concluded that this aspect of the work was well integrated. 'Uniformity and harmony of method are preserved throughout the school.'[62] It was a fitting Froebelian-style tribute.

VARIED OCCUPATIONS

In the area of varied occupations Louisa Walker's work was considered innovative and was internationally recognized. These occupations included star- and fanwinding, paper-folding and cutting, making woollen balls and chickens, straw-splitting and weaving, beadwork, drawing and shading, cane-weaving, cross stitch and darning, macramé lace, frame-work, artificial flowers, diagonal mat-weaving and chair-caning (Plates 21 a/b). Inspectors' reports observed that the production of 'knitted petticoats, towels, pinafores and other garments is deserving of great praise', and later that the occupations work proved 'great ingenuity on the part of the Mistress; observation and accuracy in the children'.[63]

On inviting Louisa Walker to contribute a series of articles on 'Varied Occupations' to *The Infants' Mistress*, which appeared between June and October 1893, the Editor stated:

Perhaps no teacher living has made a greater name than this lady as an inventor and successful teacher of new occupations.

The 'crème de la crème' of the London School Board's Chicago exhibit was the work of the little fingers of her protégés ... it is all but incredible that small hands could make useful articles of such artistic beauty as we saw.[64]

The 'Chicago exhibit' referred to the London School Board's

21a. 'Varied Occupations', Fleet Road Infants' Department: Cane Weaving, Class 1, Aged 7

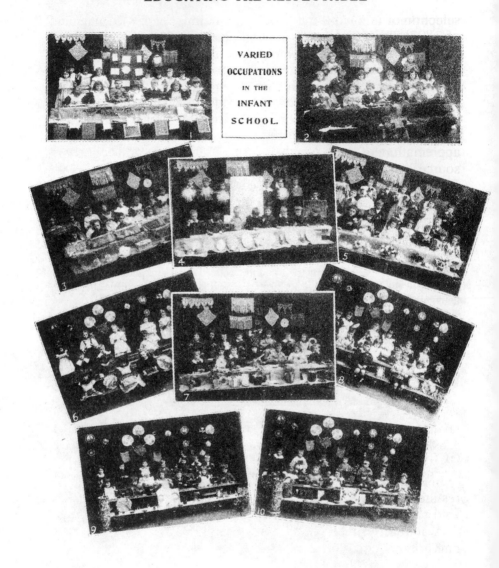

21b. 'Varied Occupations', Fleet Road Infants' Department, including string work, rug work, straw and blob work, paper-flower making, paper-mat plaiting, paper cutting and winding, bead work, and fraying, from Class X (aged 4) to Class II (aged 7)

selection of this work on varied occupations for the World's Fair of 1893. The idea was to send 'a small collection of apparatus and material which will serve to illustrate the condition of Elementary Education in this country'.[65] The kudos this brought Mrs. Walker led to a series of text-books. In 1895, Macmillan published her *Varied Occupations in Weaving*. The book was 'respectfully dedicated' to Lyulph Stanley 'at whose suggestion the work has been compiled, and whose kind interest in, and appreciation of, the Author's varied occupations have been a source of much encouragement to her over many years'.

In the preface she set out her philosophy, based on, by then, classic kindergarten principles:

From the time that I received the first elements of Froebelian principles at the Home and Colonial Training College until the present, it has been my aim to use the Froebel gifts as the basis of all teaching, and when possible to apply the same excellent methods to other work of everyday usefulness.

System and method are two essentials for gaining good results in varied occupations. The methods must be properly prepared and the teacher be well acquainted with the subject.[66]

The educational value of occupation was seen as follows:

(a) It may be utilized to teach the addition and multiplication of numbers.
(b) It is good for the cultivation of the initiative and inventive faculties, and affords scope for practical ingenuity in designing new patterns.
(c) It teaches regularity and symmetry, thus training both hand and eye to correctness.
(d) It forms an educational yet pleasant and interesting occupation for children.
(e) It teaches colour, and cultivates a taste for combining the same.[67]

In addition to their educational value, varied occupations resulted in a useful end-product which could, as appropriate, be sold to parents.[68]

A similarly practical approach was advocated in another text on varied occupations, in this case on rug-making.

Rug making is an admirable occupation for girls who are good knitters, and in mixed schools the occupation is exceptionally applicable, because the boys can be employed in the preparation of the material and be engaged in the more laborious part of the work.

The rugs and mats when finished are very durable and find a ready sale, and the money so derived can be applied to the further purchase of material.[69]

Another book on ornamental paper work and flower-making was said to be also useful for invalids, girls' friendly societies, evening classes and bazaars, as well as for school work. Once more the debt to Froebelian method was acknowledged.

In his study of little children, Froebel found that they learned many things through their play, and that their first instincts were *to see, to handle* and *to exercise their senses*. Thus he was led to arrange a system of simple employments by which children could be trained to habits of obedience and concentration, quickness of observation, and a taste for school life ... Froebel designed twenty-two gifts and occupations ... each has its individual aim of development. The first six are termed 'gifts' and the remaining sixteen 'occupations'.

The educational value was described as promoting the development of accurate observation and imitation; dexterous hands; artistic taste; appreciation of beauty; and providing an attractive introduction to botany, as a good deal of paper-folding was geared to the production of flowers.[70] This love of nature was increasingly reflected in encouraging children to grow flowers at home, in collecting leaves on nature walks to mount on return to the classroom, in holding floral competitions, and in a book of 'Nature Songs' (p. 153). For Queen Alexandra Day in 1914 Louisa Walker composed a 'Rose Song'. The children made roses and wrote letters about the activity. The best of the children's letters was chosen and sent to the Queen, and a courteous reply was received. The letter read:

We each made a rose, and sang our Rose Song. We hope you have a very happy day, and we all send our love. From the Infants of Fleet-road School.[71]

The product of the varied occupations lessons was naturally regularly on display at the public entertainments Mrs. Walker so adeptly arranged. Her texts were also well received and were adopted by the London School Board. *The Infants' Mistress* article quoted reviews of the first of them. *The Teacher's Aid* described it as 'an attractive and delightful addition to infant school work'. The *School Board Chronicle* thought the book 'one of the fullest and most complete on occupations for infants we have yet seen'. The *Educational News* was the most laudatory: 'Loving ingenuity, methodic skill, happy suggestiveness, characterise this valuable guidebook to the intellectual and industrial education of the young.'[72]

Apart from the Macmillan series, Louisa Walker produced at least two more texts of varied occupations, entitled *Rainbow Raffia Work*, illustrated by her artist daughter, Winifred.[73] By the time she retired, the varied occupations in the infant department seem to have been much less varied. A former pupil tells that while they were still doing paper-cutting, at their desks in serried ranks of 60, work with plasticine had replaced many of the more ambitious activities.[74]

ACTION SONGS AND ENTERTAINMENTS

A noteworthy incident in the new school was the introduction by Mrs. Walker of a grand piano. Mr. Stanley and the singing instructor both objected, and its removal was ordered. Mrs. Walker argued the matter, and to the objections that it took too much room, and the children must be taught to sing alone, she answered she would get a cottage piano and place it back against the wall and play it for marching and games ... It is probably to the stand made by the teacher on this occasion ... that the presence of pianos in so many Board schools may now be traced.[75]

Of all the Froebel-inspired infant school activities it is probably the action songs and games that had most appeal for Louisa Walker, and tested most searchingly her energy and organizing skills. In his book on the London School Board, Philpott stressed the value in the urban school of games and action songs, and quoted an example from Fleet Road (Plate 22).

London children do not know how to play; the old traditional games have, many of them, been forgotten, but when taught in the infant schools they are received with delight, as are many of the charming new games and songs that have been written for little children ... there is no pleasanter sight in London than an organised game in an infant school, when it is part of the daily round and not a rehearsal for an entertainment.[76]

To Louisa Walker, however, both were important, and the extra-curricular school entertainment loomed large, as well as these activities being part of the 'daily round'. She was an inveterate composer of ditties, working with local musicians, particularly Louis D. Marsden. She produced no fewer than five sets of action songs, games, dialogues and recitations for J. Curwen in the years between 1899 and 1910. These were *Mrs. Walker's Action Songs and Games for Young Children* (1899), dedicated to Lady Kekewich; *Mrs. Walker's Recitations and Dialogues* (1900); *Mrs. Walker's Merry Games for Little People* (1902), which complemented her first collection, and shared the same introduction; *Mrs. Walker's Character Songs and Games* (1903); and *Mrs. Walker's Nature Songs and Games* (1910), witness to an increasing interest in the natural world in her later years.

The detailed introductions to these compilations testified afresh to Louisa Walker's crisp and pragmatic but also imaginative approach to this type of activity, as well as her organizational skills. No stone was left unturned in explaining the detail of the songs and games to the children, and their purposes to the teacher. Teachers had to lose their inhibitions and enter into the spirit of the action song.

If teachers wish their children to be natural, they must be natural themselves, and lay aside all dignity and come down to the level of their children, and enter heartily into the fun and life of the little ones. Never mind looking ridiculous; it is the great qualification needed in a good infants' teacher that she should be able to become as one of her children. *Telling* little children is no good, *doing* is the thing required, and then exaggerate slightly what is to be done to make the children come out of themselves ... It is surprising what can be done with little children if congeniality and fun be brought into the teaching, and the children made to lose all fear by seeing their teacher enter with spirit into their games.

Entertainments had to be well managed. 'Tiresome waits between the items should never be allowed'. Children 'not fit for important parts' were to make up a 'permanent chorus' designed to 'make a pretty background' and 'give fulness to the singing'.[77] The pretty background and the dressing up were essential features of Louisa Walker's entertainments (Plate 23). Unlike Goyder (p. 133), she was not dealing with the children of the poor, and to teachers like her the concept of 'the folly of finery' would have appeared anachronistic.

'Dressing up' is the principal feature of all plays, dialogues and recitations. A child dressed in character, feels far more important, and certainly throws himself with greater gusto into his part than he would in ordinary attire. Young children are not self-conscious, and consequently imitate and follow directions more implicitly than children of older years. Lovers of children find great enjoyment in seeing a number of infants act their respective parts with that intensity and simplicity so enjoyable in young children.[78]

The tunes for the songs were generally derived from well-known music of the time, drawn from the music hall and Gilbert and Sullivan, rather than religious and Froebelian origins. Louisa Walker claimed she liked to use such music because she thought the children would more quickly learn tunes they partly knew, while

22. The Railway Game: Fleet Road Infants' Department

23. 'Dressing Up': Fleet Road Infants in 'The Coming of Spring' in aid of
The Underfed Children's Fund, 1907 (photograph from Fleet Primary
School)

at an entertainment, a popular tune is well received by the audience, who often are carried away by the effect of little children acting and singing in a tune well-known to them.[79]

The audience at the entertainment had also to be catered for, and deserved to have presented to them a polished performance. Mrs. Walker suggested also how to cater for younger members of an audience, 'killing two birds with one stone'.

Young children in the audience are a nuisance, but as it is natural that children wish to see their brothers and sisters act, it has been found expedient to have a children's night as a preliminary to the entertainment. This should partake of the form of a dress rehearsal, and all shortcomings be made note of, and remedied, before the coming night.[80]

A minority of the Walker action songs and games were Froebelian in style. The 'Living Letters' simulation (Plate 20) was a case in point. The most classically Froebelian action song she wrote was, arguably 'The Silly Fish', in which a baby fish disobeys its mother, and plays around a fisherman's hook, which gets stuck in his little gill.

> And as he faint and fainter grew,
> With hollow voice he cried –
> 'Dear mother, if I'd minded you
> I need not now have died.'
> So children, learn from his sad fate
> Never to disobey!
> But always mind your mother's word,
> And not want your own way![81]

More characteristic of Louisa Walker's individual style was an instructional game entitled 'A, B, C Duet' in which boys, dressed in appropriate hats, played dunces and girls their teachers. The boys were asked to 'look very dull and stupid' and assume grimacing and hang-dog expressions, while the girls had to show 'energy and spirit'.[82] Similarly in 'The Cat and Mouse' song children learned about articles of food and the habits of cats and mice, which demanded elaborate dressing up in costumes depicting flour bags, butter tubs and cheese sections. The 'ludicrous sight' of the little ones portraying these articles of food provided a 'comical item' which always 'calls forth an encore',[83] claimed the authoress.

A good educational starting point was the direct experience of the children, and 'The Railway Train' (Plate 22) was a prime example of building on such experience, simulating travel on the North London Line from Hampstead Heath Station. A tall boy played the engine, his hands held from behind by the driver and stoker who led the carriages, composed in turn of a double line of children, outer arms on the shoulders of those in front, and inner joined from shoulder to shoulder. The outer arms represented the carriage doors, and when opened for a passenger were lifted up by the Porter, the passenger moving into the middle between the double line forming the carriage. The Guard at the back was another tall boy, who blew a whistle and waved a green flag at the appropriate point at each stop. A 'busy, energetic boy' took the role of Porter, repeated what the Guard said, and rang a bell at the terminus, shouting 'All change here'. The Ticket Collector, like the Guard and Porter wearing a peaked cap, stood at a gate held by two boys. The actions took place between the verse and chorus of the song. Other children made up the choir, and waved handkerchiefs as the train moved off. Bridges and tunnels were simulated by children standing on forms and holding across strips of material.[84]

In this song boys' parts predominated and roles were characteristically gender-related. In 'Model Laundry Maids' the same applied with the girls, the boys being used merely to come on with a clothes-line, and present placards saying 'Hygienic Laundry' or the like. But the social situation was hardly what authentic Hampstead residents would have anticipated, for these were 'high society, model laundry maids', engaging in a Gilbertian kind of dialogue, which interspersed with the vocal lines:

Forewoman: Be silent, I beg, a customer approaches. Good morning, madam! What can I have the pleasure of doing for you?
Lady Customer: Is this the high-class laundry?
Forewoman: It is, madam.
Lady Customer: Really and truly worked by ladies of title and high degree?
Forewoman: Yes, madam.
Lady Customer: I should hardly think their dainty little hands fit for such work.
Forewoman: The fact of the matter is this, madam, that at the present time *industry* of any kind is looked upon as an honourable occupation, and therefore our society ladies are coming to the front as doctors, nurses, lady-helps, gardeners, and last, but not least hygienic laundry maids ...[85]

Here and elsewhere the little girls were incited to ape high society ladies, as in a play with action song entitled 'Five o'Clock

Tea' in which a servant grumbles about the 'At Home' day nuisance. The hostess is Mrs. Raison-Smith (wearing a tea-gown *à la mode*), in the process of entertaining three other ladies with double-barrelled surnames, all attired in the latest long-dress fashions. The conversation was Mrs. Walker's version of high-society scandalous gossip. It laid special stress on the foibles of modern servants, such as the French maid constantly neglecting her duties to go away to note down an idea for a book she was writing, and another a Salvation Army girl, who smashed dinner plates through using them as tambourines and marched round the kitchen table singing 'Follow on'. The final worry was that the ladies would have to do all the work themselves, the result of the board schools over-educating working-class girls, 'making them too grand for servants'.[86]

Mrs. Walker had obviously a soft spot for the quirks of little boys, inviting the tolerance of the audience, as when, in 'A Boy's Pocket', the protagonist goes through its over-full contents, spilling them out in a heap on the floor, complaining of his mother's unreasonableness.[87] In 'Johnny's Grievance' the grumble is that in the varied occupations boys are asked to undertake activities normally done by girls.[88] While these songs and games almost inevitably, for their time, conveyed gender stereotypes, the girls were not usually presented in submissive terms, reflecting an unchanging order of society. Indeed, like the boys, they were being conditioned to a more meritocratic way of thinking.

To the outside public, action songs and games which encouraged so blatantly ideas of academic and social climbing must have seemed wantonly perverse. Why an 'Oxford and Cambridge Boat Race' song at this age?[89] Why the enticements of 'Up-to-date Young Men' in which three young boys are dressed in undergraduate gowns and mortar boards 'and, to a Gilbert and Sullivan tune', tell how much cleverer they are than their counterparts of 50 years before.[90] The twin song was 'Nineteenth Century Girls':

> Just think of all the dreadful things
> Girls study nowadays;
> They would have made our grandmothers
> Look blank in sheer amaze.[91]

'How I got my LL.A.' was even more provocative. The LL.A.

degree was the Lady Literate in Arts of St. Andrew's University, which offered a degree for women with a comparable status to an M.A. of a Scottish university. Again to a Gilbert and Sullivan tune, Sir Joseph Porter's Song from *H.M.S. Pinafore*, the ambitious young female is taken from learning her A.B.C. 'on a tiny stool' to an academic career which culminates in both Lady Margaret Hall and Girton competing to nurse her 'budding genius' *en route* to a doctorate and an LL.A.[92]

If one part of the inspiration was Gilbert and Sullivan, the other was the pantomime. In this genre, good and evil could be vividly presented. Fleet Road children were brought up to believe they were a fortunate group, coming from supportive homes. It was their duty to help the less well off. In 'A Case of Toys', two aristocratic girls are bored with their surfeit of playthings, while in a 'lonesome garret', in the following scene, two ragged children are making imaginative use of old bits of wood and furniture to play shop. A good toy-shop fairy transports the aristocratic children to the attic, where they quickly pick up the moral of the story, explicitly spelled out to the audience by the good fairy: 'To these poor children then shall be presented, some of the toys I have invented.'[93]

Louisa Walker lived and taught through the period of the Boer War and the First World War. These were times when the imperial spirit and patriotic feelings touched new heights of jingoism, reflected in the popular press and boys' periodicals in particular, but far from absent in text-books and educational journals such as *The Teachers' Aid*. At Fleet Road, such values were not especially in the forefront, but Mrs. Walker was inspired by the Boer War to produce an action song of singular bathos entitled 'Off to the War'. In this two infants play a mother and son in the process of a tearful farewell as the son 'at duty's call' goes to 'protect Old England from a foe'.[94] During the First World War Louisa Walker was approaching retirement and her energies were naturally diminishing. The old-style entertainments were less in evidence, but her encouragement of 'dressing-up' did not wane. Fancy dress occasions, recalls an old pupil under Mrs. Walker in the latter years of the war, remained very popular. John Jones's mother lovingly recreated the uniform of his father, serving in the Royal Artillery, and later a John Bull costume (Plates 24a/b), the latter a natural first-prize winner in the circumstances of the time.[95]

24a/b. John E. Jones in Royal Artillery uniform and John Bull outfit for
Fleet Road Infants' Department fancy dress occasions, 1916–18 period

Louisa Walker's skills in adapting for school use songs from
Gilbert and Sullivan, pantomime, and the music hall in general,
encompassed also the highly popular 'nigger minstrel' entertainment, espoused in the teachers' journals as a certain success
at school prize-givings.[96] Her action song 'The Little Cotton
Pickers' conveyed one of the most prevalent social stereotypes of
the time: the simple, cheery, singing and dancing black, his
servile lot ameliorated by his uncomplaining, happy-go-lucky
nature and the sub-tropical sunshine. Mrs. Walker, in true
Froebelian fashion, used the story to force home a moral lesson
for lucky but unappreciative English children:

> From cotton pretty things are made
> Pick'd by the coon of dusky shade;
> And ev'ry child should strive to be
> As gay and active, kind as he.[97]

A more offensive symbol was the equation of blackness with dirtiness, and this was one exploited by Mrs. Walker in a recitation on the theme of 'The Dirty Boy', in which a scruffy urchin is threatened that if he does not keep himself cleaner he will end up as a little black boy. The recitation was based on a contemporary 'Pear's Soap' advert.

> He shocks and grieves his parents
> We all his state deplore,
> I tell him if he grows like this
> He'll be a blackamoor.[98]

There was difference of opinion at the time as to the educational value of action songs and games. Some felt they were valuable so long as an integral part of the school work, but were suspicious of the growing fashion for school entertainments. The Froebel journal *Child Life* made this clear in a critical review of Louisa Walker's *Action Songs and Games*. While agreeing that the text was attractively presented, and the music 'pretty and suitable', it was otherwise censorious:

Though this book contains many bright and amusing songs, it does not, perhaps, call for special notice from an educational standpont, as it is frankly compiled largely with a view to the annual entertainment, which we believe is becoming more and more a bugbear to teachers ...

Some of the songs are old friends with new faces, and several would, perhaps, never have been written but for the suggestiveness of certain light operas. Accompanying the songs are directions as to the actions, and suggestions for costumes, etc. The latter, no doubt, make the songs more popular with an ordinary audience, but rob them of much of their value in training the children's imagination. We confess, especially, to a dislike of a garden of flowers of crinkled paper, and children as lambs with tails of frayed rope; and we cannot see the advantage of turning our little ones of five into 'ludicrous sights'.

Another point to which we take exception is the somewhat flippant treatment of animal life; and we cannot think that such a song as 'Up-to-date Young Men' is in any way suitable for children. It cannot be anything but a mistake to allow our children, even in game and song, to treat the serious matters of adult life with foolish frivolity.[99]

It was clear that in her initiatives to translate Froebel's ideas of action songs into the social situation in which she found herself and of which she was part, Mrs. Walker stretched the tolerance of the orthodox much too far. Yet she herself would have claimed she was retaining the spirit if not the letter of the Froebelian approach. The last of her song books, *Mrs. Walker's Nature*

Songs and Games (1910), was less iconoclastic, though still directed towards entertainment and dressing up. Here the infant players simulated Hay-making (Plate 25), danced round the Maypole (Plate 26) or, most elaborate of all, acted out the budding of plants, in 'Flowers, awake!' (Plate 27). In this tiny girls 'of equal height for the flowers' were attired 'in long Kate Greenaway dresses of art muslin or Jap silk the colour of the flower'. The song ended with the chorus performing 'a last verse of thankfulness'.[100]

How far this return to nature reflected a reminder of her Froebelian training, how far a privileged residential location on the edge of Hampstead Heath, and how far a personal resonance with a social climate increasingly anxious about the perceived chaos and lack of moral clarity of city life, with the compensating nostalgia for a lost rural way of life, is a matter of speculation. It would not have been surprising had Louisa Walker sought a counter to the acquisitive urban values that the various departments of her school were so assiduously cultivating in their children.

THE ENTERTAINMENTS

Child Life was one of a number of organs of educational opinion commenting on the 'bugbear' of entertainments. It can confidently be inferred that nothing would have deterred Louisa Walker from running them. One old pupil described her as 'wonderful at arranging concerts'. They prompted the most elaborate preparations in school in the time leading up to the performance. The girls might make artificial flowers while the boys built cradles out of Bovril boxes, which the girls later draped. One of the occasions is described in the school's Centenary publication:

We had to have white silk dresses which were made to measure by Daniels in Kentish Town Road. The yokes were of lace lined with pale green with sashes and hair ribbons to match. In addition to the dresses which I expect cost about 4/11d in those days mothers had to take our knickers and petticoats for Mrs. Walker's inspection and if they didn't meet with her approval you were not in the concert. This was all for the concert at Hampstead Town Hall which was filled for two nights and an extra one at a church hall ...

At the concert at the church hall, Reggie McCullock, in a kilt, sang 'Goodbye Dolly I must leave you though it breaks my heart to go' to Ethel

25. Haymaking: a Mrs. Walker Action Song

26. May Day: a Mrs. Walker Action Song

27. Flowers Awake: another Mrs. Walker Action Song from *Nature Songs and Games*

Moore. He was so nervous he burst into tears just at the right moment and of course was a high success.[101]

Some of the entertainments were used to raise money for charity, as in a production in Hampstead Town Hall in 1907, 'The Coming of Spring', in aid of the Underfed Children's Fund (Plate 23).[102]

Two of the most notable public occasions took place in 1895. In the first, Mrs. Walker's infants were invited to perform their action songs at the London School Board's Vocal Music Competition at the Queen's Hall in December of that year (see Chapter 9). It was the highlight of the occasion, in the opinion of the *School Music Review*, which commented on the unanimity, enthusiasm and enjoyment of the children, and 'how wonderfully well the little actors managed their eyes'. Louisa Walker was interviewed by the reporter and clarified that the songs had been 'invented entirely by myself'. Great care was taken in ensuring the children understood the meaning of the song, that words were matched exactly with actions, and that the actions were contrived to produce effects 'very pretty in the mass'.[102] The element of 'showing off', as defined by *Child Life*,[103] was seen by Mrs. Walker as a beneficial element in the social education of her pupils.

The other red-letter day of 1895 was the entertainment

arranged in Hampstead to celebrate the 21st anniversary of Louisa Walker's arrival in the district. It took place in the Vestry Hall, and was advertised in the *Hampstead and Highgate Express*. Tickets were two shillings for reserved and one shilling for unreserved seats. HMI Fitzmaurice was to preside over the occasion, and prizes were to be presented by Mrs. Lyulph Stanley. The proceeds were to be used to arrange a tea for all 723 children in the school, with anything left over being placed in a reserve fund for deserving cases.[104] 180 infants appeared in the entertainment. Particular mention was made in the press of the striking character costumes of the actors, with little boys in Cambridge knickerbockers and white sailor jackets, and little girls in pink or Cambridge blue dresses, with white pinafores. The costumes were made by mothers on the basis of Mrs. Walker's designs and with flannelette supplied by her at cost price. In a short sketch entitled 'Playing at School' a group of scholars gave 'a capital representation of how instruction is imparted and personal cleanliness insisted on at "the Fleet-road seminary"'.[105]

The 1898 entertainment was a combined effort with Broomsleigh Street, Louisa Walker's husband's school, described as 'in every way' a remarkable occasion.[106] The 1899 prize-giving was attended by Sir George Kekewich, Secretary of the Education Department, who congratulated Louisa Walker on 'the pitch of perfection to which she and her assistants had brought that school'.[107] In 1901, the prizes were distributed by Lady Lindsay, 'the authoress of many poetical and charming works'. She said the experience had 'not conveyed to her the impression of being in a school at all, but in a delightful fairyland'.[108] At the 1902 Coronation Commemoration in Hampstead, to which Fleet Road school contributed, Mrs. Walker reminded the audience that in the 28 years she had been a Headmistress, nearly 60,000 infants had passed under her instruction,[109] which would appear an excessive claim. In 1911 the Mayor attended to distribute Coronation souvenirs, declaring the purpose of the occasion as being to make the children 'think of the great British Empire and to continue to "Rule Britannia" as in the past'.[110]

The journal *Child Life* was not alone in disliking Louisa Walker's action songs and games. Opinion in Hampstead was often critical of what was variously described as 'tomfoolery', and the indulgence of 'getting up these unnecessary ... entertainments' at ratepayers' expense, as if the object of board school education was a training for the stage, rather than what it was intended for, which was the production of a casual labour reserve content to service the comforts of local residents. A correspondent under the pseudonym 'A Ratepayer' was particularly direct.

Will you kindly make known through your columns the very grave disapproval felt by hundreds of ratepayers at the utterly useless displays that are got up by the Fleet-road and other Board school children. There are many respectable middle-class people who ... will not consent much longer to be forced to pay the yearly increasing rate ... for teaching children singing, recitations, games, dancing, for wasting their time in inventing new games and in rigging the children out in velvet knickerbockers, cream blouses, and sashes, etc. ...

The Board schools have been instituted nearly thirty years, with what result? Where is one to find a young man, or a young woman, who has been fitted for his or her walk in life? Where is one to get a laundry-maid, a cook, a dressmaker, a plumber, or any other workman who knows anything about the business he pretends to? ... The children are kept at school singing, dancing, playing the fiddle, and learning all sorts of rubbish that is utterly useless for them thereafter, until they are too old either to learn a trade or be of use to anyone.[111]

The spirit of the Revised Code regularly resurfaced in public utterances from the voluntaryist lobby in Hampstead during the 1880s and 1890s, particularly at the time of School Board elections. The action songs were doubly deplorable to such a climate of opinion. They were inappropriate not only in terms of waste of resources, but also more fundamentally as social education. The view from Hampstead found it hard to distinguish different types of Board school, which had been defined on the basis of the voluntaryist fantasy of 1870 that such schools would be for the 'education of the poor'. The children of Fleet Road had it made clear to them they were not of the poor, but were a favoured group, there to help the poor. The action songs stressed the meritocratic virtues, the need to work hard, the virtue of trying to get on in the world, and the responsibility of offering at least limited support to the needy.

These values are also present in another of Louisa Walker's publishing initiatives, a set of readers for Cassell entitled *The Robbie Books*, based on the experiences of a young boy, Robbie, reacting to the stimulus of four different holiday environments: the countryside; the seaside; London; and on the river. The emphasis, apart from the development of reading skills, was on

the constructive use of leisure time and developing an appreciation of the environment. A fairly cosy view of modern life was in
evidence, in which the benefits of a well-ordered society and of
technological advances such as the motor car and the 'gram-o-
phone' loomed quite large. There is a quick glimpse of the
seamier side of society as Robbie, on an open-topped omnibus,
witnesses poor people sleeping out on the Embankment.

'They have no homes and many of them are starving too. How sad!' said
Robbie. 'Does no one help them?' 'Yes' answered his father, 'there are kind
people who do a great deal for them. They give beds and food to as many as they
can, and to the others they give warm soup at night and a hot breakfast in the
morning.'[112]

AN APPRAISAL OF LOUISA WALKER

Louisa Walker finally retired in March 1918, having completed
44 years' teaching service in Gospel Oak, and nearly forty at Fleet
Road itself. There was, predictably, an entertainment, to which
Sir George Kekewich was invited back. He repeated his old
rating of the Department: that it was one of the best, if not the
best, in London. The Chairman reminded the audience of Mrs.
Walker's services to the area. She had lived 'within the sound of
the school bell'. People had deliberately come to reside in Gospel
Oak to secure for their children a place in her Department.[113]
Comparison was made, possibly for the last time, with Eton and
Harrow.[114] In her response, Louisa Walker stressed the importance she had always attached to getting young children to use
their hands and to respond to music. She had introduced the
piano at an early stage and had 'lived down opposition'.[115]
She implied that she had been aggressive in seeking resources,
because she wanted things to be better. It was 'only dissatisfaction that pushed on the world'.[116] One of the speakers attri-
buted her success to her strong personality and individuality,
which he accepted had not always been liked.[117] Her combative
style made enemies. There is a notable absence of reference to
cooperation with the main school. It is to be doubted whether she
was close either professionally or socially to W.B. Adams. The
infants sent a wreath to his funeral, but Mrs. Walker is not
recorded as attending. She complained bitterly when W.B.
Adams took over his wife's Department on her retirement. She
had to be instructed by the London School Board to fit in with the

new arrangement. While they shared meritocratic values and an ability to exploit the media, it may be construed they were rivals rather than allies.

Louisa Walker was not infrequently in dispute with the London School Board. While on excellent terms with its leading politicians, she had much less time for its bureaucrats. In her evidence to the Board's enquiry on methods of infant teaching, she complained strongly about the requisitions she was offered for her progressive infant work. Large numbers of submissions were refused, the colours of materials provided were crude and artistically wanting, while the system restricted the ingenuity of the teacher in laying down what could and what could not be ordered. She had on occasions not been refunded for material she had bought herself. The requisitions list might have been suitable for normal Froebel work: 'but I like to go further. I think the teacher should have a free hand, and have what she wants.'[118]

A number of confrontations occurred in 1902 and 1903. In December 1902 the Board informed her that if she and her daughter were absent to attend a wedding early the following month, their pay would be stopped.[119] There was disagreement with Adams, in the month before he died, over transfer arrangements from the Infants' to the Junior Mixed Department. Mrs. Walker was ordered to carry out the arrangement. About the same time the Board's Inspector reported[120] that portions of the Infants' Department records had been lost, and others not kept complete. He recommended that the Headmistress be reminded of her duties on these matters.[121]

She had an unpleasant confrontation with a temporary teacher towards the end of 1902. The teacher arrived on 4 December of that year and stalked out angrily on 21 January 1903. She complained that Mrs. Walker interfered with her class, distracting the children and then complaining they were not being kept in order. On 21 January Mrs. Walker entered with the school-keeper and was alleged to have said to him within hearing: 'This teacher cannot manage this class.' At this the complainant walked out and in her submission to the Board described the Headmistress as 'most insolent'. The conclusion of the Board was that while it accepted the school-keeper had been in the room accidentally, it 'viewed with displeasure' Louisa Walker's 'indiscretion'. She seems to have accepted she made the offending comment, but argued that she had been annoyed by the state of the class. She was asked to be more careful in the future.[122]

Notwithstanding her reputation as a progressive, maintaining a bright and cheerful atmosphere in her Department, Louisa Walker was also regarded as a strict disciplinarian, and on occasions used corporal punishment. In 1895 the Managers reported a complaint from a Mr. Francis about Mrs. Walker striking her son.[123] In the Centenary publication, an old pupil of 1915 recalls her as 'a kind, grey-haired lady and we all liked her'. Others make it clear, however, that she 'knew exactly what she wanted and got it ... ALL children, throughout the school, held Mrs. Walker in great awe – AND the parents! She was THE all-out disciplinarian, and I am sure we children were not wrong in thinking that the staff quaked before her too.'[124] The same publication offers a diverting cameo of Louisa Walker at one of her entertainments, 'standing behind the scenes with a cane in her hand', as little boys with blackened faces were chasing girls in their light frocks backstage.[125]

There are certainly pieces of evidence to suggest that her staff found her threatening, and were less than convinced of the value of her entertainments and action songs. Mrs. Walker's successor was Mrs. M.M. Bowler of Haggerston Road Council School. She expressed a wish to take over the Fleet Road Infants' Department. Exceptionally, the London County Council agreed to her suggestion, and she was appointed without competition.[126] John Jones, a former pupil whose aunt taught at the time in the Department, recalls family conversations which testified to the more relaxed atmosphere which prevailed in the Infants' Department under Mrs. Bowler.

Another old pupil reported that the attention paid to the making of flowers and other activities of this sort was not 'wholly appreciated in the Junior Department where one frequently heard, "Pity they don't spend the time on reading and writing!" Feeling ran high, and an inspector's judgement was invited.'[127] John Jones recalls his aunt referring to 'that silly woman and her action songs' after the pathos of 'The Silly Fish' song (p. 148) had reduced many of the infants to tears. He was told that Mrs. Bowler discontinued this activity. Louisa Walker was something of a prophetess without honour in her own country, perhaps more particularly in her later years. These criticisms were less in evidence in her heyday in the 1890s.

While 1895 witnessed triumphs for Louisa Walker, it was also a year of distress. She was unable to supply her annual report to the Managers that year because of illness at home and consequent absence. It was recorded that 'Mrs. Walker has had much home anxiety during the past year'.[128] Family history tells that her daughter Winifred was desperately ill about this time. But the reference was no doubt more specifically addressed to the fact that her husband, James Walker, had been fined by Marylebone magistrates on a charge of assault of a boy at his school, Broomsleigh Street. The boy had illicitly gone home when told to leave a classroom he was not supposed to be in. The following day the boy once more resisted punishment, tried to run off home, and was struck again on his way out. The magistrate claimed that Walker had acted in an undignified manner in thrice flogging the boy, and described the punishment as excessive. Walker was fined 10/- with 23/- costs. It was claimed that the boy had been encouraged by his father not to accept caning.

The local newspaper in its editorial, without explicitly mentioning the court case, wrote sympathetically of Walker as 'a man of modest, kindly disposition' and 'held in high esteem in the district', his school being 'one of the most efficiently taught of all the board schools'.[129] The issue was publicized in the *Westminster Gazette*, which enjoined its readers to say what they would do in the 'provoking circumstances' of a boy who had 'wilfully misinterpreted' instructions and kept trying to 'bolt home'.[130] The London School Board Teaching Staff Sub-committee took up the case, but concluded that the boy was deserving of the punishment and resolved to take no further action.[131]

On Louisa Walker's death, the *Hampstead Advertiser* reflected the view of all the other local papers.

Mrs. Walker was in the forefront of her profession, and she was always regarded as a pioneer in school methods ... To watch Mrs. Walker with her pupils was to see Education under the most advanced and successful conditions.[132]

The case of Louisa Walker's life and work provokes further investigation of a whole series of stereotypes which have come down to us about late-Victorian elementary education in general and infant education in particular. While an institution placed in the aristocracy of the board schools can hardly be taken as a norm, its achievements can legitimately be used to help to

reshape our image of a period of explosive expansion and innovation. While the Revised Code and its successors could hardly
be ignored, there were important counter-forces at work, particularly in schools such as Fleet Road. Redirecting the experience
of thousands of London children, Louisa Walker's personal
energy and style, her historical, social and territorial placings,
and her idiosyncratic interpretations and implementation of
educational trends and official regulations, are full of nuances for
the historian of the curriculum and indeed of extra-curricular
provision. The achievements of other remarkable teachers of her
time in the public sector have yet to be illumined. It is fortunate
that some of Louisa Walker's contemporaries judged her work
to be worth publicizing, while her own ability to commit her
practical ideas to print has provided enough of an historical
record to allow some redress of an important 'aspect of neglect'[133]
of late Victorian and Edwardian popular education.

REFERENCES AND NOTES

1. *The Practical Teacher*, vol. 19 (1898), p.61.
2. *HHE*, 25 Feb. 1922.
3. *The Practical Teacher*, vol. 19 (1898), pp.57–8.
4. *PRO*, Ed. 7/75.
5. *HHE*, 3 April 1915.
6. *HHE*, 25 Feb. 1922.
7. *The Practical Teacher*, vol. 19 (1898), pp.58–60.
8. LSB, *School Management Committee*, 27 Nov. 1878, p.730.
9. *Ibid.*, 23 June 1880, p.138.
10. National Society Archives, *St. Stephen's Hampstead File*.
11. LSB, *School Management Committee*, 7 May 1879, p.959.
12. *Ibid.*, 5 May 1881, p.841.
13. *Ibid.*, 12 Oct. 1882, p.564.
14. *Ibid.*, 26 Feb. 1885, p.598.
15. *Ibid.*, 29 July 1886, p.500.
16. F.M.L. Thompson, *Hampstead: Building a Borough 1650–1964* (London, 1974),
    pp.355–6.
17. *HHE*, 18 Feb. 1932.
18. LSB, *School Management Committee*, 14 Feb. 1889, p.443.
19. *Ibid.*, 19 Dec. 1895, p.241.
20. LCC, *Teaching Staff Sub-committee*, 6 July 1905 and 13 July 1906.
21. *Ibid.*, 18 July 1907.
22. *HHE*, 9 Jan. 1909.
23. *GLC Record Office*, EO/GEN/8/1.
24. LCC, *Teaching Staff Sub-committee*, 4 Dec. 1935, p.307.
25. *SBC*, 7 April 1888, p.359.
26. SBL 1470, LCC *Technical Instruction Board* Scholarship Lists.
27. *HHE*, 25 Feb. 1922.

28. H.B. Philpott, *London at School: the Story of the London School Board 1870–1904* (London, 1904), p.67.
29. *Ibid.*, p.68.
30. *Ibid.*, p.69.
31. N. Whitbread, *The Evolution of the Nursery-Infant School: a History of Infant and Nursery Education in Britain 1800–1870* (London, 1972), p.47. See also Board of Education, *Reports on Children under Five Years of Age in Public Elementary Schools* (London, 1905), Cd.2726, pp.i–iii.
32. L. Walker, 'How I came to Introduce Varied Occupations', *The Practical Teacher*, vol. 19 (1898), p.63.
33. R. Dunning, *The Phonic System of Teaching to Read Applied after the Methods of Pestalozzi* (London, 1856), pp.3–9.
34. C. Steedman, '"The Mother made Conscious": the Historical Development of a Primary School Pedagogy', *History Workshop Journal*, vol. 20 (1985), pp.149–63. See also, A.T. Allen, 'Spiritual Motherhood: German Feminists and the Kindergarten Movement', *History of Education Quarterly*, vol. 22 (1982), pp.319–39.
35. See, for example, J. and B. Ronge, *A Practical Guide to the English Kindergarten* (London, 1855), frontispiece; and E. Heerwart's introduction to F.W.A. Froebel, *Mother's Songs, Games and Stories* (London, 1888).
36. D.G. Goyder, *A Manual Detailing the System of Instruction Pursued at the Infant School Bristol* (London, 1824), p.9 and pp.49–50.
37. Quoted in *The Teachers' Times and Kindergarten Gazette*, 17 Oct. 1902, p.370.
38. J. and B. Ronge, *op. cit.* (1855), p.56.
39. Froebel, *op. cit.* (1888), p.102 and p.106. See also H.A. Hamilton, 'The Religious Roots of Froebel's Philosophy' in E. Lawrence (ed.), *Friedrich Froebel and English Education* (London, 1952), pp.166–78.
40. J. and B. Ronge, *op. cit.* (1855), p.11.
41. J.S. Laurie (ed.), *Infant Education: Descriptive Notes on the Kindergarten System* (London, 1877). Appendix illustrating the kindergarten gifts and occupations material as sold by the Central School depot in Paternoster Row.
42. M.E. Bailey, *Hints on Introducing the Kindergarten System into English Infant Schools* (London, 1876), p.22.
43. E.M. Mortimer, *Practical Kindergarten Lessons* (London, 1891), pp.35–6.
44. G. Davidson, 'Course of Lessons in the First Gift', *The Girls' and Infants' Mistress*, 14 Sept. 1901, p.5.
45. Education Department, *Instruction of Infants*, Circular 322 (London, 1893), pp.68–9.
46. *HHE*, 10 Oct. 1891.
47. SBL 717, *School Management Committee Special Sub-committee on Method in Infants' Schools*, 23 July 1897.
48. Bailey, *op. cit.* (1876), p.7. See also Mortimer, *op. cit.* (1891), p.14.
49. Steedman, *op. cit.* (1985), p.154.
50. *HHE*, 10 Oct. 1891.
51. *The Infants' Mistress*, vol. 1 (1893), p.1.
52. The comments are drawn from a series of Government Inspectors' Reports in SBL 1586 and numbers following.
53. The timetable was printed in *The Infants' Mistress*, vol. 1 (1893), p.2.
54. LSB, *Record of Examination in Scripture Knowledge*, held 27/28 Nov. 1894.
55. *The Infants' Mistress*, vol. 1 (1893), p.2.
56. SBL 717, *op. cit.* (1897), p.71.
57. Philpott, *op. cit.* (1904), p.69.
58. SBL 141, *Report of Special Committee on Subjects and Modes of Instruction in Board Schools*.
59. Education Department, *Object Teaching*, Circular 369 (London, 1895), pp.74–5.
60. L. Walker, *Cusack's Object Lessons: Part II: Mineral and Vegetable World and Common Objects* (London, 1895), pp.vii–viii.
61. LSB, *Government Reports on Fleet Road Infants' School*, 1894–6.

62. *The Infants' Mistress*, vol. 1 (1893), p.2.
63. LSB, *Government Inspectors' Report*, 1883.
64. *The Infants' Mistress*, vol. 1 (1903), p.2.
65. LSB, *Minutes*, 3 March 1892, p.658.
66. L. Walker, *Varied Occupations in Weaving* (London, 1895), pp.vii–viii.
67. *Ibid.*, p.9.
68. *Ibid.*, p.19.
69. L. Walker, *Rug Making: an Occupation for Infants and Standard I* (London, 1898), Introduction.
70. L. Walker, *Instructive and Ornamental Paper Work: a Practical Book on Making Flowers and Many other Articles for Artistic Decoration* (London, 1901), p.1 and p.50.
71. *HHE*, 4 July 1914.
72. *The Infants' Mistress*, vol. 2 (1894), p.8.
73. L. Walker, *Rainbow Raffia Work, Books 1 and 2* (London, undated).
74. For this and other information I am indebted to Mr. John E. Jones, an old pupil of Fleet Road School, in the Infants' Department towards the end of the First World War in Mrs. Walker's last years as Headmistress.
75. *The Practical Teacher*, vol. 19 (1898), p.60.
76. Philpott, *op. cit.* (1904), p.77.
77. L. Walker, *Mrs. Walker's Merry Games for Little People* (London, 1902), Introduction.
78. *Ibid.*, p.47.
79. L. Walker, *Mrs Walker's Recitations and Dialogues* (London, 1900), p.iii.
80. Walker, *op. cit.* (1902), p.ii.
81. L. Walker, *Mrs. Walker's Action Songs and Games for Young Children* (London, 1899), p.8.
82. L. Walker, *Mrs. Walker's Character Songs and Games* (London, 1903), pp.12–13.
83. Walker, *op. cit.* (1899), pp.14–17.
84. *Ibid.*, pp.18–21.
85. Walker, *op. cit.* (1903), pp.47–9.
86. Walker, *op. cit.* (1902), pp.29–30.
87. *Ibid.*, pp.1–2.
88. Walker, *op. cit.* (1900), pp.14–15.
89. Walker, *op. cit.* (1899), pp.84–8.
90. *Ibid.*, pp.89–91.
91. Walker, *op. cit.* (1902), p.9.
92. *Ibid.*, pp.16–17.
93. *Ibid.*, pp.62–73.
94. *Ibid.*, pp.101–2.
95. My thanks are due to Mr. and Mrs. Jones for copies of these photographs.
96. See W.E. Marsden, '"All in a Good Cause": Geography, History and the Politicization of the Curriculum in Nineteenth and Twentieth Century England', *Journal of Curriculum Studies*, vol. 21 (1989), pp.509–26.
97. L. Walker, *Mrs. Walker's Nature Songs and Games* (London, 1910), pp.48–51.
98. Walker, *op. cit.* (1900), p.98.
99. *Child Life*, vol. 2 (1900), p.64.
100. Walker, *op. cit.* (1910), p.11.
101. *Hundred Years Fleet School 1879–1979* (Hampstead, 1979), pp.10–11.
102. *School Music Review*, vol. 4 (1895), pp.120–1.
103. *Child Life*, vol. 2 (1900), p.64.
104. *HHE*, 23 March 1895.
105. *HHE*, 30 March 1895.
106. *Hampstead Record*, 24 Dec. 1898.

107. *Hampstead Record*, 18 Feb. 1899.
108. *HHE*, 30 March 1901.
109. *HHE*, 9 Nov. 1902.
110. *HHE*, 29 July 1911.
111. *HHE*, 4 March 1899.
112. L. Walker, *Robbie in London*, No. 3 of *The Robbie Books* (London, 1911), p.21. Mrs. Walker's eldest son was named Robert.
113. *Hampstead Record*, 5 April 1918.
114. *HHE*, 30 March 1918.
115. *Hampstead Record*, 5 April 1918.
116. *Hampstead and St. John's Wood and Kilburn Advertiser*, 4 April 1918.
117. *HHE*, 30 March 1918.
118. SBL 717, *op. cit.* (1897), pp.71–2.
119. SBL 670, *School Management Committee*, 19 Dec. 1902.
120. SBL 670, 6 Feb. 1903.
121. SBL 893, *Teaching Staff Sub-committee*, 19 Jan. 1903.
122. SBL 893, 26 Jan., 16 Feb. and 2 March 1903.
123. SBL 699, *School Management Committee*, 29 Nov. 1895.
124. *Hundred Years Fleet School, op. cit.* (1979), p.39.
125. *Ibid.*, p.10.
126. LCC, *Report of the Teaching Staff Sub-committee*, 27 March 1918, pp.211–12.
127. *Hundred Years Fleet School, op. cit.* (1979), p.10.
128. LSB, *Manager's Yearly Report*, Fleet Road, Hampstead, Board School, 1895.
129. *HHE*, 2 Nov. 1895.
130. *Westminster Gazette*, 30 Oct. 1895.
131. SBL 875, *Teaching Staff Sub-committee*, 4 Nov. 1895.
132. *Hampstead Advertiser*, 2 March 1922.
133. See H. Silver, 'Aspects of Neglect: the Strange Case of Victorian Popular Education', in H. Silver, *Education as History: Interpreting Nineteenth- and Twentieth-Century Education* (London, 1983), pp.17–34.

CHAPTER SEVEN

The Teachers and Managers

The considerations which influence mankind in the deter-
mination of each individual's social status are (1) Birth,
(2) Education, (3) The dignity or utility of professional
pursuits, (4) Extraordinary accomplishments, (5) Social
character ... We think the trained Schoolmaster can fairly
lay claim to public consideration upon the second, third and
fifth of these grounds of social gradation.[1]

The Schoolmaster, 1872

The Fleet Road Board School seems fortunate in having
twelve active managers, including the vicar and, amongst
others, a medical man, whose professional advice on
questions of sanitation and over-pressure is specially
valued.[2]

Cross Commission, 1888

The rapid growth of educational provision in the period of the
school boards, particularly in expanding urban areas such as
London, brought in its train an abundant demand for teachers,
and also for local school managers, required at the base of an
increasingly bureaucratized system of organization. The Headmaster of Fleet Road School, W.B. Adams, regularly stressed
the importance to the school of the quality of its teachers and the
support of its managers. In the latter case, he was thinking
above all of the Rt. Hon. Lyulph Stanley, one of the leading
figures on the London School Board and the most prominent and
influential member of the local group of managers. Unfortunately, most assistant teachers and managers shared in common
the fact that they were low down in the chain of command, and
records of their individual achievements and opinions are hard to
come by. In the case of Fleet Road School, for example, there is
precious little evidence of the feelings of the teachers, as distinct
from the headteacher, towards the managers, and vice versa.

The tensions between the local managers, though not specifically the Fleet Road group of managers, and the London School Board, gained a more public airing. Like the teachers, the managers were very sensitive about status.

THE TEACHERS

Teachers are a group of special interest to this study both in being self-evidently a central feature of a school biography, and also contextually. In the broader canvas of social change they embodied distinctive Victorian lower-middle-class anxieties about status. They demanded the respectability they regarded as due to a professional group, and were embittered by the low esteem in which they were regarded by the upper ranks of society. The position of earlier generations of parish school teachers was characteristically subservient, with career prospects at the mercy of the whims of the local manager. Their situation was a faithful reflection of the social placing of 'the office of educator', described by one 1840 commentator as 'of low caste, even beneath the common rank of successful tradesmen and shopkeepers'.[3]

The pupil-teacher system provided one of the few avenues of upward mobility for working-class children of the period.[4] But a profession which depended on the working class for its recruits, as the elementary system did in its early years, had a hard battle in store in the quest for an improved ranking. The school board period generated new opportunities both in economic and social terms. *The Times* saw as one of the consequences of the 1870 Act the 'boundless prospect opening up before the teaching profession'. At the same time it drew attention to the ambiguous position and the perceived narrowness of outlook of its practitioners.

They have too much education to be quite at home with small farmers and shopkeepers while they have not the knowledge or the manners which are acquired in good society. They can scarcely avoid being pedants or mere pedagogues.[5]

These were not merely the sentiments of social critics of the professional pretensions of the teachers. Thus Thomas Gautrey, a long-standing teacher union leader and also a member and an historian of the London School Board, tells that in the early years of the London School Board there was a general feeling that the elementary school teachers needed more culture: 'what we have to do is to get them into dress suits.'[6] Lyulph Stanley, very much in sympathy with teacher aspirations, none the less expressed anxiety on this score.

Now at present our pupil teachers come often from homes where there is not much cultivation. Too often the literary conversation and the elevating influences to which they have been subject are mainly in the schools. So certain a test of refinement as the tone of the voice, if applied to teachers, too often shows that they have not acquired that higher cultivation which is so much wanted to humanize the rough children committed to their charge.[7]

By the time Stanley was writing, it is likely that pupil teachers were still being drawn primarily from working-class backgrounds. But they were characteristically respectable working-class backgrounds, which makes confident placing of origins difficult. The growth of popular education in the second half of the nineteenth century was part of the great burgeoning of tertiary occupations, providing opportunities for vast numbers to rise into the lower middle-class or white-collar groups. The major socio-economic break was not between the middle class and the working class. It was between the respectable and the rough working classes. Respectable families had quite typically within them both white- and blue-collar members, and were in a situation in which not only upward mobility beckoned, but also social slippage was to be feared. It these circumstances, preoccupation with socio-economic status was understandable.

Choice of residence was critical, and necessarily responded to the delicate balance between status aspiration and economic capacity. As early as 1851 teachers were being caught up in the centrifugal ecological forces which spun people (and schools) out into the suburbs.[8] So far as inner city areas were concerned, teachers tended to become increasingly less visible within the communities served by their schools. In her testimony to the Cross Commission, Mrs. Burgwin, the formidable Headmistress of Orange Street School, Southwark, a 'school of special difficulty', felt it no disadvantage that her teachers lived well away from the catchment area of her school.

I think a teacher comes fresher to her work when she comes from a nicer home altogether, with nicer surroundings, and certainly coming into the district of this school; you could hardly want anyone to sleep in it.[9]

By 1891 the teachers had essentially become a suburban race.[10]

While residential preferences continued to be constrained by modest incomes, there was still considerable room for choice. The most popular areas for teacher residence were Fulham, Wandsworth (including Clapham), Lewisham and Hackney, all characterized by large tracts of respectable lower-middle-class housing. Generally avoided were districts at the upper end of the housing market, as in Marylebone (including Hampstead) and the West End, and also at the bottom end of the scale, as in Southwark and the East End. Within these wider areas, however, there were pockets of lower-middle-class housing attractive to teachers, as in the pink streets in the catchment of Fleet Road School. Yet the personal choice and life-chance factors were also important, and teachers' residences ranged from streets in red to those in purple in Booth's scheme.

Booth and his team in a number of instances identified and criticized headteachers who distanced themselves from involvement in the social problems of their school areas. A headmaster in Saffron Hill, Clerkenwell, was said to come and go from the school each day 'like a city clerk', and knew little of the locality of his school.[11] One School Board visitor interviewed by Booth had a jaundiced view of the social pretensions of schoolteachers.

The teachers generally are the children of artisans, and rising as they do into a different social stratum they suffer from 'swelled heads' and think more of their social position in the suburb in which they live than of the welfare of the children in their school.[12]

There is little doubt that the policies of the London School Board helped greatly to improve the lot and the status of the elementary teacher. While the National Union of Elementary Teachers obviously played a part, the salaries and career structures provided by a huge School Board offered opportunities quite beyond those generally available in the voluntary sector. There was an element of necessity in this. Spalding, Secretary to the London School Board, noted the presence of a much greater demand for than supply of teachers in the early 1870s.[13] Lyulph Stanley indicated that the Board had recognized that it would need to pay 'very liberal salaries' in order to enable teachers 'to live tidily and decently', vital if they were to be respected by parents.[14]

Stanley was critical of what he saw as the continuing patronizing attitudes of denominational training colleges towards their students. He urged that they should be treated with more courtesy.

We should endeavour to make our elementary teachers feel that they belong to an elevated order ... We want to get rid of the old tone of superiority of the clerical manager towards his schoolmaster, who was probably his clerk. We want the idea to grow that schoolmasters and mistresses are, or should be, gentlemen and ladies.[15]

In terms of salaries and professional prospects, the London School Board had the will and capacity to make its teachers the aristocrats of the elementary profession. Thus in a Merseyside town, Bootle, school board teachers earned between £82 and £105 per annum if male, and £78 and £84 if female, by the late 1890s. Their London counterparts took home between £155 to £185, and £120 to £145 respectively.

At Fleet Road, W.B. Adams was in no doubt that the key to success was the appointment of proficient teachers. On a number of occasions he credited the success of the school to the 'hearty exertions' of the staff.[16] In appointing staff, he exploited his long-standing connection with the British and Foreign School Society. Adams was particularly favourably inclined towards students from Stockwell, the British Society's female training college where his wife had been a student. In correspondence in 1879 with the Secretary of the Society, he appealed for a 'thoroughly efficient man' from Borough Road to replace a senior assistant about to leave, and mentioned that 'all the Stockwell students ... are doing well'.[17] In a follow-up letter he emphasizes the importance of finding someone of 'more than average ability' able 'to superintend in my absence a school numbering 800 children and 11 other assistants', who would need to exercise 'much tact and care' in fulfilling this responsibility. For the right man, the position would be a 'certain road to promotion'.[18]

In general, however, Adams' observations on training college recruits were less than favourable, possibly reflecting a residual bitterness towards Church of England training colleges, from whom perforce most of his staff came,[19] and to which he had been denied entry in his youth on the grounds of his family's Nonconformist allegiance. He complained to the Cross Commission that when probationers arrived 'they seemed to know everything except the art of teaching'.[20]

As Adams claimed, appointment to Fleet Road, once the

reputation of the school had been established, was an enviable prospect. Success there offered strong chances of promotion to senior posts in other schools, and also to training colleges. Thus H. J. Dare was appointed in 1880 with a starting salary of £80, and was taking home £155 14 years later, when he secured the headship of Barrow Hill Road Board School, Portland Town. Adams noted that during the whole period his work had been 'entirely satisfactory'.[21] He had first met a class of 80 pupils 'fresh from the streets, with plenty of fresh air from the Heath to make them lively'. They had taxed the young teacher to the utmost but, as Adams informed the gathering at Dare's leaving presentation, he had overcome the difficulties and made his way to the top.[22] Dare was a local boy who had attended Christ Church School, Hampstead, and had been a pupil teacher at Heath Street British School (Map 6).[23] At Fleet Road he had been responsible for the celebrated scholarship class.[24] Booth's interviewer was very impressed with him, by then well-established as head of Barrow Hill Road.

He is a man of 40 looking much younger ... He is exceedingly keen and intelligent, and as usual with schoolmasters I enjoyed my interview and walk round with him immensely, coming away with a renewed conviction that as an elevating influence the school swamps the rest.[25]

John Sadd was the first of the original teachers to move on. He soon left Fleet Road for a more senior position at Haverstock Hill Board School. Earning £90 when he left, he returned to Fleet Road to succeed Adams in 1903 at a salary of £370. Of those not promoted elsewhere, another initial appointment, Jesse Harris, gained an enviable reputation as a brilliant choirmaster (Chapter 9). Pupil teachers were also helped by having served at Fleet Road. Two special cases were the children of two of the head-teachers. As we have seen, J. W. B. Adams and Kate Walker began their successful teaching careers in their parents' respective departments, both finishing with headships.

There were notable promotions for women staff. Kate Denson, appointed in 1894 to the Senior Mixed Department at a salary of £85, was receiving £124 in 1900. She was soon to leave to be a headmistress under the Walthamstow School Board. The early Stockwell appointees did well. Sarah Emily Pratt lived at 24, Kentish Town Road. One of a family of five, her father was a copper-plate printer. Her elder sister was a dressmaker, her two elder brothers clerks, and her younger sister was still at school. By 1881 the Pratt parents, aged 60 and 58 respectively, presumably with the aid of income from four unmarried earning offspring and two lodgers, were able to afford a servant. Sarah Emily became a pupil teacher at Mansfield Place School (Chapter 2, Plate 6) prior to entering Stockwell College in 1879, gaining her certificate in 1880. Her first appointment was at the notorious St. Clement's Road Board School in Notting Dale, a school 'of special difficulty'. She was appointed to Fleet Road in 1881, at a salary of £70, almost on sufferance, 'failing a good master' becoming available.[26] She was a success and left in 1893 to become Headmistress of Choumert Road Board School in Camberwell, having always given 'excellent service'.[27] Similarly, Anne Steele, at Stockwell 1877–8, and one of Adams' first appointments, left in 1891 to become Headmistress of Dulwich Hamlet Board School.[28]

Annie Bird, another Stockwell student of 1877–8, had been a pupil teacher at High Pavement Board School, Nottingham. On an application document provided by the College, she indicated she would prefer a school in Nottinghamshire or the Midland counties, but would be willing to accept an assistantship elsewhere if in a large school, but at not less than £70.[29] At the time Adams was looking for 'a ladylike, intelligent teacher'.[30] He seemed impressed with Miss Bird, noting her 'knowledge of French would be especially useful in such a school as ours'.[31] She was appointed at a salary of £70. She later took an LL.A. degree and finally left Fleet Road for a position at Nottingham University Day Training College. Another Fleet Road appointment, Miss S. Reintjes, who joined the school in 1896 at a salary of £127, also left for Nottingham Day Training College, becoming Mistress of Method there in 1900.[32]

In the period from 1893 to 1903 all the assistant teachers at Fleet Road had gained 1st or 2nd Class certificates. In the Senior Mixed Department the number of probationers was kept to a minimum. Apart from 1894–5, there were no pupil teachers in that department over the period. By the end of the century the school was attracting graduate teachers. While on the Fleet Road staff J.B. Miles and W. Salmon gained Intermediate B.Sc. degrees and Miss Reintjes an LL.A. Mr. Begbie was appointed in 1898 with a B.A. and Mr. Peall in 1899 with an M.A. In 1902 Adams proudly announced that he had given the Misses Copsey,

Farmer and Sproxton leave of absence to attend Bangor University to receive their B.A. degrees.[33] Of five appointees to specialist posts in the Senior Department in 1903, all had qualifications beyond a teaching certificate, and one a Cambridge B.A. Honours degree and Intermediate B.Sc. of London University.

Another presumably beneficial feature was the stability of the Fleet Road staff. There was a strong core of experience. The age structure of the three departments in 1900 was as follows:

TABLE 7.1

Ages	No. of Staff	
Over 50	3	
40–49	8	
30–39	11	
25–29	16	} 22
20–24	6	

Many of the younger staff were in the Infants' and Junior Mixed departments. Of the Senior Mixed staff, Adams and Harris had been present from the opening of the school in 1879, Florence May from the end of that year, and five other staff from the 1880s. In 1903, only three of the 16 Senior Mixed staff had been at Fleet Road less than three years. In the Junior Mixed Department, Mrs. Adams had retired, but there were three out of eight who had been there almost from the beginning.

Not all Adams' appointments proved successful. In an era of accountability, headteachers were less than tolerant of weak staff. A widespread tactic was to highlight such assistants through the medium of the log book, in which weaknesses would be recorded. An accumulation of negative comments could well lead to the managers recommending dismissal. A number of instances occurred at Fleet Road. In 1895, for example, Adams noted J. Anderson's 'defective discipline',[34] literally within months of his appointment. This was soon followed by the recording of a complaint from a parent that Anderson had administered corporal punishment, the boy's back being found to be 'severely marked'.[35] The London School Board's rules on corporal punishment were strict, and it could only be administered by heads and specified assistants. Anderson was officially warned by the Correspondent that if there was any further violation of these rules, transfer would be recommended.[36] In November

1895, after eight months at the school, Anderson left. Adams noted, perhaps pointedly, that he was to become Headmaster of a Church school in Preston.[37]

The episode of Mr. W.H. Begbie was a lengthier affair. Holder of a B.A., he was appointed in 1898. Log book entries tell of an unfortunate year at Fleet Road. On 2 September 1898 Adams recorded that discipline in Mr. Begbie's class was 'weak in the extreme'. His first ploy was to talk privately to Begbie. Poor discipline continued and Adams wrote to the School Board Correspondent, for report to the managers. Further problems led to Adams calling in the School Board Inspector in October, which did not resolve anything. On 7 November Adams reported he had transferred Begbie from Standard VI to Standard IV. This had no immediate effect. Begbie was spoken to again in March 1899 following an HMI Report on his discipline. On 10 May Begbie sent in his resignation. Further fault was found with his discipline in June, and on 17 July Adams confirmed that Begbie was not returning after the summer term.

A longer-standing member of staff, H. Atkins, appointed in 1883, was, in 1900, at the age of 52, giving Adams cause for concern. Again the log book entries document his decline and fall:

7th February: Spoke to Mr. Atkins about want of punctuality in his class.
21st February: Pleased with improvement in Mr. Atkins' class.
5th March: Improvement in general work of Mr. Atkins' class.

But between then and the following year there were complaints that he had been away without furnishing a medical certificate.

7th May 1901: Order in Mr. Atkins' class unsatisfactory.
21st May   Atkins' class in bad order.
14th June: Atkins told he would be transferred to Kentish Town Board School.
28th June: Atkins left.[38]

It may be inferred that the London School Board regarded Fleet Road as in need of protection from weak teachers. Less prestigious board schools seemingly gained less support.

The log books typically record teacher absence through illness, from which even the best board schools were not protected. The Board's implementation of its rules for absence was strict, and even headteachers, as in the case of Mrs. Adams and Mrs. Walker, fell foul of the bureaucracy if they did not diligently present doctors' notes when absent. While there are more points of similarity between schools of a hundred years ago and today than is often accepted, there also existed significant differences. One was the sheer pressure of numbers. Another was the fact that both teachers and pupils lived in fear of illness and death to an extent that cannot easily be appreciated nowadays. As we have seen, Louisa Walker lost three of her own children prematurely. Many diseases were at that time incurable, and the nature of others not understood. Crowded and ill-ventilated classrooms spread infectious diseases like wildfire. The intensity of elementary school work, with huge classes and constant pressure to be accountable, manifestly created stress, especially in circumstances of debilitating illness. The evidence would suggest that Mrs. Adams felt impelled to retire early under the strain (Chapter 5). There was the additional factor of the impact of life misfortunes, family problems and the like, which could intensify difficulties to breaking point, in a period where official welfare safety nets did not exist. The case of Jesse Harris, to be described in Chapter 9, was particularly poignant.

Regrettably the opinions of the children about their teachers are not well documented, and what is remembered in oral accounts is more often the quirky and the remarkable rather than the normal. An old pupil tells of Mr. Sadd as having 'a habit of shaking his head and pinching his nose'. Another indicated that he was a good man who taught well, but 'does not forget to use the stick'.

Mr. Spary was regarded as very strict in inspecting clean hands, ears and shoes, but was well liked, not least because he allowed a period at 3 p.m. when children could bring out their own sweets. Mr. Nott was recollected as a 'kind encouraging person'. By contrast, Mr. Charles Campbell graded his class with bright pupils at the back and the less intelligent at the front. He kept a musical box on his desk, confiscated from one of the boys. If a pupil displeased him, he was brought to the front and ordered to play, the victim identified before the class as one fit only to be an organ grinder in later life. One of the victims, Mr. H.J. Newcombe, tells that he was thus called out on one occasion, and 'felt so enraged at the humiliation, that I punched him in the stomach and ran off home. On my return to class, much to my surprise, nothing was said about the matter.'

Not surprisingly, the few old pupils who have recorded

memories remember incidentals, not the central curricular experience: ceremonial occasions such as those associated with the death of the Queen; the embarrassment of having to collect both cane and punishment book if they were to be chastised; the rush for hot cakes which could be bought cheaply when the girls came out of cookery class; the construction of innumerable marble boards and pipe racks in woodwork lessons; street games; doing odd jobs outside school; a colourful character dubbed 'Old Brandy Balls' who sat at the school gates, dressed in a white apron with a basket on his lap filled with brandy balls, which he sold at play-times to the children; attending swimming lessons at Prince of Wales Road public baths; reading *Boy's Own* and the *Magnet*; the lure of Parliament Hill Fields and the fairs on Hampstead Heath, or catching the tram at a $\frac{1}{2}$d child's fare into central London; the kudos of winning certificates and junior scholarships to stay on into Ex-VII or go on to secondary school. The notion of belonging to a 'good school' and awareness of being part of a relatively favoured scholar group rubbed off on the children.[39]

As indicated in other sections, there existed in Hampstead continuing disquiet, which at times of School Board elections boiled over in open protest, at the nature of the schooling being offered at Fleet Road, and in particular the salaries that were the current norm for teachers seen as over-qualified for the task of elementary teaching.

A special aggravation at the time concerned the salaries being paid to women teachers. In Hampstead the fact that three local women headteachers, Mrs. Groome in Kentish Town, and Mrs. Adams and Mrs. Walker at Fleet Road, were second wage-earners in their respective families was presumably especially inflammatory. A local correspondent complained bitterly.

Hundreds of efficient teachers (not married women, who ought to be in their own homes taking care of their own poor children), but single women and widows in needy circumstances, could be found to teach all that is necessary for the happiness and future welfare of these children for from £40 to £50 a year.[40]

The writer urged that no candidate should be returned to Parliament at the next general election who was not pledged to limiting free education to the three R's, manual labour of every kind, reducing teachers' wages, and returning the educational rate, as originally intended, to not more than threepence in the £.

The correspondent was no doubt aware that by this time the most striking feature of staff employment at Fleet Road was the recruitment of graduates. By 1899 the most junior female assistants were being hired at a rate of over £65 per annum.

THE MANAGERS

The accolade to the managers of Fleet Road from the Final Report of the Cross Commission (ref. 2) was characteristically referred to by W. B. Adams at a school prize-giving in November 1889. The leading signatory of the minority report of the Cross Commission, which sought to mitigate some of its pro-voluntaryist recommendations, was the Rt. Hon. Lyulph Stanley who, as we have seen, was Fleet Road School's most influential publicist. No doubt his presence on the Commission occasioned this comment.

As Gordon shows, the London School Board's management system was heavily reliant on the support of the leisured classes as well as higher status managerial and professional groups, not least in well-to-do districts such as the Marylebone Divisions, as Table 7.2 illustrates.

TABLE 7.2

Occupations of Local Managers of the London
School Board, 1884

Categories	Overall L.S.B. %	Marylebone
Leisured class	31	65
Professions	$10\frac{1}{2}$	$8\frac{1}{2}$
Church	21	14
Merchant/managerial	$8\frac{1}{2}$	5
Sub-managerial	22	$5\frac{1}{2}$
Skilled workers	$4\frac{1}{2}$	–
Teachers	$2\frac{1}{2}$	2

The figures indicate major differences between school board divisions. Thus while Marylebone's managers were 65 per cent leisured ($47\frac{1}{2}$ per cent women and $17\frac{1}{2}$ per cent men), the proportion in Southwark was $15\frac{1}{2}$ per cent (11 per cent and $4\frac{1}{2}$ per cent respectively). By contrast, the proportions in the sub-managerial and skilled worker groups was 46 per cent for Southwark as against $5\frac{1}{2}$ per cent for Marylebone.[41]

London School Board's system of management was complicated. Three layers, which also came to constitute vested interest groups, were involved. Different and sometimes competing definitions of responsibilities created tensions. The three levels were:

(1) the London School Board itself, working through a School Management Committee;

(2) the Divisional members, who recommended the local managers of schools;

(3) the school managers themselves.

An underlying problem for the Board was to offer local managers sufficient responsibilities to secure a high level of commitment without divesting itself of the capacity to maintain central control. The managers were originally used to select teaching staffs, including headteachers; visit schools, check registers and examine the condition of the premises; examine complaints about the teachers; and draw up annual reports of schools, helping the School Management Committee in deciding future needs.[42] Divisional members had greater access to the centre than the school managers. The increasing politicization of school board work and issues from the 1880s heightened tensions. Sometimes divisional members were accused of having political axes to grind, and of oppressing schools in their visits, while local managers in turn were charged on occasions with showing bias in favour of teachers known to them, in appointing heads, for example. Indeed in 1889 the School Management Committee took over the responsibility for the selection of headteachers, to the annoyance of local managers.[43] The Board was concerned over the quality of some of the managers. One response to a circular on the powers and duties of school managers showed 22 out of 78 chairmen replying referring to the unsuitability of managers for their duties.[44] The general trend over the London School Board period was towards a whittling away of the powers of local managers.

The local grouping of managers in which Fleet Road was placed included first Great College Street, Camden Town and Newmarket Terrace, York Road. Later Newmarket Terrace was replaced by Brecknock.[45] Much later, Fleet Road was grouped with Haverstock Hill and two temporary schools, Mansfield Road and Wilkin Street, a grouping with a more local flavour.[46]

The managers of the Fleet Road group in 1883 were as follows:[47]

Name	Occupation
Hon. E. Lyulph Stanley	Member of Parliament
Rev. James Boyd	Presbyterian Minister
Dr. F.H. Gervis	Doctor of Medicine
Mr. T.W. Gittens	Carrier
Mr. L. Lewis	Artist
Mr. G. Tomlinson	Gentleman
Miss Adams	Poor Law Guardian
Miss Boyd	No occupation given
Miss M. Hill	No occupation given
Miss B.A. Jourdan	No occupation given
Mrs. Maitland	No occupation given

Two of this group, Stanley and Gervis, were still serving as managers in 1898:[48]

Name	Occupation
Dr. F.H. Gervis	Surgeon
Mr. C.W. Ryalls	Barrister
Mr. R. Petherbridge	Gentleman
Mrs. Rea	No occupation given
Mrs. B.M. Bates	No occupation given
Mrs. S.W. Heberden	No occupation given
Mrs. M.W. Nevinson	No occupation given
Mrs. L.J. Russell	No occupation given
Miss J. Christie	No occupation given
Hon. E.L. Stanley	Member of London School Board
G.C. Maile	Monumental Sculptor
A.B. Russell	Chartered Accountant

The 1883 managers resided both in Hampstead and Camden Town, reflecting the geographical spread of schools in the group. Those of 1898 were largely concentrated in Hampstead itself, particularly in wealthy areas of South Hampstead. The pattern was consistent with that of the Marylebone Division as a whole, with the majority either in professional occupations or leisured. The only occupations recorded of a less prestigious character were a commission agent, a carriage builder and a pianoforte maker.

The annual reports of the managers were one of the most effective ways of formally drawing attention to the achievements of the school. Among the items brought to the notice of the London School Board in the 1894–1903 period were:

(a) promotions of Fleet Road teachers to headships elsewhere;
(b) details of scholarships gained and other successes of scholars as in the examinations of the London Chamber of Commerce and the Society of Arts (see Chapter 10);
(c) success in choral competitions (see Chapter 9);
(d) details of prize days and other public entertainments (Chapter 9);
(e) reference to the school magazine;
(f) information about the boys' cricket and football teams, tennis for the girls, and a swimming club;
(g) collections for charity and an annual gift of cast-off clothing for poor East End schools;
(h) degrees gained by members of staff;
(i) successes of former scholars and pupil teachers;
(j) the use of the school by training college students;
(k) school visits, as to the Tower of London and museums.

The Report for 1895 is a typical example. It noted that five Bancroft scholarships, four Christ's Hospital scholarships and the Wells and Campden Scholarship had been won by pupils of the school. At the prize-giving, an 'admirable address' had been given by Dr. J. Fitch, late H.M. Inspector of Training Colleges. It noted the present state of the picture collection in the school hall, help given to poorer schools and the Shaftesbury Homes, prizes for sport and medals for attendance, the matriculation of two former scholars at London University, and the establishment of an exchange library for ex-VII scholars.

Just as the school log books were deployed by headteachers to carry messages to managers, so the managers' reports were pressed into service to record not only achievement, but also deficiencies that the School Board needed to put right. The most common complaint at Fleet Road was over-crowding, especially in the Junior Mixed Department. As we have seen, the managers also received a number of sallies from Louisa Walker, impatient when the decisions of bureaucrats impeded progress in the Infants' Department.

In various public arenas, whether prize distributions and concerts at the school, or in his interviews in turn with the Cross Commission, *The Practical Teacher*, and with Charles Morley, Adams identified significant individuals on the managing body as benefactors of the school, though in his evidence to the Cross Commission he stressed that all 12 managers took an interest in the school, and supposed that schools without such support were at a disadvantage.[49]

In recording his views for *The Practical Teacher*, Adams specially extolled the activity of E. Barnes, Chairman of the Managers, and obviously Lyulph Stanley, firing 'all concerned with his educational zeal'.[50] He was even more magniloquent in his responses to Charles Morley, explaining why he was such 'a lucky man'.

... what managers I have! – so broad, so elastic, so human. Mr. Barnes ... takes as keen an interest in the school as I do, I honestly believe ... Mr. Herklots, the Rector of St. Saviour's, is one of our best friends ... We are all proud of our school, sir. All of us – managers, masters, pupils ... Then Mr. Lyulph Stanley is another of my very good friends.[51]

Notwithstanding the plaudits, the managers were not just responsible for one school, and there is much evidence in the London School Board documentation of a fairly rapid turnover of managers, and some reference to unsatisfactory attendance at meetings, followed by resignations or assurances of greater regularity to come.

It is difficult to exaggerate the importance of Lyulph Stanley's role as a kind of self-appointed patron of Fleet Road School. There were other high-achieving schools in London, but few with so influential and dedicated a mentor. As the Chairman of the managers said at a school prize-giving in 1893, no one took a greater interest in the London School Board than Stanley, but 'he might say with confidence that he took an especial interest in Fleet-road Schools'.[52]

An outstanding figure on the London School Board, Lyulph Stanley was a well-known workaholic. He served on the Board from 1876 to 1904, apart from the three years from 1885, and was said to have visited every board school in London, most of them several times. He claimed this was therapeutic, a release from the committee load within the School Board offices. As Gautrey recounts, the pressure was phenomenal.

It was notorious that members were hunted from one committee room or office to another, with chops in their hands, in search of a spot where they could consume them in quiet. The chops were cooked down in the basement by the housekeeper's wife. I have frequently seen the Hon. E.L. Stanley suddenly disappear from a committee for a short period. In the interval he had eaten his chop and vegetables, in desperate haste.[53]

Another commentator records him as sitting on committee after committee, 'driving the business all the time', going without lunch and hastily swallowing a cup of tea.[54]

It would seem that, for Stanley, Fleet Road represented the quintessence of his vision for national education. This would be based on a firm elementary foundation, as represented by the Junior Mixed Department, leading to a series of more specialist, vocationally-orientated options, as offered by the Senior Mixed Department. Stanley explained that for him commercial education was an important element at this level. He envisaged a layered system with no children leaving school before 14, and with higher elementary classes for 10–20 per cent of the scholars, who would stay on at least a year longer. 'Just as schools of science had been developed, so schools giving training in commercial skills should now be built up', the abler pupils from these going on to higher institutions.[54]

It was a source of concern to Stanley that London's higher elementary schools were not ranked as highly as the higher-grade schools of the major provincial cities. Strict higher-grade status demanded designation as an accredited school of science. Only four of London's board schools were thus accredited. Fleet Road was not one of them, and it may be this which inhibited Stanley from being as confident as some of his fellow managers and members of the London School Board in publicly proclaiming Fleet Road to be the finest elementary school in the country. Commercial, not science education, was indeed the area in which higher elementary classes at Fleet Road specialized. As the next chapter will illustrate, this was far from a peripheral issue. While officially lauded for the high quality of its teachers and the effective support of its managers, Fleet Road, at the apogee of its public fame in the late 1890s, came into conflict with authority in laying emphasis on a curriculum which was increasingly defined as departing from the regulations of the elementary education acts. The school's curriculum had been irreversibly pointed in the direction of commerce as a result of the meritocratic philosophy of its Headteacher, W.B. Adams, with the full support of its most influential manager, Lyulph Stanley and, indeed, the London School Board on which Stanley was so significant a figure. It is to Fleet Road's curriculum that we now turn.

EDUCATING THE RESPECTABLE

REFERENCES AND NOTES

1. *The Schoolmaster*, 19 Oct. 1872, p.155.
2. *Cross Commission*, Final Report (1888), p.67.
3. Anon, 'The Social Position of Educators', *The Scholastic Journal*, June 1840, p.321. See also A. Tropp, *The School Teachers: the Growth of the Teaching Profession in England and Wales from 1800 to the Present Day* (London, 1957), Ch. 3.
4. F. Widdowson, *Growing up into the Next Class: Women and Elementary Teacher Training, 1840–1914* (London, 1980), p.11.
5. Quoted in *The Schoolmaster*, 22 June 1872, p.269.
6. T. Gautrey, *'Lux Mihi Laus': School Board Memories* (London, 1937), p.130.
7. L. Stanley, 'National Education and the London School Board', *Fortnightly Review*, vol. 32 (1879), p.536.
8. See H. Mayhew and J. Binny, *The Criminal Prisons of London and Scenes of Prison Life* (London, 1862, Cass reprint 1968), p.65.
9. *Cross Commission*, 2nd Report (1887), p.123.
10. For a map and discussion, see W.E. Marsden, 'Residential Segregation and the Hierarchy of Elementary Schooling from Charles Booth's London Surveys', *The London Journal*, vol. 11 (1985), pp.140–1.
11. C. Booth, *Miscellaneous Notes* (Booth Collection, London School of Economics), Group A, vol. 51, p.10.
12. C. Booth, *Miscellaneous Notes* (Booth Collection, London School of Economics), Group B, vol. 233, p.89.
13. T.A. Spalding and T.S.A. Canney, *The Work of the London School Board* (London, 1900), pp.105–6.
14. Stanley, *op. cit.* (1879), p.536.
15. *Ibid.*, p.539.
16. *The Practical Teacher*, vol. 15 (1894), p.5.
17. *BFSS Archives*, letter from W.B. Adams to A. Bourne, dated 2 July 1879.
18. *BFSS Archives*, letter from W.B. Adams to A. Bourne, dated 5 July 1879.
19. *Cross Commission*, 2nd Report (1887), p.53.
20. *Ibid.*, p.50.
21. *Fleet Road School Senior Mixed Department Log Book* (hereafter *FRLB*), 9 Feb. 1894.
22. *HHE*, 10 Feb. 1894.
23. *HHE*, 3 Feb. 1894.
24. *The Practical Teacher*, vol. 15 (1894), p.5.
25. C. Booth, *Miscellaneous Notes* (Booth Collection, London School of Economics), Group B, vol. 211, p.83.
26. *BFSS Archives*, letter from W.B. Adams to A. Bourne, 31 March 1881. In general I am grateful to George Bartle for searching out relevant Fleet Road School references in the BFSS Archives, and not least in this section on the Stockwell teachers, painstakingly searching out pieces of information from the *Educational Record* and *Stockwell Old Students' Lists*.
27. *FRLB*, 21 Dec. 1893.
28. *The Practical Teacher*, vol. 15 (1894), p.5.
29. *BFSS Archives*, School Application Form, Anne Florence Bird, 15 Oct. 1878.
30. *BFSS Archives*, letter from W.B. Adams to A. Bourne, dated 30 April 1879.
31. *BFSS Archives*, Letter from W.B. Adams to A. Bourne, Secretary, dated 9 April 1879.
32. *FRLB*, 2 July 1900.
33. *FRLB*, 13 Nov. 1902.
34. *FRLB*, 10 April 1895.
35. *FRLB*, 16 May 1895.

36. *FRLB*, 20 May 1895.
37. *FRLB*, 15 Nov. 1895.
38. The material on both Begbie and Atkins is all derived from Adams' entries in the *FRLB*.
39. For most of this oral material I am indebted to Mr. H.J. Newcombe, and also his brother Mr. A. Newcombe, who were pupils at Fleet Road before the First World War. I have also received information from Mr. L.H. Dewar who in 1987 was still living in Mansfield Road and entered Fleet Road in 1908, staying on into Standard Ex-VII with what was presumably a Junior Scholarship, leaving at the age of 15½. Other material is drawn from the school's centenary publication, *Hundred Years Fleet School 1879–1979*.
40. *HHE*, 1 April 1899.
41. See P. Gordon, *The Victorian School Manager: a Study in the Management of Education* (London, Woburn Press, 1974), pp.162–3, from which Table 7.2 is adapted.
42. *Ibid.*, p.153.
43. *Ibid.*, pp.154–6.
44. *Ibid*, p.160.
45. LSB, *School Management Department Return*, 31 Oct. 1883.
46. *Ibid.*, 3 Feb. 1898.
47. *Ibid.*, 31 Oct. 1883.
48. *Ibid.*, 3 Feb. 1898.
49. *Cross Commission*, 2nd Report (1887), p.65.
50. *The Practical Teacher*, vol. 15 (1894), p.1.
51. C. Morley, *Studies in Board Schools* (London, 1897), p.96.
52. Reported in *SBC*, 8 April 1893, p.390.
53. Gautrey, *op. cit.* (1937), p.31 and pp.50–3.
54. Graham Wallas, quoted in Gordon, *op. cit.* (1974), p.293.
55. A.W. Jones, *Lyulph Stanley: a Study in Educational Politics* (Wilfred Laurier University Press, 1979), pp.115–17.

CHAPTER EIGHT

The Curriculum of Fleet Road Senior and Junior Mixed Departments

Very good results are produced in this School on a very large scale. The ground work is solid and accurate; the class instruction is intelligent and vigorous; specific subjects have been prepared with great care. History is a feature especially deserving of notice. It is rare to find a school which is so well taught throughout. The advance of many of the scholars two Standards shows that the School is conducted with a view to what is best for the individual scholar, even when it involves additional labour to the teachers. One part of the training falls behind the high standard exhibited by the rest. Needlework is reported fair only, and the Domestic Economy papers do not exceed the same mark. I am sure there has been no conscious neglect of these subjects, but I think that it is possible in that the energies of the girls in the stimulating atmosphere of this great School have been directed more to the intellectual than the industrial side of their training. It is proposed in the coming year to add French and Algebra to their subjects, not at the expense, it is to be hoped, of things so much more essential to girls as Needlework or a practical knowledge of housekeeping.[1]

HMI Report, 1882

By the time Fleet Road School was opened in 1879, the worst effects of the Revised Code of 1862 had been mitigated.[2] Thus from 1867, in addition to the three R's, *specific subjects* such as history, geography and grammar could be offered, and later the natural sciences, political economy and languages. The 1875 Code introduced as *class subjects* grammar, geography, history and plain needlework. In class subjects, schools were assessed on the basis of classwork and not individual proficiency. English literature was added to the list of specific subjects in 1876.

Further broadening took place in the 1880s. The 1882 Code was a vital one for schools such as Fleet Road, for a new Standard VII was introduced, allowing children to stay on at their elementary school into their teens. The limits of elementary education were extended not just in terms of age, but also further specific subjects, including electricity, chemistry and agriculture. Elementary science was brought in throughout the school. For grant purposes, schools were to be classified as fair, good or excellent. A merit grant was to be paid for exceptional work. Another important landmark was the development of higher elementary and higher-grade schools. Extra grants were available from the Science and Art Department for certain types of instruction. These developments all brought the elementary sector under increased public scrutiny, and facilitated the evolution of a hierarchical grading of schools.

Apart from the residual social respectability they could depend on, the church schools found themselves at a severe disadvantage in this surge of educational progress. The Cross Commission was appointed in the mid-1880s to examine the workings of the elementary system. Its concerns included such issues as whether the new subjects were the best that could be selected; whether they could reasonably be called elementary; and whether children were getting enough grounding in the three Rs. This was also the time when the voluntary case was supported by elements in the medical profession raising the spectre of 'over-pressure' on developing minds of subjects judged to be more appropriate for older children. While there were differences of opinion on the Commission which led to majority and minority reports, the outcome in curricular terms might have been worse for the progressive lobby. There was an agreement on what the elementary curriculum should consist of:

- Reading, writing and arithmetic
- Needlework for girls
- Linear drawing for boys
- Singing
- English, 'to give children an adequate knowledge of their mother tongue'
- English history, 'taught by means of reading books'
- Geography, 'especially of the British Empire'
- Lessons on common objects in the lower standards, leading up to a knowledge of elementary science in the higher.[3]

It was agreed that the seven standards should be maintained, and flexibility and alternative curricula were recommended. The 1890 Code modified and relaxed the already much changed payment by results system. During the 1890s subjects such as manual instruction, drawing for boys, domestic subjects for girls, commercial subjects (including book-keeping and shorthand), science and mathematics gained increasing amounts of time, as the 'elementary' curriculum became more differentiated. The 1900 Code replaced the previous tripartite division of obligatory, specific and class subjects. In future, inspections would be general and not linked to an annual examination. Schools would receive block grants. A 'common curriculum' for the elementary school was worked out, with eight or nine core elements but with the possibility of choice from over 20 other subjects. Fleet Road's formative years were thus part of a period in which the most radical changes yet seen in the educational history of the country were being enacted.

The responses of W.B. Adams to the questions of the Cross Commissioners provide interesting insight not only into his personal views, but also into a developing meritocratic mode of thinking about the curriculum. At the time of the Revised Code, in the early 1860s, Adams had been working as a pupil teacher. He agreed that before this the lower classes had been neglected, the upper classes receiving 'a very large amount of attention from the head master'. The present system had led to 'a vast levelling up of the instruction over large masses of children'.

At the same time, Adams was severely critical of a number of the consequences of the Revised Code. One area on which he expressed himself strongly was dictation, which he judged as too mechanically exacting:

instead of the teacher having time to bring out the intelligent points of the reading lesson, the attention of the children is constantly concentrated on spelling lists of difficult words, words that they are not likely to meet with in ordinary conversation, or in ordinary reading books ... I should substitute for this dictation exercise an easy composition test, or a short letter, or a short abstract of the reading lesson ... I do not mean to say I would abolish the dictation test altogether, but I should make it far less exacting.[4]

A *leitmotiv* in Adams' evidence was his opposition to the crudely mechanical, the excessively difficult, and the practically useless. He was equally critical about the artificial nature of the examining in arithmetic, and the lack of uniformity in the tests set by the Education Department. In some years the questions asked were much more difficult than in others, which could lead to an unjustified lowering of the merit grant. He was asked to give examples of unreasonable questions. As he told the Commissioners:

I think it a very useless thing to ask a girl in the Fourth Standard to bring 123,456,789 inches into miles, instead of the cost of a reasonable number of yards of print to make pinafores; or asking her to find the difference between a million threepenny pieces, and some hundreds of guineas, instead of telling her to make out a washing or grocery bill for the week.[5]

Although scornful of what he termed 'Government arithmetic' Adams was not in principle opposed to some kind of payment by results system, and accepted the case for individual examination between Standards I and V.[6] Another bone of contention was the absence of a graduated scheme of classification of scholars to Standard V. Teachers faced great difficulties in coping with different ability levels. Adams identified three groups of children: those scrambling through the standard; the average child getting through at a fair standard; and 'the very sharp child who gets through at a bound'. But he could give no satisfactory response to how he would do away with uniform standards, apart from the unconvincing suggestion that a class of 60 might naturally resolve itself into three sections.[7]

So far as his own school was concerned, Adams indicated that the system of standards limited the flexibility he would have preferred. He argued forcefully that teachers and managers should be permitted to hold children back if they passed poorly, or not at all, and not have to enable them to proceed to the next standard notwithstanding.[8] He was also concerned to ensure that bright children were correctly placed. In his own school there was a reclassification process every year. In the previous year he had been able to give 93 children 'two removes'.[9] For the higher standards, that is VI and VII, he wished to abolish individual examination and give teachers as much liberty as possible. Here he would prefer a system of class teaching.[10] He proposed a sophisticated, purpose-built framework which he advocated for Standard Ex-VII boys, geared to their interests and their London situation, which involved considerable integration of history and literature teaching. He wished to develop at this stage the special individual faculties of boys and girls:

The peculiar bent of a scholar's mind is not apparent until he reaches the upper

189

standards. In London schools I would advocate instruction in the following subjects. A study of London; its great buildings, its historical associations, its manufactures in particular districts, and its commerce; I should organise visits to places of interest for scholars ... I should have those visits count as attendance ... Then I should study the constitutional history of England in a proper manner with my scholars; I should read with them far more largely from standard authors ... Lord Macaulay's magnificent first chapter on the History of England ... Sir Walter Scott's 'Tales of a Grandfather' ... Southey's 'Life of Nelson' and selections from Dickens and Thackeray. Then I should give them lessons in shorthand and book-keeping ... and I think French, because of its great commercial value. So far I am speaking of London purely.[11]

In his own situation, Adams retained a high measure of curricular control, except at the infant level, which he regarded as beyond his purview. From 1884 Fleet Road was split into Senior and Junior Mixed departments, as we have seen, his wife becoming the headmistress of the Junior Department. The object of the first two standards was, above all, to establish the basics, as Adams had advocated in his evidence to the Cross Commission. The Senior Mixed Department took children from Standard III upwards (normally age 9 plus, presuming they passed a Standard each year – some children were of course older than this before they passed Standard III). Fleet Road was a large school, with far more than the London norm in Standards V and above. At the time of the Cross Commission, there were 258 pupils in Standard III; 206 in IV; 182 in V; 142 in VI; and 113 in VII and Ex-VII.[12] This means that in less than eight years of the school's establishment, this 'elementary' school was admitting over 250 children who would be age today by attending secondary stage schooling. To the burghers of Hampstead it appeared strange and inappropriate.

The Junior Mixed Department generally gained less publicity than the Senior, but consistently received good inspectors' reports. The subjects taught included the three Rs, geography, singing, Swedish and musical drill, and needlework. As one report suggested, musical drill had been introduced 'with very happy results; it is in itself useful, and tends to lighten the monotony of the elementary work of a Junior School'.[13] The overall merit of the Junior Department, despite occasional criticisms, was annually recounted in the reports, culminating in that of 1894: 'The condition of this school, both as to tone and attainments, reflects the highest credit on Mrs. Adams and her Staff.'

Despite the suspicions of local opponents of the school, the Senior Department timetable (Table 8.1) in general retains the look of elementary provision. Each day, 35 minutes of prayers and scripture followed the marking of the registers at 9.00 a.m. The next hour was time for work in the three R's. From 10.40 to 11.00 a.m. a period of drill or singing ensued, with more work in the three R's for most of the time from then until the dinner break. This lasted for two hours, and was followed by another bout of three-R's activity, and on two days drawing or needlework. In the late afternoon, there was more variety, with some limited offering of French, shorthand, algebra, domestic economy, geography and history. The afternoon finished at 4.30.[14]

The more ambitious timetable was in the top part of the Senior Mixed Department. The Ex-VII provision was, by the time of the Cross Commission (Tables 8.2a and b), already much more flexible. It included Latin. Drawing and commercial subjects were strong points in the curriculum. For both boys and girls as much time was devoted to the commercial group as to arithmetic, or to needlework for the girls and scripture for the boys. Lack of Latin for the girls was compensated for by more history and more grammar than the boys were given. For nine periods of the week the boys were taught separately from the girls.[15]

In 1900 the Board of Education was showing considerable interest in the curriculum of Fleet Road mixed school. It queried how much was legitimate for grant purposes, and produced information on the amount of time devoted in Standards IV to VII in different subjects (Table 8.3).[16]

Fleet Road had been designated a Higher Grade School by the London Board in 1898. As we noted in Chapter 2, in most such schools in London provision for science was not strong. This was certainly the case at Fleet Road, where Adams gave clear priority to cultural transmission subjects such as history and literature, and to the French and commercial subjects needed by future clerks and typists, providing the major vocational impetus to the curriculum. The general timetable shows the Senior Department divided into eight classes. Classes 7 and 8 were at the level of Standard IV; Classes 5 and 6 at V; Classes 3 and 4 at VI; and Classes 1 and 2 at VII. Apart from the timetabled subjects, the girls attended cookery classes at the Fleet Road centre, and the boys manual training classes similarly.

TABLE 8.1
FLEET ROAD HIGHER GRADE SCHOOL. SENIOR DEPARTMENT.
TIMETABLE 1893–94

Class.	9.0—9.5.	9.5—9.40.	9.40—9.50.	9.50—9.55.	9.55—10.40.	10.40—11.0.	11—11.45.	11.45—12.
1	Regs. Markd.	Prayers and Scripture	Reptn., Ment. Arith.or Spell.	Regs. Closed	English	Drill	Arithmetic	Repetition or Ment. Arith.
2	Regs. Markd.	Prayers and Scripture	Reptn., Ment. Arith.or Spell.	Regs. Closed	English	Drill	Arithmetic	Repetition or Ment. Arith.
3	Regs. Markd.	Prayers and Scripture	Reptn., Ment. Arith.or Spell.	Regs. Closed	English	Drill	Arithmetic	Repetition or Ment. Arith.
4	Regs. Markd.	Prayers and Scripture	Reptn., Ment. Arith.or Spell.	Regs. Closed	Arithmetic	Drill	11—11.30. Reading	11.30—12.0. Dictation
5	Regs. Markd.	Prayers and Scripture	Reptn., Ment. Arith.or Spell.	Regs. Closed	Arithmetic	Drill	English	Reading
1	Regs. Markd.	Prayers and Scripture	Reptn., Ment. Arith.or Spell.	Regs. Closed	Arithmetic	Singing	11—11.45. Reading	11.45—12.0. Repetition or Ment. Arith.
2	Regs. Markd.	Prayers and Scripture	Reptn., Ment. Arith.or Spell.	Regs. Closed	Arithmetic	Singing	Reading	Repetition or Ment. Arith.
3	Regs. Markd.	Prayers and Scripture	Reptn., Ment. Arith.or Spell.	Regs. Closed	Arithmetic	Singing	Reading	Repetition or Ment. Arith.
4	Regs. Markd.	Prayers and Scripture	Reptn., Ment. Arith.or Spell.	Regs. Closed	Arithmetic	Singing	11—11.30. Reading	11.30—12.0. Grammar
5	Regs. Markd.	Prayers and Scripture	Reptn., Ment. Arith.or Spell.	Regs. Closed	Arithmetic	Singing	Reading	Dictation
1	Regs. Markd.	Prayers and Scripture	9.40—10.15. B. Reptition, Mental Arith. or Spelling G. Drawing	Regs. Closed	10.15—10.40. Arithmetic	Drill	11—11.45. Composition or Dictation	11.45—12.0. Writing (Forms of Letters)
2	Regs. Markd.	Prayers and Scripture	B. Repetition, Mental Arith. or Spelling G. Drawing	Regs. Closed	Arithmetic	Drill	Composition or Dictation	Writing (Forms of Letters)
3	Regs. Markd.	Prayers and Scripture	B. Repetition, Mental Arith. or Spelling G. Drawing	Regs. Closed	Arithmetic	Drill	Composition or Dictation	Repetition or Ment. Arith.
4	Regs. Markd.	Prayers and Scripture	Map Drawing	Regs. Closed	Arithmetic	Drill	11—11.30. Reading	11.30—12.0. Repetition
5	Regs. Markd.	Prayers and Scripture	Map Drawing	Regs. Closed	Arithmetic	Drill	Reading	Dictation
1	Regs. Markd.	Prayers and Scripture	9.40—9.50. Reptn., Ment. Arith.or Spell.	Regs. Closed	9.55—10.40. Arithmetic	Drill	English	History
2	Regs. Markd.	Prayers and Scripture	Reptn., Ment. Arith.or Spell.	Regs. Closed	Arithmetic	Drill	English	History
3	Regs. Markd.	Prayers and Scripture	Reptn., Ment. Arith.or Spell.	Regs. Closed	Arithmetic	Drill	English	History
4	Regs. Markd.	Prayers and Scripture	Reptn., Ment. Arith.or Spell.	Regs. Closed	Dictation	Drill	Reading	Arithmetic
5	Regs. Markd.	Prayers and Scripture	Reptn., Ment. Arith.or Spell.	Regs. Closed	Arithmetic	Drill	English	Reading
1	Regs. Markd.	Prayers and Scripture	Reptn., Ment. Arith.or Spell.	Regs. Closed	Arithmetic	Singing	Reading	Composition or Dictation
2	Regs. Markd.	Prayers and Scripture	Reptn., Ment. Arith.or Spell.	Regs. Closed	Composition	Singing	Arithmetic	Arithmetic
3	Regs. Markd.	Prayers and Scripture	Reptn., Ment. Arith.or Spell.	Regs. Closed	Arithmetic	Singing	Reading	11.30—12. Composition or Dictation
4	Regs. Markd.	Prayers and Scripture	Reptn., Ment. Arith.or Spell.	Regs. Closed	Arithmetic	Singing	Reading	Dictation
5	Regs. Markd.	Prayers and Scripture	Reptn., Ment. Arith.or Spell.	Regs. Closed	Arithmetic	Singing	Reading	Dictation

TABLE 8.1 (cont.)

—	Class.	2—2.5.	2.5—2.30.	2.10—2.15.	2.30—3.0.	3.0—4.0.	4.0—4.30.
MONDAY.	1	Regs. Markd.	Arith. (Slate or Mental)	Regs. Closed	Rdg. & Spll.	B. Fr.or Shtnd. G. Dom. Econ.	Singing
	2	Regs. Markd.	Do.	Regs. Closed	Do.	Do.	Singing
	3	Regs. Markd.	Do.	Regs. Closed	Do.	Do.	Singing
	4	Regs. Markd.	Writing Lessn.	Regs. Closed	Grammar	Arithmetic	Singing
	5	Regs. Markd.	2.5—2.45. Writing Lessn.	Regs. Closed	2.45—3.30. Reading	3.30—4.0. Dictation	Singing
TUESDAY.	1	Regs. Markd.	2.5—3.0. B. Drawing 2.5—3.30. G. Ndlework.	Regs. Closed		3.0—4.0. B. Algebra 3.30—4.0. G. Drawing	History
	2	Regs. Markd.	Do.	Regs. Closed		Do.	History
	3	Regs. Markd.	Do.	Regs. Closed		Do.	History
	4	Regs. Markd.	B. Drawing or Arithmetic G. Ndlework.	Regs. Closed		B. Arith. or Drawing G. Drawing	Geography
	5	Regs. Markd.	B. Drawing G. Ndlework.	Regs. Closed	3.0—3.30. B. Reading	3.30—4.0. B.Dict. G.Dwg.	Geography
WEDNESDAY.	1	Regs. Markd.	B. Drawing G. Ndlework.	Regs. Closed		3.0—4.0. B. Algebra 3.30—4.0. G. Drawing	Arithmetic
	2	Regs. Markd.	Do.	Regs. Closed		Do.	Grammar.
	3	Regs. Markd.	Do.	Regs. Closed		Do.	Arithmetic
	4	Regs. Markd.	B. Drawing or Arithmetic G. Ndlework.	Regs. Closed		B. Arith. or Drawing. G. Drawing	Collective Less.
	5	Regs. Markd.	B. Drawing G. Ndlework.	Regs. Closed	3.0—3.30. B. Reading	3.30—4.0. B. Dictation G. Drawing	Collective Less.
THURSDAY.	1	Regs. Markd.	2.5—2.30. Arith. (Slate or Mental)	Regs. Closed	2.30—3.0. Compstn. or Dictation	3.0—4.0. B. Fr.or Shtnd. G. Dom. Econ.	Writing
	2	Regs. Markd.	Do.	Regs. Closed	Do.	Do.	Writing
	3	Regs. Markd.	Do.	Regs. Closed	2.30—3.15. Compstn. or Dictation		3.15—4.30. B. Algebra. G. Dom. Econ.
	4	Regs. Markd.	Writing Lessn.	Regs. Closed	Grammar	Arithmetic	4.0—4.30. Geography
	5	Regs. Markd.	2.5—2.45. Writing Lessn.	Regs. Closed	2.45—3.30. Reading	B. Dictation.	Geography
FRIDAY.	1	Regs. Markd.	2.5—2.30. Arith. (Slate or Mental)	Regs. Closed	2.30—3.0. Writing	3.0—3.30. B. Fr.or Shtnd. G. Arithmetic	3.30—4.30. Singing
	2	Regs. Markd.	Do.	Regs. Closed	Do.	2.30—3.30. Fr. or Shtnd.	Singing
	3	Regs. Markd.	Do.	Regs. Closed		Fr. or Shtnd.	Fr. or Shtnd.
	4	Regs. Markd.	Spelling	Regs. Closed	2.30—3.15. Copybks. or Wrtng Ex.	3.15—4.0. Reading.	4.0—4.30. Ment. Arith. or Tables
	5	Regs. Markd.	Copybooks	Regs. Closed	Arithmetic	Do.	Geography

TABLE 8.2a
EX-VII TIMETABLE OF FLEET ROAD AT TIME OF
CROSS COMMISSION

FLEET ROAD SENIOR SCHOOL, HAMPSTEAD, N.W.

ANALYSIS of TIME TABLE, Boys and GIRLS.

Ex. VII.

—	Boys.	Girls.
	H. M.	H. M.
Grammar - - - - -	1 0	1 45
Arithmetic - - - - -	3 45	3 45
Shorthand - - - -	1 30	1 30
Letter writing - - - -	0 45	0 45
Book-keeping - - - -	1 30	1 30
Latin - - - - -	2 15	—
Drawing - - - - -	1 30	1 30
Map drawing - - - -	0 45	0 45
Recapitulation - - - -	1 0	1 0
Geography - - - -	0 30	0 30
Mensuration - - - -	1 45	—
Algebra - - - - -	1 45	—
Reading - - - - -	1 0	1 0
French - - - - -	1 15	—
History - - - - -	1 0	2 30
Needlework - - - -	—	3 30
Scripture - - - -	3 45	—

Presumably in addition to these classes, there were five 'specialist' options: an Intermediate (I); a Junior Commercial (JC); a Senior Commercial (SC); a Scholarship class (S); and a Candidates class for girls only (C). Table 8.4 reflects the provision for these.

The Board of Education inferred that this represented the timetable for Standards VI, VII and Ex-VII. It would appear that the five classes were separate from the eight on the main timetable. There were 12 teachers on the full-time staff apart from Adams. With 750 children on the roll of the Senior Department at the time, 13 classes would mean an average of nearly 60 children in each.

The intermediate class received the most general timetable. There was then a split for those hoping to specialize in commercial subjects and for those aiming to take scholarships, for

FLEET ROAD SENIOR MIXED SCHOOL.

Time Table for Ex. VII.

	MORNING.					AFTERNOON.			
	9 to 9.45.	9.45 to 10.	10 to 10.30.	10.30 to 11.15.	11.15 to 12.	2 to 2.15.	2.15 to 3.	3 to 3.45.	3.45 to 4.30.
Monday	Scripture.	Registers.	Grammar. Analysis. Parsing, &c.	Arithmetic.	Shorthand	Registers closed.	Arithmetic.	Letter writing.	Book-keeping.
Tuesday			Recapitulation. Standard work.	*Boys,* Latin. *Girls,* History.	Drawing		*Boys,* Mensuration *Girls,* Needlework	3 to 4. *Boys,* Mensuration *Girls,* Needlework	4.0 to 4.30. Reading. Colonies.
Wednesday			Geography.	Shorthand	Arithmetic		*Boys,* Algebra *Girls,* Needlework	2 to 4. *Boys,* Algebra *Girls,* Needlework	4.0 to 4.30. Reading. History.
Thursday			Recapitulation. Standard work.	*Boys,* Latin. *Girls,* History.	Map drawing.		Arithmetic.	Book-keeping.	*Boys,* Latin. *Girls,* Grammar.
Friday			Grammar.	Arithmetic.	Drawing.		*Boys,* French. *Girls,* Geography	3.0 to 3.30. *Boys,* French. *Girls,* Geography.	3.30 to 4.30. History.

TABLE 8.2b

FLEET ROAD SENIOR MIXED SCHOOL TIMETABLE FOR EX-VII

TABLE 8.3

Subject (Time in minutes)	IV	V	VI	VII
Algebra (Boys)	–	90	90	90
Arithmetic	270	210	195	255
Colour Drawing (Girls)	–	–	30	–
Composition	–	75	135	120
Dictation	105	60	–	–
Drawing (Boys)	210	120	120	120
Drill	30	30	30	30
English Literature	–	–	–	–
French	–	45	60	60
Geography	90	90	60	90
Grammar	30	30	30	60
History	90	90	60	90
Mapping	–	45	60	60
Mental Arithmetic	60	40	40	60
Needlework (Girls)	210	210	210	210
Object Lesson	30	–	–	–
Reading	150	150	135	120
Repetition	30	60	60	40
Scripture	150	150	150	150
Shorthand	–	–	90	90
Singing	45	45	45	45
Spelling	100	90	70	30
Writing	90	60	50	60

Source: PRO, Ed.14/41.

which, as we shall see, Fleet Road was so famous (Chapter 10), or in the case of girls, wishing to go into teacher training, a class taken by Miss Reintjes who was shortly to leave for a teacher-training institution. In the scholarship class, boys and girls followed largely the same curriculum, apart from boys taking drawing and manual training while the girls did cookery and needlework. In the candidates class, the class designed for would-be teachers, high priority was given to domestic economy and needlework. Both scholarship and candidates classes devoted periods to recitation and reading, not offered in the junior and senior commercial classes, where the vocational orientation was much stronger.

HMI REPORTS

Until 1886 London board schools were visited as a matter of course by both board and government inspectors, giving a

TABLE 8.4

Subject (Time in minutes)	I	JC	SC*	S	C
Registration	75	75	75	75	75
Scripture	150	150	150	150	150
Recreation	100	100	100	100	100
Arithmetic (Commercial JC/SC)	390**	210	210	240	210
Experimental Science	120	120	120	120	120
English Grammar/Composition	210	210	210	210	210
History (Commercial for JC/SC)	80	60	60	90	90
Geography (Commercial for JC/SC)	75	80	120	90	90
French	180	120	120	120	120
Drawing	240	120	120(B)	120(B)	120
Physical Exercises	60	60	60	60	60
Manual Training (Boys)	120	–	–	150	–
Domestic Economy (Girls)	120	–	–	–	135
Needlework (Girls)	–	–	–	120	240
Cookery (Girls)	–	–	–	150	–
Algebra	–	120	120(B)	120	–
Singing or Music	–	60	30	30	–
Book-keeping	–	120	90	–	–
Shorthand	–	120	95	–	–
Commercial Correspondence	–	75	–	–	–
Typewriting	–	–	60	–	–
Business Training	–	–	120	–	–
Political Economy	–	–	60	–	–
Recitation	–	–	–	45	30
Reading	–	–	–	80	50

Source: PRO 14/41.
Notes: * The Senior Commercial Class timetable amounted to 32 hours, taken at face value, though there may be a mistake in ascribing two 'options' to boys and none to girls.
** Included 'Mathematics' as well.

thorough twice-yearly inspection. By then, Fleet Road was basking in the approval of both. Thus, prior to its separation into Senior and Junior departments, the Board's inspector, following a visit in May 1880, was already clear that the large mixed school was 'in excellent hands', promising to become 'one of the best conducted schools in my district', and was critical only of the domestic economy which was referred to as 'not handled with intelligence'. The crowding was shown by class sizes ranging from 62 children in the smallest to over 80 in the two classes at Standard I level. The government inspector's report in December of that year indicated the instruction as 'highly satisfactory both in style and results'. The specific subjects, English literature and Physiology, were singled out for praise, while the singing was said to be 'taught with taste'. The Board inspector's report for 1882 was a particularly encouraging one:

Mr. Adams conducts this very large school with remarkable ability and success ... History is taught with unusual intelligence ... The Singing and the Drawing, particularly in the upper standards, are very good; in short, all the subjects of instruction are taught with intelligence and, generally speaking, with success.

The HMI Report of 1883 assessed the school as 'excellent':

This large and important school has passed a very successful examination. The fundamental instruction is sound, and the class work is distinguished by breadth and accuracy. History, as in past years, is most successfully taught. The Specific Subjects, viz., Algebra, French and Domestic Economy, have been taught with decidedly good results. The Singing of the School is a pleasure to listen to, and the musical tests were rendered with great ease. Two decidedly good features shown by the statistics of the examination are (1) that 40 per cent of the scholars have been examined either in the Fourth Standard or above it, and (2) that between 8 and 9 per cent have gone up more than one Standard since the last inspection. A large lending library and a chess and draught club provide for the intellectual amusement of the scholars, and a very successful cricket and football club is conducive to the pleasure of the older boys.

The following year's report was also generous in its praise, though now the Senior and Junior departments were separate. It indicated, however, that the influence on the boys would be 'decidedly beneficial' if 'the habitual tone of some of the male teachers were more subdued'.

By 1890 there was evidence of incipient streaming, the inspector commenting that backward children at Standard III, the first standard in the Senior Mixed Department, should be distributed among the four classes at this standard, and not concentrated in one. Apart from this and a slightly restrained report in 1888, there was regular praise for good basic teaching, particularly strength in history, geography and music, and a wide range of extra-curricular activities and success in outside competitions, culminating in the 1900 Report on the reunited mixed school.

This large Mixed School reflects the greatest credit upon Mr. Adams and his staff. The organisation is admirable, the curriculum is wide and well chosen. The staff are most energetic and intelligent, and scholarships and certificates of various societies furnish some evidence of the quality of the work. The Cookery and Manual Training Schools are excellent.

HISTORY AND ENGLISH LITERATURE TEACHING

One of the more distinctive elements in the Fleet Road Senior Mixed Department curriculum was the history teaching, an area in which Adams considered himself a specialist. While Head at Portland Street British Schools he had written a pair of textbooks entitled *Leading Events in English History*, sub-titled 'Adapted to the Requirements of the Code of 1871'. History had in fact been permitted as a specific subject since 1867, but the take-up had been low. In his evidence to the Cross Commission, something of a landmark in the proselytization of history as an elementary subject, Adams made clear his dissatisfaction with changed regulations which prevented it from being offered as a class subject before Standard V. It came far below geography in popularity in the elementary school, and Adams' aim was to achieve for history a similar status. It is evident that not all the Cross Commissioners were as enthusiastic as Adams for the subject's inclusion. He confidently offered a rationale.

I should recommend it on social grounds and on patriotic grounds. I think that all our elder scholars ought to know how we are governed, and how the laws are made, and that would form part of history ... I think that, perhaps, the reason why history has been made unpopular in a great many schools is, that the children had been made to swallow wholesale lists of the mere names of Saxon kings, instead of getting the life and colour, so to speak, of the great events of history. I think we should devote our attention to later times, when the nation, already formed and rooted, began to grow from within and to found a great colonial empire. I should give pictures of the daily life and manner of our ancestors, as being both attractive and useful, and sketches of the great men who have helped to give us good laws and good government.[18]

He was so sure that history was as appropriate in Standard II as Standard VI that he had placed it on the timetable on a Friday afternoon, the worst attended session of the week, and claimed the reward of 94 to 95 per cent attendance figures.[19] He agreed that in traditional texts there was too much concentration on battles and rulers rather than on the people themselves, but argued the case for retaining some constitutional history.[20] He lamented that a Committee of the London School Board on which he had been a member had rejected the case for the elementary teaching of history in London schools on religious grounds. The Commissioners picked up this point and asked how he would deal with the religious difficulty, as it was perceived at that time.

I do not think ... that the religious difficulty in teaching history need arise at all. The misfortune is that most of the text books we have in history ... have imparted a spirit of bitterness with regard to religious persecution ... a great deal has been made ... of the persecution of the reign of Queen Mary, while nothing has been said about the persecution of the reign of Queen Elizabeth. In dealing with that part of the subject myself I should tell the children that those terrible persecutions occurred at a time when the principles of religious liberty were not yet understood in this country; and then I should go on to tell them how thankful we should be that we live in the present time when everybody is allowed to worship God as they please.[21]

Adams had also a personal axe to grind, as revealed in other parts of his evidence to the Commission. As we have seen, in a minor way, but one that loomed large with him at the time, he had experienced religious 'persecution' in not being able to attend his first choice training college, and at the hands of the Unitarians at Portland Street. It was a subject he felt strongly about.

In response to questions on relations with geography he argued simply that history should be placed on an equal footing. He proposed that both could best be taught by concentrating on England and its colonies, and other countries related to us by commerce, for which purpose history was one of the most important parts of geography. Similarly, historical geography was of help to the historian, as in studies of the Hundred Years' War, or of colonial expansion.[22] More dear to him than the geography connection, however, was the link between English history and English literature, which he illustrated through a brief account of the treatment of Shakespeare at Fleet Road.

We take Shakspere [sic] in conjunction with history a great deal. One of my divisions this year took the Tudor period, and we read the play of Henry the Eighth; and another of the divisions took the York and Lancaster period, and we read Richard the Third. I think that Shakspere very much helps the study of history; certainly it introduces children to the very best literature possible. We thoroughly master and analyse a play every year in the upper standards, and I think with the best possible results. I do not think children ever forget that part of their training.[23]

He was convinced that this cross-curricular view was relevant to 9–13-year-olds, emphasizing that he always combined the study of literature and history.[24] At the same time, he accepted that the basics must be taught, and laid great stress on reading and composition as well as on literature. He was violently opposed, however, to the preoccupation with parsing and analysing of sentences, activities he dismissed as 'a great waste of time'.[25]

The fact that he wrote a text-book gives some inkling of how he translated his ideas into practice. Apart from being adapted to the requirements of the Code, he claimed that his objectives were to develop connected and intelligible writing about history, and stressed the importance of the 'connecting links' between the various case studies which largely made up his *Leading Events in English History*. The focus was on the major figures and significant historical events with which they were associated. The book was well reviewed in *The Schoolmaster*: 'This is one of the very best handbooks of history we have seen. The biographical sketches are excellent. The author is a master of terse and vigorous English.'[26]

In the text, there was a compact description of each leading event, preceded by a summary of the causes of the event, and succeeded by a cryptic statement of the results. There were in addition biographical sketches of famous historical figures such as Lady Jane Grey and Cardinal Wolsey. A brief example of the approach can be illustrated by the following account:

KING JOHN'S QUARREL WITH POPE INNOCENT III
Date – 1207–13

CAUSE. – *Dispute as to the right of nomination to the see of Canterbury*

DETAILS. King John was one of the weakest kings that grasped the English sceptre; Innocent III, one of the most powerful pontiffs. In 1205, Hubert, Archbishop of Canterbury, died; and the pope decided that the right of electing a successor lay with the monks of St. Augustine's Abbey – who were his creatures – and not the bishops of the province. In accordance with the wish of the monks, Stephen Langton was elected to the primacy, without the consent or knowledge of John, who had desired the office for his favourite, the bishop of Norwich (1207). The king retaliated by banishing the monks, and seizing their revenues. To force John into submission, the pope laid the kingdom under an *interdict* (1208). Finding this unavailing, a sentence of *excommunication* was passed on the king by the pontiff (1209). Three years afterwards, Innocent released the people from their oaths of allegiance, and entrusted Philip, king of France, with the carrying out of the sentence of *deposition*. John now gave way, acknowledged Langton, and did homage to the pope's envoy, Pandolf (1213).

RESULT. – *Increase of papal power in England.*[27]

Although it might be agreed that the language was 'terse and vigorous' what is more striking is its astonishing compression and sophistication. Presumably the teacher was expected to clarify the meaning of the technical terms in italics, such as *interdict, excommunication* and *deposition*. While there were contemporary pedagogical principles on which Adams could have drawn, these did not extend to the adaptation or translation of the language of the specialist to match with the comprehension levels of young readers. Writers such as Adams claimed it an advance to go beyond dates of kings and queens and great battles, to be learned by heart, to deal with connected events, their causes and effects. What in the event happened was that the children learned reasons and effects in addition to specific facts.

Two of the visitors to Fleet Road School wrote up accounts of the noteworthy history provision initiated by Adams, who himself took chief responsibility for that subject. He drew up a graduated syllabus and for the upper standards made carefully structured sheets of notes, copied by the 'trypograph', and put in the hands of each scholar to follow as the teacher made comments and gave illustrations. Each section contained two sheets of foolscap materials 'for a very thorough course of instruction on the Stuart period'.[28]

Both the correspondent of the journal *London* and Charles Morley appeared bowled over by the quick-fire exchanges in the question and answer sessions which Adams seemed so much to enjoy. Not here alone the visibility and responses of the girls occasioned some surprise and patronizing comment, as is evident in the reactions of the *London* correspondent.

Then the head master fired a round of questions at the class. 'Who was Henry the Eighth?' ... 'Why did he close the monasteries?' ... And so on, all answered as fast as they could be put. The change came when Henry's domestic life was touched upon. 'How many wives had Henry?' Every boy and girl had the answer. 'Who among the six was the wisest?' Ah, they were caught at last. Boys and girls alike looked at each other helplessly. Presently one pretty little maid, looking very timid, raised her hand.

'Well?'

'Catherine Parr,' she answered.

'Why?'

'Because – because' – this with a falter and a blush – 'because, unlike the others, she got the better of her husband and outlived him.' Bravo, little Board school girl; you will know how to manage a husband when your turn comes.[29]

If the following account, by Charles Morley, is taken at face value, and it may be surmised that these were set-piece events with particularly bright classes, it would appear Adams liked some banter, and relished scoring points. The repartee illustrates Tabor's point that 'smartness' was a valued trait in schools of this type. Similar questioning techniques were used in English. Morley was equally impressed with the spontaneous responses to a bombardment of questions:

'A Bishop who was banished, quick.'
'Atterbury' ...
'A naval Minister who kept a diary?'
'Pepys.'
'Whose reign?'
'Charles the Second and James the Second.' ...
'The Scotch lady who secured the safety of the Young Pretender?'
'Flora Macdonald.'
'A Queen whose memory will always be remembered by sailors?'
Here there was a pause. And a number of shots.
'You're guessing.'
'Can no one tell me? Ah! then I've floored you ... Mary the Second, wife of William III, who founded Greenwich Hospital,' and Mr. Adams burst into a fit of Homeric laughter. Every week it is his custom to pop into various rooms and shell them with questions upon all manner of subjects. But not every week does he succeed in getting a floorer, clever as he is.[30]

In English Adams would ask questions linking novels and plays with historical events, seeking the opinions of children on the books they had read, and why they had liked them.

'Who reads Charles Dickens?'
Great show of hands.
'Which book of his do you like best?'
Great show of hands and loud cries of – 'OLIVER TWIST.'
'And what part of Oliver Twist do you like best?'
'When he is in the workhouse' (note – boys and girls in this part of the world don't call it 'workus', and their aspirates are remarkably well-placed), say some. 'When he's with the old Jew,' say others.
'Who was *he*?'
'Fagin.'
'Why do you like Oliver when he was in the workhouse?'
'Because he ASKED FOR MORE.'
There was universal laughter at this.
'The best answer I've had to-day,' cried Mr. Adams, hugely delighted.[31]

Both correspondents were impressed by the high quality of the recitation, paying particular tribute to that from the girls. The *London* correspondent, having found a class 'smart and accurate' in their answers to questions on the Ganges and Himalayas, asked if they could also recite. A girl led off with the opening cantos of *The Faerie Queen*, 'said with all due inflections and proper feeling ... Girls, I have been told, could generally recite better than boys. I believed it when that little lady sat down.'[32] Morley was overwhelmed by a recitation from *Henry V* by a girl of 13 'with a most intellectual headpiece' who 'threw out her chest, tossed back her head' and performed in tones of 'depth and fire', bringing applause from masters and pupils alike.[33]

Examples were given by both visitors of the written follow-up to visits to Westminster Abbey and the Tower of London, combining history and literature. Miss Reintjes produced some of the essays stimulated by work on eighteenth- and nineteenth-century literature, and included an essay which compared critically contemporary writing with that of the earlier century, exciting the warm approval of the *London* interviewer, who enjoyed the precocious judgements:

Writers of the last century expressed their thoughts in the simplest manner. In the nineteenth century thoughts are often hidden in very extravagant and obscure language, and it is not at all unusual to have to read a paragraph twice before understanding the author's meaning.[34]

Morley approved the competitive element which followed the outside visits, the best essay receiving the 'honour of PRINT', a 'most artful combination of business and pleasure; of powder and jam'. The prize essay was included in his account.[35]

As was characteristic of the period, history and literature, and no doubt geography as well, were politicized in the sense of being used to underline Britain's greatness as a colonial power and fount of liberty. While there is no real evidence that by the standards of the time this was unduly stressed in the Fleet Road curriculum, neither did the school neglect its patriotic duty in inculcating a love of country and empire celebrating, for example, great events such as the relief of Ladysmith in 1900:

The whole school assembled in the Hall at 3.45 and sang 'God Save the Queen'. Three cheers were given for General Buller and Sir George White. Also for Lord Roberts. The Hall was decorated with flags.[36]

The local newspaper printed a Fleet Road scholarship boy's four-verse eulogy of the Queen on her eightieth birthday, which Adams pasted in the Log book. Two verses are quoted:

Rejoice all true and loyal Britons
Scattered o'er our Empire wide
'Tis eighty years since Queen Victoria,
Came our destinies to guide ...
Long her life and great her goodness
May she yet continue long
Thus to stand as THE PROTECTOR
Of the right against the wrong.[37]

One of the hidden agendas in all these accounts is the underlying status of Fleet Road School. While publicized as the finest elementary school in Europe, the classes visited by these correspondents and cited as evidence of the excellence of the school were often made up of older children staying on at school to what would today be classified as in the secondary phase. The schoolboy writer of the eulogy to the Queen was no less than 15 years old. The girl providing the essay for Miss Reintjes was presumably in the specialist 'Candidates' class (p. 196), geared to those intending to go on to teacher training.

Adams' teaching style and curriculum planning were considered advanced for their time. The basis for the older children at least was a Socratic dialogue in which great weight was attached to the ability to recall facts, but some room was left in which to elicit more open responses. Certainly his pedagogy was expansive when compared with earlier catechetical treatment of the teaching of history.

How successful Adams was in his attempts to extend the teaching of history in the elementary school is uncertain. While many saw its advantages as a patriotic subject, the tension provoked by continuing religious differences in education inhibited history from growing apace. While some improvement took place after the time of the Cross Commission, the attitude of the London School Board was apparently less than enthusiastic. When the Cross Commission sat, there were only 15 boys' and three girls' departments taking history as a class subject. The number rose slowly to 26 in 1889, 60 in 1892, and 128 in 1895. Even then it remained at the bottom end of the popularity league among the class subjects.[38] In 1898, only 26,761 out of 581,976 London School Board children took history: about 5 per cent of the total.[39] Yet Adams made publicly clear his satisfaction and conviction that it was his evidence to the Cross Commission that had led to history being recognized as a subject of instruction in all classes of the elementary school.[40]

RELIGIOUS INSTRUCTION

In religious instruction the syllabus followed was that approved by the London School Board. This was entirely based on the Bible and contained no hint of denominational teaching, a circumstance no doubt appealing to Adams as a Congregationalist. It was also seen as reassuring parents that instruction was not purely secular. An advantage for Fleet Road School was the incitement to competition that the prize system of the London School Board in scripture knowledge offered. In 1881, for example, two years after the founding of the school, Fleet Road scholars were winning well beyond the average percentage of prizes (Table 8.5).[41]

TABLE 8.5

1881 Entries from Standard IV to VI

	Number Entered	Gaining Prizes	%	Gaining Certificates	%
London School Board	7,244	1,164	16	2,720	38
Marylebone Division	703	108	15	238	34
Fleet Road School	61	26	43	19	31

Source: SBL, 1884.

Thus of the 61 children entered in this year, nearly three-quarters gained a prize or a certificate. In 1886, for the second year in succession, Fleet Road took first place in the whole of London, on this occasion over 90 per cent of those entered gaining prizes or certificates. At the prize-giving at the school, one of the clerical managers expressed satisfaction that 'a good sound Scriptural education was given in the Board schools' on this evidence.[42] Fleet Road was also preeminent in the following year, all the girls entered gaining prizes or certificates, leading to the Marylebone Division HMI expressing the fear that this continued success might 'extinguish rivalry'.[43] The prizes, offered by a private benefactor and the Bible Tract Society, were bibles and other appropriate literature. Apart from the competitions, the London School Board ran annual examinations in scripture knowledge, which generated quarterly internal tests, designed as practice sessions. There was generally very favourable comment from School Board inspectors on the standard of hymn-singing and conduct of short morning services, including that in the Junior Mixed Department under Mrs. Adams.

DOMESTIC ECONOMY

Prior to 1890, Fleet Road children had to attend the London School Board Cookery Centre at Great College Street, Camden Town, which served 13 schools.[44] From this time, Fleet Road had its own Cookery Centre which became a model of its kind. Such centres were regarded as vital to the health and moral well-being of the next generation of urban people. The London School Board's efforts, and particularly the 'practical good sense' of 'some of the women members', were applauded by Mary Tabor, who also noted the enjoyment domestic economy lessons provided for the girls. There was widespread belief that they were the front-line troops in the battle against the moral and physical decay of the urban population.

The beginnings of good are here. The deepest and best instinct, lying back of everything in the woman heart, the desire to 'make home comfortable,' is reached and brought into play ... Many things are taught at these cookery centres besides cookery itself – cleanliness, neatness, precision, despatch. The observing faculties are brought into play, the latent womanliness developed ... Training in the domestic arts is the best thing we can give to girls of this class, needful before all else if we are to raise their standard of living.[45]

While this social justification was less compulsive at Fleet Road, the moral reasoning was equally at the heart of the educational philosophy of the school, in which there was a desire to balance cultural transmission with a useful education. Domestic science promoted care, tidiness (and Adams was a martinet so far as the dropping of litter was concerned), order and thrift, as well as beneficial skills. The dinner illustrated on Plate 29 was not only wholesome, but also economic, two courses feeding six people for 1/8d. The homily on the wall offered John Ruskin's words of wisdom on the subject:

it means carefulness and inventiveness and watchfulness and willingness ... it means the economy of your great-grandmother and the science of modern chemists; it means much tasting and no wasting; it means English thoroughness and French art and Arabian hospitality; and it means, in fine, that you are to be perfectly, and always, ladies.

The lesson on Plate 28, also written up on the blackboard,

28. Fleet Road Domestic Economy class, early 1900s

shows diets for different types of people: children; outdoor workers; indoor workers; and invalids. As one of a huge number of schools photographs commissioned by the L.C.C. during the Edwardian period, a particular aspect of the socialization process in progress is made clear.

Charles Morley was predictably very impressed with the domestic economy provision at Fleet Road. It included more than the actual technicalities of cookery: knowledge of pots and pans, kitchen ranges, the value of different foods in the diet, of soaps and sodas and cleaning materials; the pros and cons of different ways of cooking meat. For example:

Stewing has many advantages, among which are the following: It saves time, labour, fuel and money. Any old pieces can be used up. All nutrition is obtained from meat, bones and gristle. It is very satisfying.

Frying makes the meat very indigestible, and some of the nutrition goes up the chimney or in the pan.

29. Fleet Road Domestic Economy:
preparing a dinner for six people costing 1/8d

Morley found that among the topics to be covered were:

What food to give a baby three months old.
What food a labouring man could digest.
Why his organs were likely to be healthier than those of his masters.
What food I should give to an adult suffering from fever.
Why food should be cooked at all.

209

Morley's 'school meal' prompted middle-class masculine speculation about the consequences of mixing cooking with algebra for the next generation of housewives and servants, having appreciated the chop 'grilled to a turn, and a dishful of beautiful mealy potatoes, steaming in their jackets', brought by a 'neat little girl' who 'dropped a pretty curtsey to the master' before informing him the meal was ready.

'Cooked by the children', says Mr. Adams, regarding the viands with a critical eye. 'We turn out excellent cooks, I assure you. And now they teach their mothers – they often write to tell me so.'

Lunch is over – let us ... just listen for a minute or two to a lesson on Domestic Economy. Surely the sternest lady in the land, the most unbending foe to Board schools and their ways, can raise no objection to such a course. A profound acquaintance with algebra and the mysterious ways of x's *may* tend to make a brain-proud hussy. We need no symbols to enable us to dispense the ingredients of a plum pudding. It *might* possibly be painful for a mistress to come down into her kitchen and find her young and highly intelligent cook absorbed in the pages of 'Euclid,' instead of seeing to the roasting of the meat.[47]

COMMERCIAL EDUCATION

In April 1893 it was reported that Maud Farr of Fleet Road School had gained a Fellow's Certificate for excellence in the Script system of shorthand typing, the first certificate of its kind to be won by a scholar in an elementary school.[48] For Adams it was a long-standing article of faith that a sure way of promoting advancement in life was to provide a commercial type of education. As early as the time of the Cross Commission he had seen French teaching in this context. The subject was given a practical orientation, with an emphasis on correspondence, based perhaps on letters in French brought from London offices, and on conversation, for which the school introduced a native French speaker on Friday afternoons.[49]

Morley needed no persuasion on the value of commercial education, and described the work of the commercial class equally favourably as the other activities he had witnessed:

It was a lesson in script shorthand. The words are conveyed to paper in neat symbols at the rate of sixty words per minute. What useful boys these will be ... One of them came up and read out the above passage from the dots and crook-backed curves in his note-book as quickly as though it had been plain print. He, and some of his fellows, are about to enter the Civil Service – the Telegraphs, the Post Offices.[50]

The Practical Teacher correspondent indicated that the Script system of shorthand had been quickly picked up by both boys and girls. He found that in more than one of the classes the blackboard notes of history and geography lessons were written partly in shorthand, to economize space.[51] Lyulph Stanley also applauded the commercial bent of the school, and spoke favourably of the possibilities of taking Junior and later Senior Certificates of the London Chamber of Commerce through evening classes at the Fleet Road evening continuation school under one of the Fleet Road teachers, a ladder of opportunity which would mean they would rise above 'the position of a mere quill-driver'.[52]

FLEET ROAD AS EPITOME

Fleet Road epitomized most of the activities which brought the London School Board into conflict with the powerful and reactionary voluntaryist lobby. It took pride in the proportion of its children in the higher standards taking specialized, advanced and manifestly post-elementary courses. Its staff were highly qualified and, by the standards of the time, highly paid. On top of this, it expended a lot of energy on publicizing these activities and suggesting they should become the norm. It attracted a disproportionate number of lower-middle-class pupils, often from far outside the normal catchment of a board school. It provided an educational experience well beyond the capacity of local voluntary schools to match. The success of schools like Fleet Road sowed the seeds of downfall of the school boards, as has been amply documented. One of the vital issues on which the opponents of the London School Board were quick to seize was that of commercial education. Why something so manifestly appropriate to a capital city helped to lead to the 'grave disaster' of the demise of the school boards[53] needs probing.

The Board of Education was distinctly unsympathetic to two concepts promoted by the London School Board. One was that of the higher elementary school which, instead of being seen as a new route in educational development, was hastily dismissed as something of inferior character, the end of schooling and preliminary merely to manual or industrial occupations.[54] The perverseness of such an interpretation in a great commercial city such as London can only reasonably be explained by an over-

riding political will to cut off in midstream a trend to what
The Practical Teacher had seen as a new direction in 'that
organisation of secondary education and its correlation with
primary education which is a crying need of our times'.[55] The
London School Board stressed the need in the London situation
for commercial subjects to be regarded as of similar status to
scientific education in industrialized parts of the country.[56] The
Board of Education, however, regarded shorthand and book-
keeping with much suspicion and typewriting as quite beyond
reason. Yet schools such as Fleet Road were subsuming typewriting under shorthand and commercial correspondence. The
latter were approved subjects but typewriting, illogically, was
not. In addition, Fleet Road was one of two schools which had
bought typewriters, seen by one member of the London School
Board as 'a monstrous innovation'. John Taylor, an official of
the Hampstead Branch of the Church of England Voluntary
Defence Union, was undoubtedly aware of the Fleet Road case.
At the same time he was part of a lobby which in 1898 began the
process against the London School Board for misappropriation
of the rates, culminating in the Cockerton Judgment of 1899
which confirmed the illegality of the Board's expenditure on
higher elementary education.[57] Prior to this, in 1897, the Board of
Education had been alerted by a Report from the local HMI, G.
Fitzmaurice, recorded in the Fleet Road Log Book. Fitzmaurice
accused Adams of not following an approved timetable, and
indicated that the scholarship classes were being worked under
'unsanctioned' arrangements. He was critical that no records of
children's attainments in geography, history, mental arithmetic
and recitation had been kept, and of the results in arithmetic in
Standards III and IV. Adams was told he needed to 'exercise
more supervision to see work was not being over-marked'. It was
the most negative report Fleet Road had ever received. To an
extent Fitzmaurice was overruled by a more ameliorative statement from his superior Rev. T.W. Sharpe, Chief HMI for
England and Wales, though Sharpe requested that the timetables 'should not depart from the time-honoured arrangement'.
For Adams the letter was a lifeline. Fitzmaurice tersely observed
that Sharpe's suggestion 'had better be followed'.[58]

The revealing memoranda[59] circulating round the Board of
Education at this stage suggested little room for comfort on the
part of Fleet Road or the London School Board. The Board of

Education had demanded the Fleet Road timetables (pp. 196–7). These timetables caused some consternation. The interpretation was that the main sheet (summarized on p. 196) referred to the real timetable, and the separate set of typed sheets (summarized on p. 197) to 'extraordinary' classes tacked on to the school proper. The officials thought the main timetable within the Code, but the commercial classes with their special timetables outside it. 'But do we pay grants for them?' was the critical question asked. It was even thought possible the classes were entirely separate from the main school.

The advice of Fitzmaurice was sought. He reassured the Board that the commercial classes were not separated from the rest of the school, and indeed were not taken into account for grant purposes. There was, however, official concern that three of the teachers took no part in the elementary instruction of the school.

In 1901 the London School Board urged the recognition of Fleet Road as able to receive higher elementary grants without the need to change the curriculum deemed suspect.[60] After this the recorded discussion comes to an end. It would seem Fleet Road had served its purpose and provided valuable ammunition in the campaign to foreclose on the board school system and what it stood for. In advancing individuality as a virtue, Adams had earlier identified his own school as being particularly 'keen on literature and history' and on commercial education. He speculated that his successor might be keener on science, and of a mind to turn the hall into a workshop. This might be equally valuable. What was more important, he felt, was that 'there was room enough in this great capital of ours for every variety of instruction'.[61] Not in the elementary sector, was the view of more powerful forces.

REFERENCES AND NOTES

1. SBL 1586, *Government Inspector's Report, Fleet Road Mixed Schools*, 12 Dec. 1882.
2. For a convenient summary of changes in the Codes over this period see P. Gordon and D. Lawton, *Curriculum Change in the Nineteenth and Twentieth Centuries* (London, 1978), pp. 12–21.
3. *Cross Commission*, Final Report (1888), p. 146.
4. *Cross Commission*, 2nd Report (1887), p. 45.
5. *Ibid.*, p. 46.
6. *Ibid.*, p. 55.

7. *Ibid.*, p.55.
8. *Ibid.*, p.64.
9. *Ibid.*, p.47.
10. *Ibid.*, p.52.
11. *Ibid.*, pp.47–8.
12. *Ibid.*, p.45.
13. SBL 1589, *Government Inspector's Report, Fleet Road Junior Mixed School*, 23 Dec. 1885.
14. The timetable was reproduced in *The Practical Teacher*, vol. 15 (1894), p.6.
15. The Ex-VII timetable details were given in *Cross Commission*, 2nd Report (1887), p.1016.
16. PRO Ed. 14/41, 64603.
17. The Government Reports for Fleet Road School were printed in the records of the *School Management Committee* of the London School Board and can be found in the former GLC Archives from numbers SBL 1583 onwards.
18. *Cross Commission*, 2nd Report (1887), p.46.
19. *Ibid.*, p.55.
20. *Ibid.*, p.56.
21. *Ibid.*, p.62.
22. *Ibid.*, p.47.
23. *Ibid.*, p.52.
24. *Ibid.*, p.62.
25. *Ibid.*, p.46.
26. Quoted in *The Practical Teacher*, vol. 15 (1894), p.4.
27. W.B. Adams, *Leading Events in English History* (London, 1872), p.16.
28. *The Practical Teacher*, vol. 15 (1894), pp.3–4.
29. *London*, vol. 7 (1898), p.154.
30. C. Morley, *Studies in Board Schools* (London, 1897), pp.92–3.
31. *Ibid.*, pp.94–5.
32. *London*, vol. 7 (1898), p.154.
33. Morley, *op. cit.* (1897), pp.91–2.
34. *London*, Vol. 7 (1898), p.154.
35. Morley, *op. cit.* (1897), pp.103–4.
36. *Fleet Road Senior Mixed Department Log Book*, 1 March 1900.
37. *Ibid.*, 25 May 1899.
38. See J.D. Corbett, 'History in the Elementary School Curriculum, 1807–1914' (unpublished University of Liverpool M.Ed. Dissertation, 1988), pp.38–40.
39. See H.L. Withers, *Memorandum on the Teaching of History in the Schools of the London School Board* (London, 1901), p.2.
40. *HHE*, 4 May 1895.
41. SBL 1588, *School Management Committee*, 17 July 1884.
42. *HHE*, 16 Dec. 1886.
43. *HHE*, 1 Oct. 1887.
44. PRO Ed. 14/37.
45. M. Tabor, 'Elementary Education' in C. Booth (ed.), *Labour and Life of the People: London, Vol. II*, p.503.
46. The collection of photographs referred to is in the City of London (former GLC) Record Office in Northampton Road, London, EC1.
47. Morley, *op. cit.* (1897), pp.95–9.
48. *SBC*, 8 April 1893, p.390.
49. *Cross Commission*, 2nd Report (1887), pp.52–3.
50. Morley, *op. cit.* (1897), p.101.
51. *The Practical Teacher*, vol. 15 (1894), pp.3–4.
52. *HHE*, 3 March 1900.
53. T. Gautrey, *'Lux Mihi Laus': School Board Memories* (London, 1937), p.169.
54. D. Reeder, 'The Reconstruction of Secondary Education in England, 1869–1920' in D.F. Muller, F. Ringer and B. Simon (eds.), *The Rise of the Modern Educational*

System: Structural Change and Social Reproduction 1870–1920 (Cambridge, 1987), p.147.
55. *The Practical Teacher*, vol. 15 (1894), p.7.
56. PRO Ed. 14/102.
57. A.I. Taylor, 'The Church Party and Popular Education 1893–1902' (unpublished University of Cambridge Ph.D. Thesis, 1981), pp.278–81.
58. *Fleet Road Senior Mixed Department Log Book*, 2, 9 and 22 March 1897.
59. PRO Ed. 14/41, 64603.
60. PRO Ed. 14/102.
61. *HHE*, 4 May 1895.

CHAPTER NINE

'Red Letter Days':
The Fleet Road Image

There are many 'red-letter days' in the calendar of Fleet
Road Board Schools, but Imperial Purple should be the only
adequate colour with which to denote Friday, the 23rd of
September, 1892 ... for on that day did Sir David Evans,
Lord Mayor of London, visit the schools in order to distribute the Scripture prizes to the scholars, and the whole
school put on its gala attire to receive him.[1]

Hampstead Record, 1892

While the celebrity of William Bateman Adams' scholarship
pupils and Louisa Walker's kindergarten innovations convinced
influential figures that a sea-change in elementary school provision was being brought about at Fleet Road, an equally important factor in building up the public image was the adroitness
with which the two headteachers controlled external relations,
whether in dealing with occasional visitors to their departments,
or in laying on set-piece occasions.

In the contemporary educational debate which advocated the
importing of the public school spirit into the elementary sector,
as a means of improving the tone, Adams could be regarded as
one of the converted. Similarly Mrs. Walker, who introduced her
young charges to this more privileged world through the action
songs described in Chapter 6. The development of sporting
prowess was an important part of the process. While success in
this area was not one of Fleet Road's chief claims to fame, the
senior boys won local football competitions in 1898 and 1900. On
the latter occasion, the winning team was 'entertained by Mrs.
Adams at her residence',[2] another derivative of the public school
ethos. In 1899 Fleet Road was the champion school team in the
Marylebone Athletic Association's meeting.[3] The girls won the

London School Board swimming shield in 1902.[4] In 1901 it was reported that over 350 scholars had joined the school swimming club, and 150 had gained certificates. Inspectors' reports approved these activities as contributory to the corporate life of the school. As in the public school sector, and as Hampstead children, Fleet Road scholars were encouraged to regard themselves as privileged, and that duty was the other side of this particular coin. From the early 1890s, for example, the Junior Mixed school collected 'spare halfpence' to send as regular monthly remittances to the 'Shaftesbury Homes', while the Senior Mixed school annually collected used clothing to send to a poor East End school, Northey Street, Limehouse. Sometimes Adams recorded letters of thanks in his log book. 'Your scholars may rest assured that some of their poorer fellows are warmer, their days made a little more endurable, and their comfort greater, by their kindness.'[6] Contributions were also made, as appropriate, for charity overseas, as in a collection in 1899 for a fund for famine relief in India.[7]

While contributing to the building of an *esprit de corps*, these were activities engaged in by many schools in similar situations. They were undertaken as a matter of course as a purposeful extra-curricular endeavour. They did not constitute any particular claim to fame.

THE SCHOOL HALL

Though Fleet Road's buildings were externally unprepossessing, most visitors expressed initial surprise and pleasure on seeing the impressive school hall, decorated by an extraordinary collection of pictures and engravings, donated by distinguished visitors, supportive officials of the School Board, and also by parental subscription.[8] The correspondent of *The Practical Teacher* wrote at length about the hall:

The central hall is a delightful room, measuring 72 feet by 40. It is not lofty, but has a very pleasant appearance, being extremely well-lighted from a skilfully constructed glazed roof. Its chief charm, however, is the remarkable collection of engravings, etchings and photographs which adorn its walls. These number considerably over a hundred.[9]

The interviewer from the journal *London* was also curious about the provenance of the exhibits in the collection.

'Gifts'! said the master proudly. 'They have been given by old scholars who retain pleasing memories of the school, or by parents whose children have won scholarships, or by friends who take an interest in our work here.'[10]

The hall was not only deployed for public occasions. In so crowded a school it was regularly in use for classes, for vocal rehearsals and singing lessons and, of course, for drill. Not for the first time, Morley found his stereotypes threatened by the Fleet Road girls. Like all visitors, he was taken to the hall to see the prints and photographs. Here he encountered 100 girls from eight to 13 'marching round and round in pairs, all eyes on the mistress'.

Did ever regiment march better? Were evolutions more accurately carried out? Shade of Napoleon, Frederick the Great, the Iron Duke. Do Board schools breed Amazons, then? I surely began to think so as I watched the hundred at their marching and wheeling, and mazy windings. Certainly in a few years I think the race of wife-beaters will have disappeared from the land. (I only trust we shall not develop a race of husband-beaters.) Flat-footed women will be seen no more. Nor flabby muscles! Nor pigeon-breasts![11]

THE SCHOOL CHOIR

The school hall was the arena for Fleet Road's celebrated prize-givings and concerts. It was also the home of the school choir, which over a period of nearly ten years developed an enviable reputation as a result of its repeated successes in the London School Board's Vocal Music competitions, held between 1889 and 1898.

The 1880s and 1890s were decades in which interesting developments were taking place in elementary school music provision. Music had been slowly introduced into such schools from the 1840s, but was confined to singing, a useful support for religious instruction. The system used, on the grounds that it was easily comprehensible to young children, was the 'fixed-doh' method. But it was readily followed only if the music was written in the key of C Major. An alternative, and much more flexible, method was the 'Tonic-Sol-fa' system, concurrently invented by John Curwen. It was disseminated from the Tonic Sol-fa School, later the Tonic Sol-fa College. This instituted graded examinations, the simplest of which could be passed in the junior school.

The system helped to democratize singing and this and the domestic piano created an enormous interest in communal and family music-making. The number of professional musicians and music teachers grew from 6,600 in 1841 to 39,300 in 1901.[12] The presence of a piano in the home was an important index of social status, and music was almost a required accomplishment for women in genteel society.[13] The musical evening became an important part of the social activities of many respectable homes. The choral mania spread into working-class communities and brass band activities burgeoned as music diffused down the social ladder. It has been shown that Fleet Road's catchment covered part of the heartland of English piano manufacturing. Private music schools and music teachers abounded in the vicinity also.

Prior to the school board period, however, musical education in the elementary sector had stagnated, not helped by the impact of the Revised Code. The new urban school boards took a more positive line, and established the tonic sol-fa as the accepted method of teaching singing.[14] The expanding music publishing industry supplied large amounts of material for school use. But even though the London School Board appointed a Music Superintendent of Schools in 1872, development was uneven. One limitation was the lack of trained teachers. Another was the absence of pianos. Mrs. Walker's infiltration of a piano into her school was, as described in Chapter 6, a piece of private enterprise, not at first officially appreciated.

When later the Board proposed to purchase 100 pianos, it was seen as monumental extravagance. 'The Great School Board Piano Question' raged for two years or more. Opponents scathingly attacked the notion that children of the lower orders might be taught to play Beethoven Sonatas,[15] one of the more blatant failures to grasp the social realities outside. While George Bernard Shaw could be cited as proposing the life condition of the labourer's son as not one likely to engender an appreciation of Beethoven, he also found this absent at the other social extreme, and argued that the 'maximum relish for art' existed among the middle, and lower-middle, and 'the more comfortable membership of the artisan class'.[16]

The pressure on the School Board from below was inexorable. Most keen schools had already side-stepped the piano problem by using the proceeds of school concerts to buy their own instruments. While the reactionary lobby on the Board was denouncing the promotion of music in elementary schools, it was itself carrying on an elaborate competitive vocal music competition for school choirs. It was on no mean scale, the contests being held once each in the Royal Albert Hall and at the Crystal Palace, and three times each at Exeter Hall and the Queen's Hall. The first took place on 17 July 1889, and the 'scene presented' in the Royal Albert Hall was described as having probably 'never been equalled in that noble building'. The choirs had to perform a sight-singing test and then a part-song. On this occasion 50 schools had been visited and eight, including Fleet Road, invited to partake in the competition. Crawford Street was judged to be the 'best all-round choir' and took away the large copper Challenge Medallion (Plate 30), large enough for the insertion of ten names of winning schools. Fleet Road was one of four other choirs 'highly commended'.[17]

[By kind permission of Messrs. Curwen.]

Presented by Mr. J. R. DIGGLE, M.A.; Dr. GLADSTONE, F.R.S.; Mr. ROSTON BOURKE. F.E.I.S.; and Mr. SPENCER CURWEN, President of the Tonic Sol-fa College.

30. The London School Board Vocal Music
Competition Challenge Medallion

The Fleet Road Choir was again a contestant in 1890, the competition this time being held, together with a 'great concert', at the Crystal Palace. Choirs had to perform a common test piece, a 'very difficult' sight-singing test, and an own choice piece. *The Board Teacher* counted the occasion a great success. It spoke 'volumes for the teaching that not a single choir broke down' in the sight test. Fleet Road's performance in this was considered 'correct', with the 'phrasing, especially in the staccato section ... very good'. But Fleet Road again was only 'highly commended'. The announcement of the award was 'received with enormous cheering'. The winning school was Beresford Street.[18]

The heady mixture of competition, entertainment, and pride in the standards being achieved generated widespread interest. More and more schools wished to enter. For 1891, the Board laid down the ground rules very carefully. There were to be preliminary competitions held locally in March, and the final in July.

Each choir will be limited to 60 voices in the Preliminary Competitions, and also in the Final Competition. The choir may consist of Boys or Girls, or Boys and Girls mixed ... The adjudication will be made on the following points:
(a) Correctness in tune and time.
(b) Quality of tone and pronunciation of words.
(c) Preservation of pitch.
(d) Expression.

Knowing public interest was great, the Board permitted the hire of public halls if school halls were too small, and a small charge for admission. It stressed it had no legal power to incur expenditure itself, and hoped teachers would assist the Board 'in their endeavour to encourage and improve the instruction in Vocal Music in their Schools'.[19]

The 1891 Final Competition was held on 16 July in the Exeter Hall. This was to be Fleet Road's year of triumph. The choir both looked and sounded well. As *The Musical Herald* reported:

Fleet Road (Hampstead) girls attracted the eye by their lavender blouses and cream skirts, dotted with the dark material of the boys; they satisfied the ear too, by the perfection of their singing. Resonant and rich were the voices. Blending and balance were beautiful. The crescendos were gradual, the words clear, the expression varied, the sight-singing confident and correct, and, above all, the voice-training was delicious. Such boys are expected only in cathedrals. The audience stamped their hall-mark of approval on the choir with feet and hands and hurrahs.

The *Herald* was less impressed with 'the dreary hour of speeches' from School Board members in various votes of thanks which following the singing.[20] In response to the thanks to the judges, W.G. McNaught, for some time in charge of music at Homerton College and an assistant inspector of music under the Board of Education, then editor in turn of *School Music Review* and *The Musical Times*, and a well-known adjudicator at competitive festivals,[21] questioned if any country in the world could have produced better singing. He said the medallion had been awarded to Fleet Road School above all on the perfection of their voice training. 'He did not know the trainer, but he must be a genius in voice training.' This would seem to have been a rhetorical comment for on a later occasion it was revealed that the choir-master, Jesse Harris, had been a pupil of McNaught. The London School Board received a report from McNaught praising in particular the 'general excellence' of the Fleet Road Choir, and commending above all their voice production.[22]

The 'attendant circumstances' of the fourth competition, also in the Exeter Hall, were an 'overflowing audience, the sale of tickets stopped, and money refused at the doors'.[23] The first choir to sing, Haselrigge Road, produced 'an instant revelation to outsiders' who 'evidently had no idea of the marvellous pitch of excellence to which these selected choirs had been trained'.[24] *The Musical Herald* argued that the standard, apart from Fleet Road, had not advanced this year, largely due to the exacting nature of the sight test, and quoted extracts[25] (reproduced below) which caused trouble to all the choirs, except for Fleet Road.

The *Herald* gave details of the character and quality of performance of the Fleet Road Choir.

In this choir there were 14 boys and 34 girls, so that the brunt of the work fell upon the fair sex. Some ten boys with real contralto voices, the low notes evidently trained, gave out quite a sonorous 'bass' to the three-part harmony. No other choir had such a foundation. The four remaining boys were first sopranos, the middle part being taken by girls. Girls are chosen because they are more enthusiastic, and can be better relied on for work than boys. The choir had held two practices a day for three weeks, and had read at sight a quantity of music – anthems, etc. Full sustained tone, pure voice production, and true intonation which is its result, were conspicuous.[26]

Fleet Road won with 154 marks, far ahead of the other commended choirs, Haselrigge Road with 127, and Great College Street with 120. The *School Music Review* provided the

full adjudicator's report on the performance. The compulsory piece, a three-part glee entitled 'See the Chariot at Hand' was

almost faultless from any standpoint ... Expression chaste and perfectly appropriate. The pp passage was simply enthralling ... there was that oneness in the execution seldom attained except by the finest adult choirs.

In the sight test, the slow pace at which it was taken 'made me tremble, but there were no mistakes'. It gained full marks, 40/40, with the second choir in this part of the test ten marks behind. The overall conclusion was adulatory.

Every detail of sight-singing and execution had received its proper proportion of attention. The expression was never exaggerated, and the tone, though full and sweet, was never forced. It seemed that all the vowels were performed with the mouth roofed as round and high as possible. Hence the extraordinary resonance and ease with which the power came.[27]

The choir returned in triumph to Hampstead, pursued by *The Musical Herald*, who attended the follow-up concert, performed before a packed audience. It was revealed that six or seven of the choir stayed on at school beyond the time they were intending to leave to be able to sing in the competition. It was also noted that Jesse Harris, the now celebrated choir-master, was 'an out and out Sol-faist' and was once a pupil of Mr. NcNaught.[28]

But *The Board Teacher* on this occasion introduced a more critical agenda, querying the competitive edge given to the Fleet Road choir by the age, number and social character of the scholars on which it could draw. Another choir had only three children from Standard VII, 11 from VI, 16 from V, 16 from IV, and four from III, boys only, with an average age of $11\frac{1}{2}$ years. One correspondent waxed sarcastic about the Fleet Road entry, requesting a reply from the medical fraternity to the query: 'Will the careful training of a female's vocal organs tend to so develop other portions of her body that height, width, depth and apparent age should cause railway officials to demand adult fare from N. London to the neighbourhood of Exeter Hall?'[29]

The 1892 contest was also attended by George Bernard Shaw, then an eminent music critic. He commented on the vast audience of 'friends, relatives and partisans of the competitors, and the contingent from the London School Board', including the Revd. Diggle 'who listened moderately', and the Revd. Headlam, 'who listened progressively'. The children included 'dreamy, poetic, delicate-featured boys and girls; docile, passively receptive ones (with medals − I despised them); little duchesses whom I should have liked to adopt, little dukes who would have been considerably enriched if anyone had cut them off with a shilling'. There were also the pupil-teacher choirs, 'large bodies of picked young women, all of them survivals of the fittest, resolute, capable, and with a high average of good looks', before whom, as a mere critic, he quailed. The competition was 'more or less a humbug', the Shield going to the choir which had been trained 'single-heartedly in the art of getting the highest marks, which is not the same thing as the art of choral singing'. The sight test was unfairly conducted, in Shaw's view, because the choirs singing later could hear what was going on before: 'the reading of the upper part got better as the afternoon wore on, the little pitchers using their long ears to pick up the tune ...' The winners sang last and must have heard the 'sight test' sung seven times before, unless their ears had been plugged with cotton-wool. Shaw referred to the 'senseless syncopation' on the word 'death' and claimed he would have awarded extra marks to choirs which made the mistake, and deducted from the 'unintelligent plodders who passed unconsciously and safely through the danger'.

Jesse Harris was referred to as 'a very competent gentleman' but criticized as playing for safety and making sure that his children were more secure on matters of fact than matters of taste. Shaw further attacked the unfairness of a system which so depended on the quality of the choir-master, 'since children, in the lump, are all alike', except in the sight test, where the choir might be fortunate enough to have in its ranks 'an absolute pitcher'. The trainer could then adopt a 'follow-my-leader plan'. Shaw concluded:

The really tragic feature of the exhibition, however, was not in the pedagogic method, but in the little snatches of sweet and delicate singing which occasionally came from the mass of sound of which, in the main, no musical adjustment could disguise the vulgarity. It was not quite so bad as an ordinary oratorio chorus – the remnants of the charm of childhood saved it from that extremity.[30]

The following June the Fleet Road choir took part in the School Board's 'Great Triennial Fete' at the Crystal Palace. A combined School Board Choir of 4,249 scholars and 651 pupil teachers, drawn from 230 board schools, performed. There had been 150 rehearsals in 15 centres. The choir was accompanied by the Handel Orchestra. Part of the extravaganza was an action song entitled 'The United Kingdom', with four 40-strong choirs dressed in appropriate national costume singing a patriotic song and carrying a flag representative of the four constituent countries. The Fleet Road Choir, not unexpectedly, represented Wales, and sang 'Men of Harlech'. *The Musical Herald* described the Fleet Road 'Welsh girls in their conical hats, small shawls, baskets and knitting' as 'very pretty'. The culmination was the massed choirs rendering the National Anthem.[31]

The fifth annual Vocal Music Competition, held at Exeter Hall on 13 December 1893, was a relative disaster for Fleet Road, who slumped unexpectedly to fifth place, owing to what one commentator described as 'a fatal tendency to sink'.[32] The choir gained only 127 marks as against the 146 of the winner, Haselrigge Road. *The Musical Herald* agreed with the verdict, saying of the Fleet Road performance:

The superiority of the choir was evident from the first, but the 'one dark blot' of flattening (a fourth) was also generally noticed. It was probably due to temporary causes, and the long wait to perform, the damp weather, the cold hall, were sufficient to account for it. Everyone will sympathise with Mr. Harris, the conductor, in losing the trophy, for he has proved a phenomenal voice trainer. The change in the 'fortunes of war', however, will put heart into other choirs who had begun to fear him.[33]

The sixth competition took place in 'the beautiful new' Queen's Hall, Langham Place, on 18 July 1894. The move coincided with a drop in attendance,[34] and indeed the competition was not again to achieve its public popularity of the early 1890s. On this occasion the commentators were, not for the first time, critical of the over-exacting nature of the sight-reading test, in which unexpected stumbling blocks were encountered, and not negotiated by any of the choirs: 'the audience watched the result with increasing amusement.' *The Musical Herald* remarked that the Fleet Road Choir was younger this year, 'but excellently proportioned and trained'. Many thought Fleet Road would be placed first, but in fact they were second, eight marks behind Lyndhurst Grove: 'the quiet reception of the verdict contrasted strongly with the applause accorded in previous years.'[35]

The 1895 competition, again at the Queen's Hall, was the most controversial of all. A titanic struggle between Lyndhurst Grove and Fleet Road ended with the former coming first by just one mark. But of the Fleet Road performance one correspondent wrote: to 'find faults in this choir was like looking for a needle in a haystack.' On a number of counts it was the best. 'No choir was more popular with the audience, judging by the applause.'[36] The Fleet Road Choir secured better marks in both compulsory tests, but only 56 against the 60 of Lyndhurst Grove in the own choice piece. Lyndhurst Grove selected 'The Lord is my Shepherd'. On behalf of the adjudicators Sir John Stainer summarized the reasons for the narrow verdict.

We desire to express our high commendation of the performance of 'When winds breathe soft', by the Fleet Road choir, and also for the general refinement and delicacy of their performance. It was, however, impossible to withhold the first prize from a choir capable of giving such a beautiful rendering of the motet 'The Lord is my Shepherd', bearing in mind that the results of the other parts of the competition were so nearly equal.[37]

George Bernard Shaw was again present, and on this occasion apparently in a more mellow frame of mind. He was appreciative of the quality of the singing, but remained critical of the competitive element.

The seventh annual musical display by the London Board Schools ... would have been altogether commendable but for the element of competition induced by the challenge medallion. Only six school choirs had been chosen to compete; but a glance at the addresses of the schools and at the dress and physique of the children was sufficient to show that nothing but an odious and elaborate system of handicapping would have made the competition even approximately fair.

It was soon apparent that the prize must go to Lyndhurst Grove or Fleet Road, 'both of them starting with considerable advantages in the way of home polish on their raw material'. On the musical side, Shaw was obviously very struck by the Fleet Road choir, only inferior to Lyndhurst Grove in 'mass and balance of tone';

on the other hand, it was more spontaneous and expressive, it showed much greater variety of excellence; its show piece was not all one thing ... in the test piece ... it greatly surpassed its competition in crispness of pronunciation and vivacity of execution; above all, its artistic spirit was wonderful ... every individual child in it was swaying with enthusiasm as it sang.

Shaw made it clear he thought the result was an injustice, and that the reward should have been the applause of an 'unusually discriminating' audience. But he did not appreciate the feeling of a 'football match'. Next year the occasion 'should be a concert and not a competition'.[38]

The Guardian critic was also present and he too was more impressed by 'the really beautiful quality of tone emitted by the Hampstead choir' than by that of Lyndhurst Road. Lyndhurst Road had won because of the judicious choice of the Schubert Motet which had 'impressed the judges favourably on the score of taste, besides being very easy and effective'.[39]

W.B. Adams was upset by the decision, and was no doubt encouraged by these reviews to write to *The Musical Herald*.

We greatly appreciate your kind remarks about the performance of our choir. I should also like Mr. Bernard Shaw's suggestion to be carried out, as the choirs under present conditions cannot come out of the contest on equal terms. When once a selected piece has been accepted, it should carry the same weight as any other piece, or an informal handicapping is the result. To say that a choir won who selected a piece most pleasing to the adjudicators is really to utterly condemn the present system of award ... I do not wish to detract in the slightest degree from the admirable rendering of 'The Lord is my Shepherd' by the Lyndhurst Grove choir, but bearing in mind that we led in the 'compulsory piece' and in the 'sight-test', it is not unreasonable to think that had we sung the same piece as the Lyndhurst Grove choir, the result of the competition might have been different ... I do not think, therefore, that we shall again enter the competition under existing conditions. But we shall not relax our efforts in our endeavours to attain the highest possible musical standard ... I feel certain that the musical training in our schools would be benefited rather than injured by this change, and it would put an end to much natural heart-burning and dissatisfaction. Please make what use you like of this letter.[40]

The withdrawal symptoms did not last, and it was more true to type that, when the whiff of competition was in the air, this time 18 months later, Fleet Road entered for the eighth contest, held once again in the Queen's Hall. *The Musical Herald* recorded a further drop in interest on the evidence of a smaller audience, and a noticeable lowering in the standard of performance. Lynd-hurst Grove, under a new conductor, slipped back to fourth place. Fleet Road, while winning the medallion for the third time, scored only 132 marks, as against the 152 the previous year when they had been second. *The Musical Herald* was still reasonably impressed.

This thrice champion choir has had the advantage of the same conductor, Mr. J. Harris, from first to last. A continuity of conductor means a great deal when that person is born to rule as Mr. Harris is. The credit of success this time is all the more due to him because he had by no means as good material to work upon as he had some years ago; the children were smaller and their tone harder and less developed than formerly. Nevertheless there was improvement in the keeping of pitch ... The failure in the sight-singing was less pronounced than that of those heard before, but was not so good as demonstrated by the next choir ... A happy choice of piece was made, Smart's 'How lovely are Thy dwellings' ... not too difficult, but delightfully tuneful and expressive. A major second was lost in pitch, but the rendering was altogether pleasing. Our only objection to Fleet Road is that we thought they were excelled in voice-training and sight-singing. More boys and bigger ones are wanted in the choir, which is a mixed one with a large majority of girls, big and little.[41]

On its return to Hampstead the champion choir was photo-graphed (Plate 31), the picture appearing in the journal *London*'s feature on the school. Mrs. Adams entertained the choir to tea. Jesse Harris, who can be seen on the opposite side of the medallion to Adams, was presented with 'a handsome desk

31. 'The Champion Choir': W.B. Adams, Jesse Harris, and the 1897 prize-winning choir, in the great school hall, showing part of the famous collection of prints and photographs

and writing table'.[42] He had guided the choir to eight finals, won on three occasions, come second on two, and been highly commended on all the others, a unique record.

In 1898 the competitive element, as Shaw had advocated, was abolished. A non-competitive concert took its place. The London School Board suggested the removal of the competition would make the occasion 'especially interesting'.[43] It was held in the Queen's Hall on 19 June 1898. The Board decreed no choir taking part in the competitions of the last three years was to be invited, in order 'to extend the influence of singing over a wider field'.[44] Seven choirs and a string band performed. There appears to have been no such occasion in 1899, but in 1900 nine choirs were brought together on 4 July in the Queen's Hall to sing Handel's *Judas Maccabeus*. Fleet Road supplied some sopranos and altos, and teachers were used for the bass and tenor parts.[45]

Throughout the 1890s the Fleet Road Choir was in regular demand for giving concerts. In 1893 it provided a demonstration of Harris' training methods at the Tonic Sol-fa College.[46] In 1894, Spencer Curwen, son of the founder of the tonic sol-fa system, presented a portrait of his father in recognition of the choir's successes.[47] In 1895 it was invited to perform at a garden party at Sir Richard Temple's residence in Hampstead for leading supporters of the women's suffrage movement.[48] In 1896 it sang to members of the London School Board at its offices.[49] Its members were much in demand to join church choirs after they left school.[50]

The *Magazine of Music* dispatched a correspondent to Fleet Road in 1893 to explore the reasons for the choir's success. Like other visitors, he was greatly impressed by the school hall, the fine Erard grand piano, bought from the proceeds of school concerts, 'and the best collection of pictures I have yet seen in a Board school'. The correspondent was then taken to see one of Jesse Harris' lessons.

Mr. Harris I may say, is a red-hot enthusiast. Mr. Adams seems to have absolute faith in him, and doubtless it is chiefly owing to his untiring industry that Fleet Road is first in singing. Rehearsals are got in at all sorts of unexpected times: in the morning before most of us are out of bed, and in the evening when one would expect the children to be anxious to get out to play. But they are not. Mr. Adams and Mr. Harris have hypnotised them, and the youngest member of the choir is all anxiety about the success of any forthcoming concert ... Amongst the pieces performed at these concerts are Rossini's 'To Thee, Great Lord', Handel's 'And the glory of the Lord', the Bridal chorus from 'Lohengrin'; but indeed all the great masters, and a lot of the little ones, are drawn on to supply the large repertoire of the choir. In four-part choruses a few gentlemen are got to supply the tenor and bass, but the altos and trebles are all drawn from the school.[51]

Harris was less resilient in the face of personal tragedy. In 1900 his wife became seriously ill. In February 1901 Adams recorded his alarm at Harris' mental condition, referring to his 'serious frustration' and 'unfitness for work'.[52] He was away in March and April, and the autumn term saw more absences. On 8 January 1902 Harris was absent because of the death of his wife. On the 13th he returned to school, but was unable to teach. 'His manner was strange', wrote Adams.[53] Harris continued to turn up, but unfit for work. On April 7, Mrs. Adams was called in on supply to take the place of Harris, who the School Management Committee had, cruelly, decided to transfer 'to one of the ordinary schools of the Board'.[54] Harris himself died on June 9 after what was described as 'a long illness'. Adams commented laconically: 'He was a member of the original staff, and during the whole time had charge of the school choir.'[55] The *School Music Review* in its obituary noted that his wife's death had left him depressed and prone to disease. Harris was survived by seven children, not well provided for.

Whether or not Harris was of an innate nervous disposition cannot be demonstrated, but there is some evidence of concern that the vocal music contests, apart from what some regarded as the unseemly competitive element, were a source of unnecessary pressure. In 1898 *The Practical Teacher* approved the abandonment of the competitive aspect and hoped the contests would be a thing of the past 'since they involved so intense and injurious a nervous strain'.[56]

There were many tributes to Harris after his death. The *School Music Review* referred to the 'extraordinarily high standard of excellence' he had set at the time of his choir's first triumph in the vocal music competition, showing 'what was possible with school children'.[57] Harris' successor was T.H. Hodges of Hugh Myddleton Higher Grade School, Clerkenwell, one of the few prestige board schools in an inner area of London. He was choirmaster at that school and a specialist musician of considerable experience. One of his first tasks was to prepare a concert on behalf of the destitute children of Jesse Harris, at which £100 was raised. It was reported that the concert maintained the previous standards of choral excellence.[58]

VISITORS TO THE SCHOOL

The reputation of the choir was one of the factors attracting large numbers of visitors from home and overseas to Fleet Road. They included Count Franchi Verney of Valetta, who had been sent by the Italian Minister of Public Instruction to report on choral singing in the schools of France and England. Adams copied extracts from his report in the school log book. Franchi concluded that musical training in French schools 'grows pale' compared with that he had found in England. At Fleet Road he noted the presence of an upper elementary school for 'youths of both sexes' from ten to 14 years. He attended one of Harris's music lessons.

Sol fa-ing, reading at sight, chorus singing, solo singing at the piano, writing of music, in fact, all the exercises which are with us prescribed for the examinations for the post of Singing Master, in the Normal Schools, were successively executed with astounding quickness and self-confidence.[59]

The 1890s in particular witnessed a stream of visitors to the school. They included interested individuals as well as official foreign dignitaries, from the U.S.A., Canada, Siam, Brazil, Uruguay, Australia, New Zealand, and no fewer than 11 European countries. The most celebrated visitor (see also Chapter 6) was probably the Prince of Siam. The visit had been recommended by HMI J.G. Fitch. The Prince was accompanied by R.L. Morant, a one-time diplomat in the Far East and now in the Education Department. They saw exhibitions of musical drill, and heard a geography lesson on Siam.[60] Subsequently Adams received a warm letter of thanks, and a framed engraving of Queen Victoria to be hung in the hall.[61] In 1894 the Secretary of the Uruguayan Legation and Director of the Pedagogic Museum in Montevideo made a similar visit, and witnessed Swedish drill, a chemistry demonstration, a lesson on model drawing, and the shorthand class. Specimens of work were taken back to Uruguay.[62]

Among the many nationals visiting Fleet Road were representatives of other school boards, universities, secondary schools and training colleges. Edinburgh, Swansea, Walthamstow, West Ham and Willesden school boards sent deputations. Representatives from Oxbridge included members of Caius, Lincoln,

Magdalen, Newnham, Pembroke and Queen's Colleges. There were also visitors from Manchester Grammar School, Marlborough and South Hampstead High School, and from Bangor, Hammersmith, Nottingham, Stockwell and Swansea training colleges. A number were personal connections of Adams. As already noted (Chapter 7), two of the staff were appointed to Nottingham. The school was regularly used for teaching practice, by Borough Road, Maria Grey, St. Katherine's (Tottenham), and Stockwell training colleges, and by J.W. Adamson's students from King's College, London University.

Even more publicized than the Prince of Siam's visit was that of the Lord Mayor of London, who came in 'picturesque official attire' in September 1892, accompanied by 'the usual mounted escort of city police'.[63] As a Welshman, Sir David Evans, the Lord Mayor, joked about the success of the school reflecting Adams' Celtic background. The choir predictably sang 'Men of Harlech'. An inscription had been placed over the platform which the local newspaper reported as 'Croesawid Calonog in Chwi a Des Heddwch', and complained: 'the mystic import of which we leave to our Welsh readers to unravel, it being too much for our mental capacity.' Unravelled, it should apparently have read 'Croeso Calonog i Chwi. A Oes Heddwch?' The latter is a phrase from the chairing or crowning ceremony of the National Eisteddfod, and the whole means: 'A heartfelt welcome to you. Is there peace?' Safe in London, Adams was happy to make capital out of his Welsh origins, albeit from the 'little England beyond Wales'. The memory of his hasty departure from the Principality when finding himself working in a Welsh-speaking community (Chapter 5) was presumably suppressed in his subconscious. But this occasion was a great success, the civic party, 'evidently delighted with their visit', driving away 'amidst the cheers of a large crowd of spectators'.[64]

PRIZE DAYS AND CONCERTS

As early as the mid-1880s, the prize days and concerts of Fleet Road School, at which scholarship awards, scripture prizes, sporting trophies, attendance medals, and so on, were awarded, and the vocal music medallion, when available, was displayed, were attracting wide attention. In 1885 the *School Board Chronicle* described the rehearsal for such an occasion at which a

Cantata entitled 'Red Riding Hood's Rescue' was performed, with the young Adams supporting as accompanist, and at which children danced quadrilles and teachers sang glees. Mrs. Adams provided fruit and buns for the children and entertained distinguished visitors to tea 'in a prettily decorated classroom'.[65]

As in public schools, the prize days at Fleet Road were treated as glittering social occasions. They were not usually marked by false modesty, though at one of them, in 1891, Lyulph Stanley cautioned the audience that the scholarships should be regarded as being for the benefit of the children and not 'as a means of advertising the school'. Fleet Road saw no harm in gaining the dual benefit. Other mentors of the school were less reticent than Lyulph Stanley. It was probably at a prize-day entertainment that the 'Eton of the Board Schools' tag was attached. Thus in a vote of thanks at this 1891 prize-giving, the proposer suggested to the children that one day 'they would all be as proud of having been a pupil in the Fleet-road Board School as the Old Etonians were of Eton'.[66] In his speech, W.B. Adams exhorted the children 'to do all in their power to keep up the fame of Fleet-road Schools'. A letter was received from Sir Richard Temple, M.P., apologizing for his absence, and expressing his regret at not being able to hear the champion choir 'of what is, in my opinion, probably the best elementary school in Europe'. The regaining of the trophy had inspired one of the staff, Miss Howarth, to verse:

EXCELSIOR

Lost they the battle twice
Downhearted never;
Plucky FLEET-ROADERS
Excelsior ever.

Rushed to the fight once more
Victory gaining;
Gallant FLEET-ROADERS,
TROPHY attaining.[67]

In reporting a concert in 1893 the local newspaper revealed that Mrs. Adams had had her musical sketch 'Haymakers' published by Novello.[68] It may be conjectured that Adams enjoyed the public reading of the eulogies in letters from notables unable to attend as much as he revelled in the hyperbole which characterized the votes of thanks and readily won the cheers of the audience. A letter from one School Board member was headed 'Semper Floreat Fleetonia'.[69] At the 1895 prize-giving,

Novello presented a large portrait of Purcell for the hall in recognition of the choral prowess of the school.[70]

While by the 1890s school prize-days had become something of a vogue, even in the elementary sector, those of Fleet Road had a special aura. Surely in few other board schools was the attention-seeking so single-minded and so pretentious? Invitations were carefully contrived. Invitees typically included the Vice-Chairman of the London School Board, the Secretary of the Education Department, HMI, principals of training colleges, the Secretary of the British and Foreign School Society, and members of the School Board, the Marylebone Division, and the school managers. Lyulph Stanley, who donated prizes for the scholarships, was regularly present, and Sir George Kekewich, Chief Secretary to the Education Department, was an important and reasonably frequent 'catch'. Two events of 1896 were typical.

At the first, in a fulsome address, Lyulph Stanley extolled the school as 'a splendid instrument of education'.

Mr. Adams had succeeded in stirring up in the neighbourhood a feeling of pride in the school, and amongst the scholars there was an *esprit de corps* and a feeling which was something akin to the feeling which a public school-boy had for the place in which he was educated. That in itself was a good result, and one which would bear good fruit in the future.[71]

Later in the year, Kekewich, in seconding a vote of thanks to the Chairman, said he considered Fleet Road to be 'the very best elementary school in England'[72] though Stanley, who was on record as admiring the higher-grade schools of places such as Bradford and Leeds, went no further than ranking it as 'one of the best schools in the County of London'.[73] The following year the Chairman made a by-then-almost-statutory reference to Fleet Road as 'Eton without payment' and to its scholars as the 'aristocracy' of London School Board children.[74]

Charles Morley paid a second visit to the school to attend one of the concerts. Among other impressions, he was particularly intrigued by the moral underpinnings of the playlets and action songs, as in one 'proclaimed with fervour' by a 12-year-old, 'of ascetic features', who had won a Band of Hope prize. It was a temperance song of a type embodying public anxieties about the state of the urban race, prevalent at the time. Morley was surprised that a Hampstead school considered 'such fierce denunciations' necessary.

Drunk in the street!
A woman arrested to-day in the city!
'Comely and young', the paper said –
'Scarcely twenty', the item read;
A Woman and wife,

Drunk in the street!
Yes; crazy with liquor; her brain is on fire!
Reeling and plunging, stagg'ring along,
Singing a strain of a childish song –
At last she stumbles and falls in the mire ...

... Would you stand still?
Is it nothing to you that such things be?
You who have sons who will soon be men,
And daughters to live in a future – what then?
Is it nothing to you – be they bond or free?

Work! Night and day!
Nail up the doors where liquor is sold!
Rescue your land from its load of death;
Add no more to the ghastly wreath
Of widows and orphans, whose knell is toll'd.[75]

Joining Harris in conducting the choir was the redoubtable choral competition adjudicator, Dr. McNaught, who apparently shared the social anxieties outlined in the song. Morley recounted how McNaught, in introducing the sort of 'good old songs' he thought should be taught in board schools, was disparaging about the music provided by popular culture outside:

'Ladies and gentlemen, I am trying my best to introduce these delightful songs into the Board schools. Our children *will* sing, and surely our good old songs – so sweet, so tender, so gay, so spirited – are better than –:' and then the doctor paused to give his words effect – ' "Her golden hair's a-hanging down her back." You know that vulgar ditty which has had such a vogue on the organs. And of all songs ... none can beat the old sea songs. Surely we should never let them die out of our hearts and memories!'

This was prelude to a performance, conducted by McNaught, of 'The Arethusa', given as an action song.

Come all ye jolly sailors bold,
Whose hearts are cast in honour's mould,
While England's glory I unfold
Hurrah for the 'Arethusa'.

In Morley's description: 'Every bosom was at once filled with a warm patriotic glow at the sound of these stirring words and the lilting air.' The 'brave frigate' was set upon by four sail of

'Frenchies', and 'the brave bluejackets thereupon fought till not a stick would stand ...'

But they drove the foe ashore, and then, in true British fashion, each filled a glass to his favourite lass (though presumably not the one with the golden hair a'hanging down her back) ... I am sure you will agree with Dr. McNaught that such a ditty is almost as worthy of attention as the street songs which boys and girls of the great metropolis borrow from organ and music-hall.[76]

The musical diet of the school concerts was, as the *Magazine of Music* suggested, an amalgam of well-known excerpts from the great masters popular at the time, such as Handel, Mendelssohn, Rossini and Wagner, and of ballads, anthems and patriotic songs of the many Victorian composers striving to keep up with a large and increasing demand for music. Most reflected 'high culture' if sometimes of an ersatz variety. The songs were interspersed with recitations and interrupted by prize-givings and speeches. Programmes were usually pasted by Adams in his Log Book. The February 1898 occasion is not untypical. At this, Lord Reay, Chairman of the London School Board, presided, and Mrs. Lyulph Stanley presented the scholarship prizes sponsored by her husband.

Programme of Proceedings

Under the Direction of the Head Master

CHORUS	'O Lord Supreme in Splendour' (Mose in Egitto) CHOIR	Rossini
AIR	'O for the Wings of a Dove' CHARLES HUDSON	Mendelssohn
CHORUS	'O Lord of Glory' (Tannhäuser) CHOIR	Wagner
RECITATION	'Henry VIII' FLORENCE MOTT AND ETHEL WARD	Shakespeare
PART SONG	'O Who will o'er the Downs' CHOIR	Pearsall

MUSICAL DRILL BY JUNIOR SCHOLARS
Distribution of Scholarship Prizes by Mrs. Stanley

ADDRESSES BY CHAIRMAN AND OTHERS

PART SONG	'O hush thee, my Babie'	Sullivan
PATRIOTIC CHORUS	'Victoria, our Queen'	Barnby

The conductor was of course Jesse Harris and the accompanists two members of staff, Messrs. H. Atkins and J. B. Miles.[77]

The impact on Morley himself appears to have included a reinforcement of his stereotyping, characteristically late-Victorian, of girls as a potential civilizing influence on society.

It is the boys of London who spread these ... 'Golden hairs a-hanging down their backs,' like an infection. Mr. Harris ... tells me that the average boy prefers MARBLES TO MUSIC. The barbarians! It is the girls of London, with the sweet, soft voices, with golden hair a-hanging down *their* backs – enthusiastic lovers of good music – to whom we must look then for reform in the direction which has been sufficiently indicated ... Will they succeed in softening the manners of their comrades?[78]

Fleet Road was caught up in the late nineteenth-century re-creation of a world of leisure. The popularity of the concerts and prize-givings was ample testimony to the public appetite. But its diffusion down the social gradient was seized upon by the higher orders as of dangerous precedent. It was the tightly prescribed work-schedule of the basic curriculum that was needed to reverse this trend. School entertainments fuelled temptation by contrast.

Not all Hampstead residents were thus as impressed with the activities at Fleet Road as its influential sponsors. A series of critical letters appeared in the *Hampstead and Highgate Express* in March and April 1899 from anonymous correspondents such as 'A Ratepayer', 'An Indignant Ratepayer', 'An Overburdened Ratepayer' and 'Another Ratepayer', all complaining of the extravagance and inappropriateness of the displays at Fleet Road. 'Every right-minded person must be sick of hearing the tomfoolery enacted at the Fleet-road and other Board schools and the twaddle written about them' one wrote, criticizing 'the manufacture of little velvet breeches and other articles of evening dress for poor children ...'. Much support, as well as counter-argument, was forthcoming:

Permit me to express my hearty approval of the opinions advanced by A Ratepayer in the letter you publish in this week's issue respecting the waste of public money sanctioned by the School Board in getting up these unnecessary displays and entertainments at Fleet-road and other Board schools.

I was present at one given at the above achool a short time since, and, as a hard-working ratepayer, was unpleasantly surprised at seeing how much time and money had been lavished in teaching these children of working people to act, sing, and dance, as if training for the stage.[79]

The upper middle classes were already anxious about the threat to public order perceived to be brewing in the slums. Was the meritocratic school also going to be a hazard in giving the respectable working classes ideas above their station? The fabric of privilege was demonstrably under attack, and where could that more damagingly take place than in Hampstead?

All must agree that school-life ought to be a preparation for work in every class, and it appears to me a pity to employ the hard-earned money of ratepayers in pursuits rather tending to a life of pleasure (to which, of course, children will naturally take quite readily) than to the really useful training for manual labour which was never so much needed in England as at present. Where ... can we hope to find, among the young people who have been so expensively trained at these Board schools at the cost of the over-taxed middle-classes, any decently capable cooks, housemaids, general servants, or skilful and industrious workmen?[80]

These more hard-line views can fairly be said to reflect the dying throes of an earlier way of thinking. For while there remained bitter resentment against providing rates for board schools, Hampstead had moved on and contained many influential residents who were aware of and admired the achievement of Fleet Road, including some of the local clerics. By the end of the Adams era the school was for some a source of civic pride. Mrs. Walker's concerts at the Vestry Hall were celebrated events well beyond educational circles.

Yet the Hampstead public found it hard to comprehend what was happening to the children 'down the hill', for Fleet Road as a street retained its earlier poor social image. It was difficult for the old-established middle classes to take on board the nuanced lower-middle-class/upper-working-class differentiation. The safest way was to regard all board school children negatively, as an environmental hazard. 'Long-suffering of Hampstead' was as worthy as 'Disgusted of Tunbridge Wells' of gaining the status of a music-hall joke.

School children and children of the lower middle class and of wage-earners roam the streets shouting at the tops of their voices as if the town belonged to their parents ... Now does it ever occur to those in authority that quiet should reign in this town above all others? In the first place, this is a health resort. There are many weak, nervous people here often sent by physicians to enjoy and profit by the pure air. Then there are many retired professional and business men, who are trying to find quiet for study, and perhaps the cultivation of music and some other art.[81]

Just as the Board of Education was discerning Fleet Road

School (and others of its type) as a kind of Trojan Horse in curricular terms, so members of the Hampstead public regarded the extra-curricular activities with equal suspicion. They were correct to scent trouble, if protecting of social barriers was the priority. For meritocratic schools were busily preparing pupils to climb the hurdles through the scholarship system, as well as widening their cultural insights and status aspirations through generating a new type of socializing ethos, consciously drawn from the Public School sector.

REFERENCES AND NOTES

1. *Hampstead Record*, 24 Sept. 1892.
2. *Fleet Road Log Book*, 12 Oct. 1900.
3. *Hampstead Record*, 4 March 1899.
4. *Fleet Road Log Book*, 18 Nov. 1902.
5. LSB, *Fleet Road Managers' Yearly Report*, Sept. 1902.
6. *The Practical Teacher*, vol. 15 (1894), p.3.
7. *Fleet Road Log Book*, 19 Jan. 1899.
8. *Ibid.*, 11 June 1894.
9. *The Practical Teacher*, vol. 15 (1894), p.2.
10. *London*, vol. 7 (1898), p.153.
11. C. Morley, *Studies in Board Schools* (London, 1897), p.114.
12. N. Temperley, 'The Lost Chord', *Victorian Studies*, vol. 30 (1986), p.7.
13. M. Burgan, 'Heroines at the Piano: Women and Music in Nineteenth-century Fiction', *Victorian Studies*, vol. 30 (1986), p.51.
14. B. Rainbow, 'The Rise of Popular Music Education in Nineteenth-century England', *Victorian Studies*, vol. 30 (1986), p.40.
15. I. Taylor, 'Music and the Victorian Elementary School', *History of Education Society Bulletin*, vol. 18 (1976), pp.44–52. See also D. Rubinstein, *School Attendance in London 1870–1904* (Hull, 1969), pp.31–2.
16. G.B. Shaw, *London Music in 1888–89 as Heard by Corno di Basetto* (London, 1937; New York 1973 reprint), pp.137–8.
17. *The Board Teacher*, 2 Nov. 1889, p.120.
18. *The Board Teacher*, 1 July 1890, p.104.
19. LSB, *School Management Department*, 18 Dec. 1890.
20. *The Musical Herald*, 1 Aug. 1891, p.235.
21. E. Blom (ed.), *Grove's Dictionary of Music and Musicians*, vol. 5 (London, 1954), pp.481–2.
22. *The Board Teacher*, 1 Sept. 1891, p.130.
23. *The Board Teacher*, 1 Dec. 1892, p.271.
24. *The Schoolmaster*, 26 Nov. 1892, p.957.
25. *The Musical Herald*, 1 Dec. 1892, p.369. See also *The Musical Times*, 1 Dec. 1892, p.730.
26. *The Musical Herald*, 1 Dec. 1892, p.369.
27. *School Music Review*, 1 Dec. 1892, p.99.
28. *The Musical Herald*, 2 Jan. 1893, p.369.
29. *The Board Teacher*, 1 Dec. 1892, p.271.
30. G.B. Shaw, *Music in London 1890–94*, vol. II (London, 1931; New York reprint, 1973), pp.209–13.

31. *The Board Teacher*, 1 July 1893, pp.161–2.
32. *School Music Review*, 1 Jan. 1894, pp.130–2.
33. *School Music Review*, 1 Aug. 1894, p.132.
34. *The Musical Herald*, 1 Aug. 1894, p.248.
35. *Ibid.*, p.249.
36. *The Musical Herald*, 2 Dec. 1895, pp.358–9.
37. *Ibid.*, p.359.
38. Quoted in *School Music Review*, 1 Dec. 1895, p.122. The original review was published in *The Daily Chronicle*, 14 Nov. 1895 under the heading 'A State Concert – New Style', and is reproduced in D.H. Laurence (ed.), *Shaw's Music: the Complete Musical Criticism of Bernard Shaw, Vol. 3, 1893–1950* (London, 1981), pp.356–8.
39. Quoted in *ibid.*, p.133.
40. *The Musical Herald*, 2 Dec. 1895, p.360.
41. *The Musical Herald*, 1 June 1897, pp.172–3.
42. *Fleet Road Log Book*, 24 May 1897.
43. SBL 901, Letter to Head Teachers, 7 June 1898.
44. *School Music Review*, 1 Aug. 1898, p.40.
45. SBL 901, 6 April 1900.
46. *Fleet Road Log Book*, 19 May 1893.
47. *Ibid.*, 27 Aug. 1894.
48. HHE, 22 June 1895.
49. *Fleet Road Log Book*, 20 Nov. 1896.
50. *London*, vol. 7 (1898), p.152.
51. *Magazine of Music*, vol. 10 (1893), p.129.
52. *Fleet Road Log Book*, 1 Feb. 1901.
53. *Ibid.*, 13 Jan. 1902.
54. *Ibid.*, 7 April 1902.
55. *Ibid.*, 9 June 1902.
56. *The Practical Teacher*, vol. 19 (1898), p.57.
57. *School Music Review*, 1 Aug. 1902, p.45.
58. HHE, 26 July 1902.
59. *Fleet Road Log Book*, quoting letter from Rome dated 5 Aug. 1897.
60. HHE, 26 July 1902.
61. SBC, 17 Oct. 1891, p.430.
62. *Fleet Road Log Book*, 3 March 1894.
63. HHE, 24 Sept. 1892.
64. *Hampstead Record*, 24 Sept. 1892.
65. SBC, 11 April 1885, p.363.
66. HHE, 17 Jan. 1891.
67. *Hampstead Record*, 19 Dec. 1891.
68. HHE, 23 Dec. 1893.
69. HHE, 15 Dec. 1894.
70. HHE, 14 Dec. 1895.
71. HIIE, 21 March 1896.
72. HHE, 19 Dec. 1896.
73. HHE, 21 March 1896.
74. HHE, 20 Feb. 1897.
75. Morley, *op. cit.* (1897), pp.112–13.
76. *Ibid.*, pp.117–18.
77. Insert of Prize Day Programme in *Fleet Road Log Book*, 23 Feb. 1898.
78. Morley, *op. cit.* (1897), p.119.
79. HHE, 11 March and 1 April 1899. See also pp.157–8.
80. HHE, 1 April 1899.
81. HHE, 10 April 1909.

CHAPTER TEN

Fleet Road School and the London Scholarship Ladder

... this Bill was part of a great whole, which, when perfected, would give to this country what it had never yet had – a national system. It commenced with the elementary schools, advancing to the middle class, proceeding to the public schools, and ended with the universities; a plan by which, he trusted, it might be easy for any clever child to ascend the ladder of merit, helped where he needed it, and hindered by no test, or unequal conditions, from the English village school to the honourable places of the universities of the land.[1]

Hansard, 1870

This vision of Sir Charles Reed, who was later to become Chairman of the London School Board, was offered in a speech to the Commons as part of the debate over the 1870 Act. Reed was clearly piqued at the subsequent attribution of the ladder metaphor to Thomas Huxley.[2] As we have seen (Chapter 2), the London School Board refused to restrict its role to merely filling in the gaps in voluntary provision. From the first, Huxley sought a much wider responsibility.

I believe no educational system in this country will be worthy of the name national, or will fulfil the great objective expected of it, unless it be one which establishes a great educational ladder, the bottom of which shall be the gutter, and the top of which shall be those Universities of which we are justly so proud.[3]

A Committee of the Board was appointed in 1871, under Huxley's chairmanship, to explore the feasibility of setting up such a system.[4] A critical element was obviously the capacity to provide scholarships for deserving pupils. While the Board did not have powers to fund scholarships, Huxley's Committee was able to recommend that the Board should enter into discussions with the Endowed Schools Commissioners. But this approach did not bear fruit, and instead private individuals and public companies were successfully persuaded to finance a system of scholarships for elementary school pupils, to be administered by the London School Board.[5] By 1897 the Board had 75 recurring and 428 terminable scholarships to administer, varying in value from £20 to £50, and tenable for terms of from two to five years. The most important of these numerically were the scholarships of the Mitchell Trust (104), the Draper's Company (103), Christ's Hospital (73), Gardiner's Trust (35) and the Clothworkers' Company (28).[6] The provision of the London Livery Companies was just one part of their overall contribution to education in the capital.[7]

A more systematic scholarship scheme was introduced in 1893 by the Technical Education Board of the London County Council. Every year it awarded seven or eight Senior, 100 Intermediate and 600 Junior scholarships. The latter were for children under 13 years of age, allowing them to continue their education for two years at a secondary school, or at a higher elementary school approved by the County Council. In addition to fees, £8 maintenance allowance was offered for the first and £12 for the second year of the scholarship. The Intermediate scholarships were open to boys and girls of less than 16 years of age, and were eligible where the parents earned less than £400 per annum. They covered fees and a maintenance grant, averaging £27/10/0d per annum until the scholar reached 18. In 1903, 61 out of 100 scholarships were awarded to children who had previously won a Junior scholarship. Philpott regarded the Intermediate scholarships as 'the goal of School Board studies'.[8]

The culmination of the system involved a marked narrowing of the ladder in the Senior County scholarship, enabling a very few promising scholars to attend university or a higher education institution of similar rank. As Philpott noted, while the ladder had been erected, 'the chances of success diminish at each step, the ascent becomes more and more difficult, and it is only a small minority that reach the summit'.[9] In addition to the tuition fees, Senior scholarships carried a maintenance allowance of £60 per annum for three years.

THE LONDON SCHOOL BOARD SCHOLARSHIPS

The scholarship system was a tremendous stimulus to higher elementary education. In London what were at one stage called 'Higher Standard' schools were later translated, not without controversy (Chapter 8) into 'Higher Grade' schools. It was from these elite schools that most scholarship winners emerged. The scholarship system demanded a test, and the London School Board set a common test for a whole range of scholarships they administered. The questions provide some insight into the levels of knowledge and understanding expected of the candidates. These were competitive tests and manifestly generated great pressure on pupils striving for success.

Before entering the scholarship examination, children had to have achieved Standard V (say at age 11 or 12). They were required to face questions such as these, taken from the 1886 examination, by which time the system was well-established.

Arithmetic

Q.1. What is the number which, if it be subtracted from one million fifteen thousand and seven, will leave a remainder that is exactly divisible by twenty-seven thousand and eight?

English Grammar and Composition

Q.1. Analyse fully the following:
      'Be good, sweet maid, and let who will be clever
      Do noble things, not dream them, all day long;
      And so make life, death and that vast forever
      One grand, sweet song.'

Elementary Science

Q.10. Describe the various ways in which the heat from a fire spreads through a room, and give other illustration of the same modes of transmission of heat.

Geography

Q.11 It is said that the sun never sets on the Queen's Dominions. Taking a line from London eastwards, denote the points which would make this statement fairly correct.

English History

Q.8. What would be thought now of the Crusades, Trial by Ordeal, and the Smithfields Fires?

Q.9. What do you mean by Free Trade, Protection, Home Rule, Vote by Ballot, National Debt?[10]

In the 1888 examination one of the English questions was:

Give the meaning of the words preposterous, remonstrate, delegate, artificial, recreation, gazette, paradox, discord, action, prevaricate, plausible, and introduce these words in sentences of your own.[11]

An element of topicality was introduced into certain questions in the 1889 examination. Thus candidates were asked in Geography: 'Which parts of our Colonial Empire are best suited for emigrants? Give reasons for your answer'; and in Elementary Science: 'Describe the construction and action of any form of electric telegraphic instrument.'[12] In the following year titles for the essay questions were:

(i)   The importance of a good character
(ii) The choice of a business or profession
(iii) The sagacity of animals.[13]

The range of questions in the scholarship examinations thus reflected an odd amalgam of factual recall and more searching items. Some were more typical of those found in secondary school examinations and were queried when applied to the elementary sector. The phenomenon was an integral part of the stretching of the bounds of elementary schooling in which the London School Board was involved.

THE SCHOLARSHIPS OF THE LONDON COUNTY COUNCIL

By the time the Technical Instruction Board of the London County Council entered the arena, the scholarship system had acquired high credentials. By the turn of the century both the London School Board and the London County Council were each administering over 700 scholarships.[14] The introduction of Junior scholarships opened the floodgates. The demand was so huge that the Technical Instruction Board instituted a Preliminary Examination. The 1900 Regulations indicate its scope. The subjects consisted of arithmetic, English composition, geography and history, 'with special reference to social conditions', drawing (for boys), and elementary mathematics, including algebra, up to and including quadratic equations, and geometry, covering the subjects of the first book of Euclid. Candidates normally had to satisfy the examiners in each subject, but excellence in one area could compensate to a certain extent for deficiency in another. The examination was a qualification for the final examination and the marks did not count in the final result. Holders of second-class honours in either the Oxford or the Cambridge Local Examinations were exempted from the preliminary examination.[15]

For those who leaped this first qualifying hurdle, the test became more competitive and wide-ranging. It included obligatory subjects: English, a modern language, pure mathematics for boys and elementary mathematics for girls, and elementary experimental science which included some alternative questions on domestic science for girls. There were in addition 15 optional subjects. These included modern languages, mathematics, sciences, drawing, needlework and manual training.

The competition greatly intensified beyond the Junior level. The sophisticated nature of the Intermediate Scholarship examination, let alone the Senior, can be illustrated from the 1900 Regulations. There was again a Preliminary Examination.[16]

Here the subjects were arithmetic, English, geography and history, drawing and, for boys, elementary mathematics. In arithmetic, English, drawing and elementary mathematics, the syllabus was similar to that of the Junior Examination. In English, candidates had to write a short essay on one of the three given subjects; a paraphrase of a passage from a classical English author; and an analysis of a similar passage. In history, there were general questions on English history, then a more specialist approach to one historical period: the earliest historical times to 1485; 1485–1688; or 1688 to the date of the examination. In geography, apart from general physical, economic and regional coverage of the United Kingdom, candidates could select one of the colonies and dependencies; Europe; or Asia, Africa and America.

The final examination became both wider-ranging and more competitive. The split between obligatory and optional subjects continued. In the obligatory subjects, more detailed specification was provided. Thus in English, apart from essay and composition, paraphrasing and analysis, there were set works, which included one of Shakespeare's *As You Like It*; *Henry V* or *The Merchant of Venice*; Scott's *Marmion* and Kingsley's *Westward Ho!*. There was a compulsory foreign language, either French, German, Spanish or Italian. Here candidates were expected to translate passages by classical authors from and into the language; have knowledge of the accidence and fundamental rules of syntax; and take a dictation test.

The optional subjects could include a second foreign language, Latin, a special pure mathematics paper for girls, applied mathematics, experimental mechanics, experimental physics, chemistry, botany, plain needlework and dressmaking, and manual training in woodwork or metalwork. A large amount of detail was given as to content. The scale of the operation was reflected in the publicity given in the *London Technical Education Gazette*.

In response to requests from headteachers, the Technical Instruction Board agreed to publish the previous year's papers in the *Gazette*, with the proviso that this implied no commitment in future years to the same syllabus or type of questioning. In fact the format did not change significantly, and from this practice no doubt developed an early example of an assessment-led curriculum, again stretching the boundaries of what had hitherto been defined as 'elementary'. The variety of questions used echoed those of the London School Board scholarship tests.

Thus in the Preliminary Examination of 1894, one of the arithmetic questions read:

What income will a man derive from investing £6,720 in the purchase of shares, the selling price of which is £96 each, and which pay a dividend of £4 per share, allowing for a deduction of 7d in the £ for income tax?

Such items symbolized a socialization process exactly in tune with the meritocratic principles of such head teachers as W.B. Adams. The English language and literature, history and geography questions were also aligned to a more ambitious approach than could be contemplated under the normal elementary codes. In the English Literature examination, ten compulsory questions made up a three-hour examination, among which pupils were asked to make an outline of one of Shakespeare's plays, and offer remarks on the plot and the characters. In a combined two-hour English history and geography paper, more traditional factual knowledge questions were evident, such as:

Give the dates, names of commanders on each side, and chief results of the following battles – Plassey, Copenhagen, Vittoria, Navarino and Tel-el Kebir.

Such questions were typical of the Preliminary Examination.

In the Final Examination a compulsory foreign language paper had to be taken. One of the questions on the French paper, made up of nine compulsory items, was: 'Write out in full the present indicative of *devoir*; the present subjunctive of *être*, the pluperfect indicative of *se laver*; the future of *mourir*; and the imperfect subjunctive of *avoir*'. To finish the paper, candidates had to translate into French the following:

The Normans, as the Danes (*Danois*) were called on the continent, had seized the part of France which is on both sides of the Seine, in the same way as the Danes had seized the north of England. Their chief, Rollo, became Duke of the Normans. After some time the Normans learned to speak French, and to live as Frenchmen lived. But they did not become subjects of the French king as the Danes in England became subjects of the English king. The French king was weak and could not conquer Normandy. The Norman duke treated him with respect as his Lord.

Among the optional subjects, physiology and physiography were quite popular. In the former, one question was based on an explanation of the terms 'contractility', 'irritability', 'secretion', 'digestion', 'cell', 'function' and 'chyme'. In physiography the students were asked, for example, 'Why does ice float on water? Why do pipes often burst when water within them freezes? State the property of water which is the cause of these effects.'

For the girls, cookery and domestic economy, and dressmaking and needlework were predictably popular. In the former examination in 1894 one of the questions asked was: 'What is oatmeal? Why is it a valuable food for poor people? Give a receipt for making porridge.' Another was: 'What is tea? How is it made? When is it injurious, and when beneficial?' In dressmaking and needlework the girls were asked: 'How would you mend – (a) A thin place in a woven woollen garment? (b) A rent in a tablecloth? (c) A hole in a flannel bodice? (d) A very old sheet? (e) A tear in a dress?'[17]

The Intermediate Examination became another symbol of the ambitious expectations of the schools which the London School Board had designated as Higher Grade. The optional nature of a significant portion of the provision could obviously be construed by opponents as going beyond the bounds of elementary practice, although the codes did of course allow a choice of subjects. Presumably to legitimate its provision at this level, the London School Board in 1899 submitted a regulated timetable to the Board of Education (see Table 10.1).[18]

TABLE 10.1

Time Available	*30 hours per week*
Registration	1 hr 15 mins
Scripture	2 hrs 30 mins
Recreation	1 hr 40 mins
Time remaining for secular instruction:	*24 hrs 35 mins per week*
Minimum time for compulsory subjects (girls):	*19 hrs 30 mins*, including
1. Arithmetic and mathematics	$3\frac{1}{2}$
2. Experimental science	2
3. English subjects (including composition)	$4\frac{1}{2}$
4. History and geography	2
5. One foreign language	2
6. Drawing	2
7. Systematic physical exercises	1
8. Needlework for Standard VII	2
9. Singing	$\frac{1}{2}$

Total: $19\frac{1}{2}$ *hours*

For the girls this left little over five hours of unallotted time, which could be used for optional subjects. For the boys it was over eight hours, as they spent one hour less on English subjects, and did not have to take singing and needlework. There was therefore some scope for 'specialist' classes.

The existence of two types of scholarship system added complexity and overload to an already pressurized situation. It created timetabling tensions and conflicts of priorities within the elementary sector. The more ambitious board schools had in the event not only two scholarship systems to administer. They also had to institute internally arrangements separating those for whom the scholarship ladder was a realistic prospect, and those for whom it was not. W.B. Adams' evidence to the Cross Commission (Chapter 8) suggested that headteachers such as he regarded such separation as desirable. Others were less confident.

CRITICISMS OF THE SCHOLARSHIP SYSTEM

Sadler claimed that the scholarship system was one of the least controversial innovations of the School Board period. He described scholarships as the 'threads which, however inadequately, attached the separate parts of what should have been our national system'.[19] Sydney Webb referred in 1903 to the

London County Council scholarships as 'one of the most success-ful developments of the last decade',[20] though the London School Board scholarships had by then been in existence for over 30 years.

In fact the scholarship system was much more controversial than these statements suggested. The churches in particular were hostile, a predictable response on the evidence of their lack of involvement in the scholarship stakes. As we have noted (Chapter 2), the non-Catholic voluntary sector in general attracted a more respectable social intake than the board schools.[21] The board sector, however, left the church schools trailing in the quest for scholarships. While open to all scholars, only 90 out of the 721 scholarships available in 1893–4 were won by voluntary school pupils. In 1897 there were 3,157 entries from board and 581 from voluntary schools. A mere 12 per cent of the scholarships went to voluntary pupils in that year. Of the top 57 junior-scholarship-winning schools during the 1896–99 period, only three were voluntary schools.[22]

The School Guardian, the voluntaryist counter to the *School Board Chronicle*, was quick to point out that it was children from comfortable homes who gained the advantage in the competitive scholarship race:

a much larger proportion of parents ... belong to what would be described as the middle classes, shopkeepers, and such like ... the number of children belonging to the hard-labouring classes is a decided minority.[23]

This anticipated the later findings of K. Lindsay's inter-war research on the workings of the scholarship system in urban areas, particularly London. He confirmed that winning scholar-ships was related 'with monotonous regularity ... to the quality of the social and economic environment'.[24] While the motivation of *The School Guardian* in offering this view may be queried, there were at the time other bodies which for a variety of reasons were beginning to draw attention to the social consequences, among them the Metropolitan Board Teachers' Association. In a letter to the Technical Instruction Board the Association quoted the case of Deptford, described as two-thirds 'villadom' and one-third either slum or 'entirely poor'. Of 37 scholarships won by Deptford Schools in 1896, 33 were from 'villadom', and mostly from three schools, while four winners came from social fringe locations, but none from the poor areas. The Association urged that the present competitive system should be discontinued and the scholarships tied to individual schools. It summarized the disadvantages faced by poorer families who (a) could not afford the special coaching often hired by more well-to-do families to improve scholarship chances; (b) were inhibited about visiting teachers' houses after hours for coaching; (c) did not have the necessary access to special scholarship classes and teachers tailoring the syllabus to the system; (d) required in any case higher grants than were on offer to keep children at school beyond the normal age limits.[25]

To be able to enter for scholarships, children had to have achieved Standard V, a feat beyond the majority. Mapping the top 25 schools in the London School Board scholarship stakes from 1893 to 1903 establishes in almost every case their suburban location, in the less crowded northern, western and southern fringes of the metropolitan area.[26]

Some of the examiners were keenly aware of the problems brought in their train by the ever-increasing competition and pressure on the children. One of them was the Rev. William Jowett, who was concerned that it was only a small minority who could be successful:

It is pleasant to feel oneself of use in securing these scholarships to those who are most likely to benefit by longer and higher school training, but it is not pleasant to feel that unsparing competition is entering so early into the lives of these children, and that one's award must bring disappointment to many.[27]

In the evaluation of the impact of the system on the pupils it was argued that girls suffered more strain than boys and, indeed, performed less effectively. Fewer scholarships were offered for girls than boys, and one examiner indicated that, had absolute standards prevailed, girls would have won even less than this smaller quota, concluding that scholarships did not provide the same stimulus for girls as for boys: 'it is unlikely they convey an equal benefit'. He was particularly critical of the performance of the girls in arithmetic: 'old-fashioned and mechanical' with more 'reliance on memory than on understanding'.[28]

There was further questioning as to whether the narrow 'gutter to university' concept was the appropriate metaphor for the time. An Edwardian social commentator, J.L. Paton, condemned the late-Victorian values which underpinned the notion:

I have spoken of the educational ladder. It is the cant phrase, but not one that I love ... It suggests the picture of a few favoured spirits, who climb up into a far-away and solitary Paradise, and for the most part scorn the base degrees by which they did ascend. It is, at bottom, a selfish and individualist ideal ... while we have provided for the few the ladder from the elementary school to the University, we have not yet provided the ladder of continuity between the elementary school and those industrial and commercial occupations on which the very existence of our country depends.[29]

It is doubtful whether W.B. Adams would have shared these misgivings or even acknowledged the distinction. While the ladder to the university was exceptionally narrow, the idea of junior scholarships was to allow children to stay on at school for longer to enable them to acquire the credentials needed to become clerks. The meritocratic principle underpinned the provision for both high-fliers and steady achievers.

Under headteachers such as Adams, it was certainly the case that a new genre of school, the 'scholarship school', was born. These were to become in the twentieth century the high-status schools geared to gaining 11+ successes. The principle was established in the School Board period. Lindsay identified them as a distinct species after the First World War. Their success varied according to the social environment, but there was more to it than this:

Most important of all would seem to be the scholarship tradition which clings in individual schools. Whether or not there is actual speeding up undoubtedly the pace is set by the school tradition, more active masters are secured, and it is impossible to dissociate active preparation from scholarship winning.[30]

Had such an accusation been made against Fleet Road School in the 1890s it could not have been denied. It might well have been interpreted as a compliment.

THE SOCIAL BACKGROUND OF THE SCHOLARSHIP HOLDERS

There was considerable contemporary focus on the scholarship holders and the social background from which they came. Which particular groups were successful in rising up the ladder of opportunity and how far? The Cross Commission provided information on the occupations of parents of the London School Board scholarship holders in the period from 1873 to 1887 and, where known, the subsequent careers of recipients in the years from 1873 to about 1881. Of the first 73 scholarship holders, only

3 per cent came from traditional middle-class occupational backgrounds. The lower middle class, such as clerks, shopkeepers and teachers, furnished 33 per cent, and 43 per cent were from superior artisan groups, including those labelled 'tradesmen' and 'artisans'. Only six per cent of winners had parents in the unskilled labouring category. The remaining 15 per cent of cases were not known.

The figures are less complete in their information on occupations followed by scholarship holders on completion of their courses, and in indicating the degree of mobility achieved. About 38 per cent of the cases were in the 'not known' category. If university entrance is taken as equivalent to achieving true middle-class status, a rough interpretation of the basic information is suggested in Table 10.2.

TABLE 10.2

Mobility		Per cent
One-step	Lower middle to middle class	8.1
	Upper working to lower middle class	20.2
Two-step	Upper working to middle class	13.5
	Lower working to lower middle class	5.4
No change	Lower middle class remaining	13.5
	Upper working class remaining	1.4

While these approximations need to be treated with caution, there is every evidence that scholarship winning did promote occupational and social mobility. The step most frequently climbed was that between the upper working and the lower middle class, essentially from blue to white collar occupations. In circumstances in which many families had members in both these categories, this is not surprising. There was not, however, evidence of downward mobility among the scholarship holders, as must have happened within the broad 'middling' cohort of society. More surprising was the fact of ten students jumping two steps, children from upper-working-class families who achieved university entrance.[31]

One of these was the first scholarship winner under the London School Board scheme, William Barker, son of a trunkmaker and a pupil of a National School in Marylebone, who won a Mortimer Scholarship to the City of London School, and six years later a scholarship to Trinity College, Cambridge.[32] In 1881 he came first in the Classical Tripos Examination.[33] This dazzling success created at the time a favourable initial image for the system, but it was not repeated by many who followed him. After taking his degree, Barker 'was then appointed to a position in the Board of Trade'.[34] Of the London County Council scholars one of the most celebrated was E. Cunningham, educated at Canal Road, Hoxton, then Crouch End board schools. From Crouch End he obtained an entrance scholarship to Owen's School, Islington, where he later won an Intermediate scholarship. He finally gained entrance on a Senior scholarship to St. John's College, Cambridge, with the help also of an open Mathematical Scholarship, and became Senior Wrangler in 1902.[35]

The *London Technical Education Gazette* provided useful detail on the occupations of parents of Junior scholarship holders. Four years are taken (Table 10.3) – 1896, 1897, 1902 and 1903.[36]

TABLE 10.3

Occupation	% of Scholarships			
	1896	*1897*	*1902*	*1903*
Trades (mostly journeymen) and unskilled labourers	50.5	53.2	57.5	60.9
Officials and servants	19.0	16.9	16.3	16.6
Shopkeepers and shop assistants	10.6	8.3	9.2	3.6
Clerical and subordinate professional occupations	16.7	17.7	13.2	14.9
Unspecified	3.2	3.9	3.8	4.0

Unfortunately the collective categories do not equate with more recent formulations. Thus in the first group white- and blue-collar workers are mingled. On the basis of information on individual occupational sub-categories within the above classification, it would appear that 50 out of 300 Junior scholarship holders in 1896 were children of unskilled labourers, by no means a negligible total. As previously suggested, more affluent middle-class parents would not be well represented, for even if they sent their children to elementary schools, they would be earning too much to be eligible for the scholarship grants. The upper-working- and lower-middle-class groups were predictably those gaining most benefit from the Junior scholarship system. Bearing all this in mind, it is interesting to try to translate the details of these contemporary tables into more recent socio-economic categorization, on the basis on the classification given in Chapter 4. Table 10.4 shows the resulting figures for junior scholarship holders in 1903.

TABLE 10.4

SEG	%
II/IIIA	26.7
IIIB	57.9
IV/V	11.4
Unspecified	4.0

At this, the lowest rung of the scholarship ladder, therefore, advantage of the system was being taken by blue-collar families, approaching 70 per cent of the holders coming from categories IIIB/IV/V. Over a four-year period, the biggest single category was the building trades, with 308 holders. The largest lower-middle-class, white-collar, categories were clerks, with 298, followed by shopworkers and salesmen with 153.

In the Intermediate scholarship area, however, the distribution skews upwards. With the higher salary threshold, children of more well-to-do parents were eligible to enter for this examination. The 1896–97 analysis is shown in Table 10.5.

TABLE 10.5

SEG	%
I	2.7
II	13.6
IIIA	40.0
IIIB	31.4
IV/V	5.9
Unspecified	6.4

While these figures are based on a smaller sample, there does not seem much doubt that the social balance differed significantly. Of the Intermediate scholarship holders 37.3 per cent came from blue-collar families, as against nearly 60 per cent of the Junior. On the other hand, 56 per cent were from socio-economic categories IIIA and above, as against only 26.7 per cent from these groups in the Junior scholarship holders.

The Senior scholarship sample is far too small to be statistically significant, but it suggests unequivocally that, while the scholarship system promoted a degree of social mobility, the 'gutter to university' characterisation was inapt. None made the potential three-step leap indicated in Table 10.2.

THE CASE OF FLEET ROAD

As one of the leading schools in the various scholarship competitions, a rich vein of evidence is available for Fleet Road which offers vivid illustration of the detailed functioning of the system. Fleet Road's entry into the board school scene was well-timed in a number of ways. As we have seen (Chapter 4), it was able to take advantage of relatively up-market residential development in its catchment area. About the time this happened, the London School Board scholarship system was fully in operation. The school effected a happy match between the two circumstances, crucial to its prestige. Then as its fame was building in the late 1880s the London County Council scholarship scheme provided fresh impetus.

In his evidence to the Cross Commission Adams made it quite clear that his special interest was in higher elementary education. He would have preferred running a school from Standard V upwards.[37] Adams was also committed to the scholarship principle, looking to the state to pay for exhibitions enabling children to move from lower to higher standard schools.[38] He was thus arguing for an intermediate or middle school type of institution.

While this was not achieved in his lifetime, Adams worked the scholarship system with huge success. As Maps 9 and 10 showed, most of Fleet Road's intake resided within a quarter of a mile of the school. But this inner zone included the 'best pink' streets of Booth's classification, those mainly responsible for gaining for the school its 'prestige and scholarships'.[39] Of the 203 County scholarships won by its pupils between 1894 and 1903, 195 were at the junior level; 156 of these resided within the area covered by Map 10. This meant, however, that a significant minority travelled from a relatively long distance to the schools (see pp. 94–6). Of those resident in the area of Map 10, on the basis of Booth's classification, nine per cent lived in 'red', 76.3 per cent in 'pink', 14.7 per cent in 'purple', and none in 'yellow', 'blue' or 'black' streets. Over this period Mansfield Road was the scholarship street *par excellence*, providing 27 successes. Almost half the holders residing on Map 10 came from homes in Mansfield Road and the streets to its north as far as the North London Railway line.

Converting the occupations given for the Fleet Road holders into socio-economic categories, Table 10.6 offers a rough breakdown.

TABLE 10.6

SEG	Number	%	
I	–	–	
II	51	25.1	
IIIA	32	15.8	} 61.6
IIIB	93	45.8	
IV	20	9.9	
V	1	0.5	
Others (e.g. widows)	6	2.9	

While this is not a refined calculation, it is sufficiently meaningful to confirm Adams' contention that his school had a mixed social intake. It could also, however, be used as evidence by his opponents who claimed he admitted a disproportionately high number of lower-middle-class and a low number of rough working-class children. While taking in a large number of children of blue-collar workers, Adams also ensured that the majority of these were from respectable families. Indeed many came from fringe families including both blue- and white-collar earners. Categories IIIA and IIIB together make up over 60 per cent of the total (Table 10.6). The fact that there was a higher percentage from SEG II than from IIIA suggests that the school was popular among lower professional groups because of its scholarship reputation.

Recollecting the controversies in Hampstead over the wide geographical catchment of the school (Chapters 3 and 4), there is again enough in the statistics to be used to support the arguments of either side. The large majority of the scholarship holders lived near the school. However 23.2 per cent came from outside the area of Map 10, taking advantage of the access offered by the railway system to seek the benefits its specialist scholarship classes offered.

When the scholarship winners over this ten-year period are

classified into groups of occupations the social fringe component is again evident. The leading eight occupations are shown in Table 10.7.[40]

TABLE 10.7

Occupation	No. of Holders
1. Building trades	28
2. Transport	26
3. Clerks	23
4. Retail/wholesale trades	18
5. Printing	13
6. Teachers	12
7=. Gardeners	8
7=. Piano manufacturing	8

The list faithfully reflects the occupational stress of the middling socio-economic categories in the district. An anomaly was that most of the winners from teachers' families lived outside the district, suggesting it was this group, with its heightened awareness of the system, that calculated that the advantage of getting their children into Fleet Road more than compensated for the expense and wear and tear of travel.

Through matching the addresses of scholarship winners with directory information, more detailed pieces of information about the link between home and school can be gained.[41] Thus F. C. Watkins, who won a scholarship in 1896, was the son of a gasfitter and one of the few successes from Fleet Road itself. Florence Clements, of 82, Park Road, was the daughter of a gardener. Ada Goodman lived with her mother, a grocer on her own account, at 5, Agincourt Road. Gertrude Pooley of 21, Agincourt Road was the daughter of a gardener; W. C. Strachan of 35, Agincourt Road, the son of a journeyman jeweller; and Robert Prior of 46, Agincourt Road, the son of a provision assistant. The occupations of parents of scholarship winners from Constantine Road included cabdrivers, builders, gardeners, carpenters, clerks and sanitary inspectors. These examples come from predictable groups. There were additionally many unrecorded names from such groups who were not allowed to enter the scholarship stakes. The aggregate appraisal, in averaging out the variations, conceals the fact that differential parental attitudes and beliefs, changing domestic circumstances, size of and placing in the family, as well as intrinsic ability, resulted in some children being favoured and not others, not only between but also within families.

It was, however, the older-established London School Board scholarship arrangements which firmly established Fleet Road as a leading school. Adams milked the publicity value of scholarship winning for all it was worth. He had certainly grasped its potential by 1887 when, in a letter to the British and Foreign School Society, he appended the comment that the Society would be pleased to know that 'out of 314 candidates we have the *two first* boys and the *two first* girls'.[42] The italicizing was that of Adams.

Continued scholarship successes captured the attention of the *School Board Chronicle* in 1888.

The remarkably large number of Scholarships recently gained at the Fleet-road Board schools, Hampstead, calls for special attention. The competition was open to all the voluntary and Board schools in London. This year there were seven open Scholarships for boys, out of which the school won four, and the first two places on the list.

It was noted that the first two scholarships were those awarded by the Drapers' Company, and were worth £30 per annum for four years. Another boy who 'stood conspicuous at the head of the list' had won a Bancroft Foundation Scholarship of the value of £60 for four years. One of the girls was seventh on the girls' list and was to be awarded a Mitchell Scholarship. In all the value of the scholarships won by Fleet Road in 1888 was £779.[43] Like research grants in the university sector one hundred years later, a performance indicator was implanted: the cumulative value of scholarship grants.

The image of success conveyed by scholarship winning was valuable to a school because so readily understandable. As a matter of course the *Hampstead and Highgate Express* printed details of local scholarship successes, including their pecuniary value. It noted in 1890, for example, that the scholarships won by Fleet Road since 1882 amounted in total to £2,462.[44] Following further successes in 1891, and the capture of over half the competitive scripture prizes in the Marylebone Division, the paper emphasized that such consistent success could only be due to 'the skill and enthusiasm with which the work of this school is conducted'.[45]

The Practical Teacher was impressed by the two large honours boards in the great hall of the school, one full and one half-full of the names of previous scholarship winners. By this time elementary schools were adopting various features of the public school system with the objective of establishing a school *esprit de corps* (see Chapter 9). In this case the Etonian–Fleetonian homonym was heaven-sent. W.B. Adams regularly pasted press cuttings in his log books, and meticulously listed each year's winners. As the 1890s progressed his school was capturing the attention not only of the local and educational, but also of the national, press. In 1896 the *Daily Telegraph* drew the attention of its readers to the successes of Fleet Road.

Fleet-road Board School, Hampstead, must either have exceptionally clever masters and mistresses, or phenomenally brilliant scholars ... During this year no fewer than nineteen scholarships have in all been won by children educated there.[47]

In the following year, the *Daily News* ran a major feature entitled 'The Educational Ladder: London Scholarship Record: From the Board School to the University: the Most Successful Schools'. The paper analysed the combined results of the scholarships of the London School Board and the Technical Instruction Board of the London County Council. These showed Fleet Road to be the 'champion school', leading the Technical Instruction Board lists, coming second in the London School Board, and first overall, over the period 1894–96.[48] The *Hampstead and Highgate Express* summarized the results, which showed 13 schools with over 20 scholarships, six with over 30, and, at the top, only two with over 40, Medburn Street with 45 and Fleet Road with 51, on the Technical Board junior scholarship list. Wilton Road with 44 School Board scholarships, led Fleet Road with 37. The combined total of 88, however, lifted Fleet Road ahead of Montem Street, Finsbury, with 58, and Wilton Road, Hackney, with 50.[49] It was clearly the 'Champion School'.

Similar publicity accrued in 1898 when the *Daily Chronicle* reported that Fleet Road had produced the top boy and top girl in the London School Board scholarship examination, and the largest number of County Council scholarships. Cumulative prize money from 1882 totalled over £10,000.[50] In 1898 37 and in 1899 49 junior scholars took up their places at Fleet Road, one of 12 elementary schools at which such attendance was allowed. It was yet another accolade. Also in 1898 Fleet Road gained the first three places on the girls' list and the first two on the boys', an unprecedented achievement which prompted the London School Board to present the school with 'a beautiful memorial picture'. The local newspaper also recorded that two 'old Fleetonians' had matriculated with honours at London University and three others in the first division.[51]

In 1902 the *Hampstead Record* published its own appraisal of the local working of the scholarship system. It paid due tribute to the efforts of Fleet Road, but stressed that not all was well with Hampstead as a whole. It examined the results of three schools – Fleet Road, Broomsleigh Street, and Heath Street British School, the latter one of the best-regarded voluntary schools in Hampstead, and these results are shown below.

TABLE 10.8

Entries for and Successes in the Junior Scholarship Examinations, 1901

School	Entries	Passed	Scholarships Gained
Fleet Road	67	37	23
Broomsleigh Street	7	6	2
Heath Street	1	1	0

The *Record* condemned the attitude of the local voluntary sector towards the scholarship system. It compared Hampstead unfavourably with other parts of London. In a ranking which must have been based on the voluntary figures only, it was shown that among the London County Council divisions in 1900 Hampstead ranked low, in 36th position. By 1901 it had improved to 15th. The paper asserted that children of the working classes in London were gaining distinction in higher education, in science and in industry. 'Why', it asked, 'should Hampstead any longer lag behind?' Those opposing the opening of new Board schools (see Chapter 3) would be wise if they woke up the voluntary school managers first.

The present state of affairs does not of necessity prove that the teaching in the voluntary schools is less efficient than in the Board schools, or that the children who attend them suffer from greater ignorance or stupidity. It simply proves that those in authority over the voluntary schools are so indifferent to the future welfare of the children, whose education they have undertaken to supervise, that they do not attempt to give them the slightest chance of mounting the scholarship ladder provided by the Technical Educational Board for the children of London.[52]

In his interview with Charles Morley, Adams talked of his special pride in the 'Exempt 7th' class, the scholarship winners and the positions they later assumed. Morley enquired about the amount of money the scholarships represented for the current year.

'Thirteen hundred and twelve pounds,' said the master in a moment, with justifiable jubilation. 'But the scholars are not so many in number as you might think. What becomes of them? Many take up teaching as a profession ... A boy who was a born mathematician would probably go into a business where brains, sharpness, and exactness are badly wanted – a bank, say.'[53]

This choice of illustration, and juxtaposition of a discussion of scholarship winnings with detail of later occupations of pupils, gives a clue to Adams' success. He was not over-ambitious. He knew that for the general run of brighter pupils the achievement of a Junior scholarship, two years' extra schooling, then a job as a clerk, or as an elementary schoolteacher, was what most of his clientele was looking for. Few of the successes were aiming at university. Fleet Road was a step on the ladder from blue- to white-collar occupations rather than from gutter to university, although that was the metaphor used for popular consumption in the local and national press. Just a few of the scholarship winners who proceeded to secondary schools were later recorded as having matriculated at London University. Adams' own son, who later went to Oxford, was an exception. The phenomenal success in the scholarship stakes which so intrigued the journal *London*,[54] and others, was largely a quantitative achievement. At the time, of course, quantity was important. It affected more (albeit a large minority) of children and happened more often, increasing coverage in the press. To local parents it was more than enough evidence that in enrolling them at Fleet Road they were giving their children a better than average prospect of getting on in life.

Not all were so impressed. It is very difficult to judge how exceptional a school Fleet Road was in comparison with the London School Board's other 'flagship' schools. As the *Daily News* survey showed, while Fleet Road could on numerical grounds be designated the 'Champion School', and the long-established record of winning School Board scholarships was clearly outstanding, it was not unique of its kind. Thus Wilton Road in Hackney, Medburn Street in St. Pancras, Bloomfield Road in Plumstead, Montem Street in Islington, and Burghley Road in St. Pancras were also leading schools on these criteria.[55]

Some schools did particularly well with a lower-status social intake. As we have seen, most of Fleet Road's scholarship winners came from lower-middle-class and/or skilled artisan families. Between 1896 and 1898 only four per cent were the children of unskilled labourers. At Sherbrooke Road in Fulham, 31 per cent were from lower-middle-class families, 44 per cent were skilled artisan, and as many as 21 per cent from unskilled worker.[56] In the Intermediate Scholarship examinations of the Technical Instruction Board, Fleet Road had not a particularly impressive record. Intermediate scholarships were often won by children who had already gained Junior scholarships. On the face of it Fleet Road should have done better. For Intermediate scholarships Medburn Street was the most successful school, winning 33 in the 1896–99 period, as against three at Fleet Road.

Neither was Fleet Road to become one of London's prestige science schools. These were only four in number: Blackheath Road in Greenwich, Bloomfield Road in Plumstead, Medburn Street in St. Pancras, and Thomas Street in Limehouse,[58] areas where an industrial training was thought to be more appropriate. Thus in the Science and Art Department examination for 1897–98, Fleet Road earned only £4/11/10d for Science and £7/19/3d for Art, and all this at elementary rather than advanced level. By contrast Burghley Road earned £250 and Medburn Street over £530 for Science alone.[59] Adams took the general London School Board line that it was a commercial rather than an industrial training that the socio-economic context of the school required. Nor did his own cultural and intellectual preferences incline him in the direction of science. In national terms, not being a 'school of science' implied less than a leading status. Adams would have claimed high effectiveness, as a 'school of commerce' was equally applicable, and indeed more important, in the capital city. Unfortunately for Fleet Road, as Chapter 8 has shown, it was not possible for commercial schools to count as a special category, let alone a prestige category, under the Department of Science and Art. The Board of Education's suspicion of this type of provision was also a critical disadvantage.

Fleet Road was to become something of a test case. To an

extent Adams' propensity to extol so publicly the successes of his school rebounded. As part of the evidence in the build-up to the Cockerton Judgement, The Board of Education required HMI G. Fitzmaurice to gather intelligence on Fleet Road's specialist upper classes. Though, and perhaps because of being, a regular attender at Fleet Road's prizegivings and concerts, he appears less than enthusiastic about the direction the school was following. On an internal memo he wrote:

Fleet Road is an ambitious school and has been most successful in obtaining scholarships, but I have always felt that bright children (I may be wrong) were ... unduly pressed in order to run for scholarships ... It is a school that advertises itself (?unduly) [crossed out].[60]

For Adams the scholarship system epitomized the 'new education': not a revival of the basics nor inculcation of religion; nor a progressive child-centred ideology. Moderately anti-establishment, he had enjoyed a reasonably advantageous start in life. At the same time, he would have claimed that he and his wife had risen in the world on the basis of hard work and ability. Other children of ability should be given this chance. He could well have been brought up on the writings of James Booth, Treasurer of the Royal Society of Arts at the time of Adams' formative years as pupil teacher and student. A potent force in the establishment of an examinations system, Booth provided some of the seminal thinking on the advantages of a meritocratic system.

The first was a matter of principle:

Is it not a wise and conservative policy that promotion in the state should be sought by science rather than sedition, by competition rather than conspiracy? That men should endeavour to pass muster at the gate, rather than clamber surreptitiously over the wall?[61]

The second was more pragmatic and utilitarian, outlining the need to motivate children by making clear the vocational advantages of the system.

Though you catch your boys and impound them in your school-rooms, you cannot force them to learn. But once hold out to your pupils the inducement that every hour they give to hard labour, to real head-work, will tell on their future advancement and prospects of life; mark what a face of reality it will put upon all they are doing, and their attention will be awakened.[62]

Similarly for parents: the great mass of the public was seen to hold education 'not an end but a means to an end; for its intrinsic advantages they are little solicitous; to its adventitious adjuncts they chiefly look'.[63]

Booth's final advantage was one Adams would surely have accepted: that examination successes testified to the quality of a school. They were a measure of public accountability, which could of course be used by the fittest in the race to their cumulative advantage. In Booth's words, the examination

would foster a spirit of laudable emulation between the schools of the same educational circuit. The proportion of candidates, coming from any given school ... would become in the estimation of the public the test of the quality of education given there.[64]

While twentieth-century commentators were to identify with some confidence the perilous social consequences of the competitive scholarship system, in the 1880s and 1890s the emphasis was on the positive advantages it conveyed, particularly in comparison with previous lack of opportunity, as an avenue of social mobility.

Fleet Road's scholarship successes reflect its placing in a particular location at a particular time of rapid social change. They formed a significant response to a surging demand for skilled employees, especially in booming tertiary occupations. They were made possible by a new and bureaucratized educational system, highly sophisticated and well-resourced by the standards of the time, in tune with the socio-economic needs of the great city. All these factors combined to provide Fleet Road School with the opportunity for engagement in the forging of the meritocracy. Other schools, however, had a similarly advantageous placing. Even if cautiously interpreted, Fleet Road's achievement was considerably above the run of schools of its type. As a catalyst it needed a leader who was both a passionate advocate and an effective implementer of the meritocratic spirit.

After Adams' death, Fleet Road continued to be highly rated as a scholarship school. But it was clear that by the 1920s it had slipped back, at least relatively speaking. While it remained in the top 25 of London County Council schools between 1920 and 1930, winning 115 scholarships, its overall ranking was as low as 19th.[65] It could no longer count itself the 'Champion School', a desirable ranking if the 'spirit of laudable emulation between the schools of the same educational circuit' was the guiding principle.

REFERENCES AND NOTES

1. *Hansard*, 3rd Series, vol. 202 (1870), col. 821.
2. Letter to *SBC*, 17 May 1879, p.473.
3. Quoted in *SBC*, 18 Feb. 1871, p.7.
4. P. Gordon, *Selection for Secondary Education* (London, 1980), p.148.
5. H.B. Philpott, *London at School: the Story of the London School Board* (London, 1904), pp.154–5.
6. *The Daily News*, 11 Aug. 1897.
7. See M.E. Bryant, *The London Experience of Secondary Education* (London, 1986), pp.368–74.
8. Philpott, *op. cit.* (1904), p.169.
9. *Ibid.*, pp.170–1.
10. SBL 1470, *School Management Report Appendix*, 28 June 1886.
11. *Ibid.*, 22 March 1888.
12. *Ibid.*, 31 Jan. 1889.
13. *Ibid.*, 30 Jan. 1890.
14. Philpott, *op. cit.* (1904), pp.167–8.
15. *The London Technical Education Gazette*, November 1900, pp.348–9.
16. *Ibid.*, November 1900, pp.350–2.
17. Details from the London County Council examination papers have been taken from *London Technical Education Gazettes* of the 1890s.
18. PRO Ed. 14/41, 64603.
19. M.E. Sadler, 'The Scholarship System of England to 1890 and Some of its Developments', in International Institute Examination Inquiry, *Essays on Education* (London, 1936), pp.75–6.
20. S. Webb, 'London Education', in E.J.T. Brennan (ed.), *Education for National Efficiency: the Contribution of Sidney and Beatrice Webb* (London, 1975), p.116.
21. See W.E. Marsden, 'Residential Segregation and the Hierarchy of Elementary Schooling from Charles Booth's Surveys', *The London Journal*, vol. 11 (1985), pp.131–2.
22. Based on lists in the *London Technical Education Gazette*.
23. *The School Guardian*, 23 July 1887.
24. K. Lindsay, *Social Progress and Educational Waste* (London, 1926), p.8.
25. Found in PRO Ed. 14/3.
26. See map in W.E. Marsden, 'Education and the Social Geography of Nineteenth-century Towns and Cities', in D.A. Reeder (ed.), *Urban Education in the Nineteenth Century* (London, 1977), pp.64–5.
27. SBL 1470, *School Management Department*, Report of Rev. William Jowett on the examination for scholarships held December 1887.
28. SBL 1470, *School Management Report Appendix*, 30 Jan. 1890.
29. J.L. Paton, 'The Secondary Education of the Working Classes', in C. Norwood and A.H. Hope (eds.), *The Higher Education of Boys in England* (London, 1909), pp.551–3.
30. Lindsay, *op. cit.* (1926), pp.88–9.
31. These tentative conclusions are based on material in the *Cross Commission*, 2nd Report (1887), pp.1057–67.
32. *SBC*, 3 May 1879, p.425.
33. *SBC*, 25 June 1881, p.619.
34. *The School Guardian*, 23 July 1887, p.487.
35. Philpott, *op. cit.* (1904), pp.171–2.
36. *The London Technical Education Gazette*, April 1897, pp.62–4; March 1898, pp.31–3; May 1902, pp.91–3; May 1903, pp.111–13.
37. *Cross Commission*, 2nd Report (1887), p.66.
38. *Ibid.*, p.67.

39. C. Booth, *Police Notes, District 20* (Booth Collection, London School of Economics), Group A, vol. 38, p.22.
40. The figures are based on material in the *London Technical Education Gazette* for the period.
41. This information is based on matching families in local directories with the addresses given in the *London Technical Education Gazette*.
42. *BFSS Archives*, letter from W.B. Adams to A. Bourne, dated 25 Feb. 1887.
43. *SBC*, 7 April 1888, p.359.
44. *HHE*, 18 Jan. 1890.
45. *HHE*, 25 July 1891.
46. *The Practical Teacher*, vol. 15 (1894), p.2.
47. *The Daily Telegraph*, 24 July 1896.
48. *The Daily News*, 11 Aug. 1897.
49. *HHE*, 28 Aug. 1897.
50. *The Daily Chronicle*, 26 Feb. 1898.
51. *HHE*, 4 March 1899.
52. *Hampstead Record*, 4 Jan. 1902.
53. C. Morley, *Studies in Board Schools* (London, 1897), pp.88–90.
54. *London*, vol. 7 (1898), p.154.
55. *The Daily News*, 11 Aug. 1897.
56. See W.E. Marsden, 'Schools for the Urban Lower Middle Class: Third Grade or Higher Grade?', in P. Searby (ed.), *Educating the Victorian Middle Class* (History of Education Society, Leicester, 1982), p.52.
57. BPP 355 (1900), LXXIII, 'Return of Scholarships awarded by County Councils in England and Wales in the Financial Year ended 31st March 1899'.
58. T.A. Spalding and T.S.A. Canney, *The Work of the London School Board* (London, 1900), p.184.
59. SBL 1470, *School Management Department Report*, Return of Science and Art Examination, 1897–8.
60. PRO Ed. 14/41, 64603.
61. J. Booth, *Systematic Instruction and Periodical Examination* (London, 1857), p.39.
62. J. Booth, *How to Learn, What to Learn* (London, 1857), p.22.
63. *Ibid.*, p.24.
64. J. Booth, *Examination: the Province of the State* (London, 1847), p.20.
65. LCC Records, EO/PS/16.

CHAPTER ELEVEN

Conclusion

No great methodological insights are required to demonstrate the limitations of using a single case history as an explanatory contribution to the study of late nineteenth-century urban education, particularly one of a school that was rather larger than life. On the other hand, if it is considered important to redress some of the 'aspects of neglect' in the history of education of this period, then more attention needs to be given to the detailed happenings in schools and the communities they served. This study is therefore much more about experiences than events. Taking some of Harold Silver's examples of neglect, the attempt is made to explore the reactions to and the quality of school experience and, more ambitiously, the complex interfaces in what Silver has described as the 'total social relationships' of schooling: the 'ways in which schools, pupils, teachers, educational activities in general, related to wider social experience'.[1]

The study is also intended to expose the not entirely lost gross stereotyping of late Victorian educational provision. Many of the histories until recent times, and even certain history-using theoretical texts of today, portray it as dominated by payment by results, reactionary, simple, symptomatic of a more primitive stage of educational development, peopled by rudimentary decision-makers: a system serviced by careworn and submissive subordinates socializing either forlorn or threatening waifs and strays into the intended docile citizens of an industrial society. While in every stereotype lurks some truth, it is appropriate to consider a counter generalization of the late Victorian educational scene as complicated, thrusting and radical in spirit, academically sophisticated, serviced by people individualistic and even arrogant in their opinions, and as promotive of social change as it was of social reproduction. This too, of course, is not an entirely well-balanced framing.

An element of serendipity has to be introduced in explaining Fleet Road School's success: the right people in the right place at the right time. It found itself in a period of rapid population growth, made up of a relatively youthful and socially aspiring cohort in the Gospel Oak area, resulting in a steeply rising demand curve for schooling, reinforced by stricter attendance legislation. Accommodation in well-regarded schools was at a premium. These local events were concurrent with the increasing need for well-educated recruits for the tertiary occupational revolution: for shop assistants, clerical workers, ranging from typists to high level clerks, local authority officials, elementary schoolteachers, salesmen, and supervisory staff on transport systems or in manufacturing industry requiring highly skilled labour. In many of these occupations a promotion ladder was present or in the process of erection. Schools such as Fleet Road reacted quickly and effectively to the vocational needs these developments uncovered.

Occupational ratings were closely linked with social class and status distinctions. The crucial thresholds were between, at the one extreme, the rich and the respectable and, at the other, the respectable and the rough, or the 'common'. In the respectable, large and growing central area, there existed a spectrum from those who were, in Booth's terms, on the verge of being 'well-to-do' and those on the margin of comfort and poverty. The finely-tuned status disparities were faithfully translated into territorial segregation of residence, then in turn into a graduated system of elementary as well as secondary schooling.[2] The mechanism of grading was the school fee. Within this central respectable social whirlpool[3] there was more than enough status variation to offer the prospect of social advance, and merit was seen as the way of achieving it. Movement beyond this whirlpool was more difficult, though not impossible.

It has been shown, in the case of the Adams family, that connections and even a degree of nepotism remained, but in general this acted as a fillip to meritocratic advance, and not as a substitute for it. The Adams and the Walker families with their double incomes were able to make the jump to true middle-class, servant-keeping status. For most, the newly-fashioned scholarship system allowed more modest but still real progress. The majority of scholarships enabled children to be kept on at school for at least two years beyond the statutory limit. This materially improved the prospects of an office job. A small number were able to continue into secondary schooling, but precious few made it further into university education. For the many, then, the key generational shift was from the upper working into the lower middle class. This meant considerable status complications in that members of the same family might in occupational roles be in either of these groups. Lack of success in schooling, or chance circumstances such as the death of a bread-winner or the failure of a family business could, on the other hand, occasion a dreaded downward shift in economic security and thus respectability. While respectability was a cultural attribute, it was hard to sustain without a steady income. This fear of failure was as much the engine of aspiration as the prospect of improvement.

The socio-economic context of Fleet Road was characteristic of suburban London of that time. It was a product of forces of urbanization rather than industrialization, in so far as these can be distinguished. Of course there was important manufacturing industry in the catchment of the school, but this was mostly of the service, consumer-oriented variety. In a different way, rapid technological change had an impact on the school. Fleet Road was a beneficiary of the growth of urban transport systems. The access these provided brought into the area the sort of parents regarded as desirable by an ambitious school. The children of commuters figured strongly among the scholarship winners of Fleet Road. The railway was used in both directions, the trains bringing in each day yet more potential scholarship children.

Fleet Road School also took more cognizance than most of the social trend towards increased leisure time. It thrived on the developing public taste for entertainment. Demand for tickets for school concerts regularly outstripped supply. The choral training offered by the school provided performers both for domestic musical evenings and for local church and chapel choirs. The rise in the influence of the music hall coincided with a loosening hold of religion on leisure time. This and the perceived licence of the entertainment industry reinforced concerns about the moral state of the population of great towns and cities, concerns fuelled by the interventionism of Social Darwinists. The schools were regarded almost as a last hope of moral rearmament. Such was an unlikely possibility when it is borne in mind that most teachers were implicated in the urban forces combining to raise fears of an irreversible descent in public morality. The dramatic social changes were reflected both in the curriculum and extra-curricular activities of Fleet Road School. One of the most interesting features of the curriculum history of Fleet Road is the way in which Louisa Walker moved away, though not wholly so, from the strict moral teachings of Froebel. The messages which emerged from her songs and games were less than clear. On the one hand they extolled the virtues of hard work and obeying rules, and accepting the superior wisdom of teachers and parents. Yet the hard work was geared to individual ambition and social change, not to subordination and social reproduction. The classic Froebel activities were secularized, urbanized, and as much infected by the debunking spirit of Gilbert and Sullivan, and even the vulgarities of the music hall, as by the solemn missives of the mainstream promoters of the kindergarten movement, most of whom stressed the imperatives of received religion.

The underlying values transmitted at Fleet Road were therefore those of the growing third force in English society. The general spirit was individualistic and, for its time, liberal. The pupils were taught that they were a fortunate group, who enjoyed the benefits of good parents and a good school. They in turn should be nice to others, especially to those less well placed. They were certainly not taught uncritical respect for establishment values or for the leisured groups in society. Fun was poked at the pretensions and life-styles of the carriage-folk of Hampstead. In return, the ratepayer faction did not take kindly to Louisa Walker's action songs or W.B. Adams' prize-givings, an antipathy not lessened by the regularity with which these features were kept in the public eye. At the same time, the wares of the school were ritually displayed before the professional establishment, to which some reverence was seen as due.

While the curriculum of Fleet Road obviously could not escape the narrowing quality of the Revised Code and its successors, it was able to take advantage of the ameliorations of the 1880s and 1890s. Indeed it was the underlying social forces that created Fleet Road which at the same time generated a more expansive view of the elementary curriculum than that held by the reactionaries. While the Junior Mixed School in particular appears to have been the power-house for training in the basics, the Infant Department was pioneering the application to mass urban education of kindergarten methods, while in the Senior

271

Mixed Department specialization was the order of the day. There seems little doubt that this secondary type specialization formed part of the Trojan Horse of illicit expenditure which brought the downfall of the London School Board.

Another progressive feature of the school was its commitment to coeducation. While this did not go so far as overturning the social mores of the time, the Fleet Road approach, from the Infant Department upwards, lent support to the idea of girls legitimately following a meritocratic course and finding a career, in marked contrast to the ancestral view that the job of the board school was to turn out reliable domestic servants. Indeed one inspector's report noted that the domestic training seemed to have been neglected in favour of the intellectual. As previously noted, visitors to the school were prone to offer surprised comment on the confidence and independence of the Fleet Road girls. It may be that the presence of two career women head-teachers promoted a more positive view towards female employment than was current at the time.

In fighting its corner against attacks on its perceived extravagance (and the rates it demanded were high), the London School Board required evidence to prove that the money was well spent. It was a body with a mission, and just as the merchant navy took out missionaries to convert foreign peoples, so the London School Board mobilized a flotilla of board schools as the key element in its social conversion operation. The flotilla needed its flagships, in order to create a favourable image in the public mind. The brightest pennants of any of the flagships were those flown by Fleet Road. By the end of the period, even the *Daily Telegraph* was commending the efforts of the Board.

The resources provided by the London School Board ensured that these flagship schools were staffed by the best-qualified teachers in the country. Both W.B. Adams and Louisa Walker attached high priority to attracting good assistants. Their success created a problem for them in that Fleet Road quickly became known as a stepping stone towards promotion. Some of their best teachers moved on. Among the most interesting aspects of the Fleet Road research has been the light thrown on the career patterns of the teachers of the time. The Adams and the Walker families are not entirely typical, in so far as the level of success they achieved was beyond the normal expectation. They both held a clear conception of their mission, knew their market and played to it. Their complementary styles of leadership (which would seem not to have extended into their personal interaction) gave Fleet Road a unique quality. The cynical might have said that what they had learned best was skill in disseminating a favourable public image.

The aspiring parents of Fleet Road's intake would quickly have seen through empty gestures, however. The school had to deliver the goods. One important measure the public could understand was favourable inspectors' reports. This Fleet Road School took in its stride. More significant was the scholarship reputation it was probably the first London school to establish. Adams seized every opportunity for entering children for some competitive activity or another, and the spirit of emulation accrued. To repeat an earlier point, the Adamses and the Walkers were in themselves in the vanguard of the upwardly aspiring, and knew exactly what the parents of the generation which followed them wanted. Both of them indeed set examples in using the system for the benefit of their own children.

Fleet Road Board School was opened in 1879. One hundred years later the British people elected a new government and a new Prime Minister, the daughter of a grocer. Had she been born earlier, she could well have emerged from an educational environment such as that of Fleet Road, meriting Charles Morley's accolades on the way. Conjecturally, she would have lauded its values and successes. Some have argued that current official preoccupation with Victorian values and standards reflects a longing for an accountability device as powerful and restrictive as the Revised Code. This is less convincing than an interpretation relating it to a desire to resurrect meritocratic virtues, of the type Fleet Road promoted. This may be a barbed compliment. It would be wrong to conclude that the school was narrowly devoted to an expedient response to persistent consumer demand. While that may have been part of the story, the educational experience of the Fleet Road children told them that there was more to life than work. The school had a broader cultural aim as well. It paid much more attention to literature and music, for example, than was normal for that time or later, and than could have been justified on a merely utilitarian reckoning. Fleet Road and its two famous headteachers helped to spearhead an educational change that extended the public awareness of the scope of elementary schooling.

REFERENCES

1. H. Silver, *Education as History: Interpreting Nineteenth and Twentieth-century Education* (London, 1983), p.22.
2. The underlying theme in W.E. Marsden, *Unequal Educational Provision in England and Wales: The Nineteenth-Century Roots* (Woburn Press, London, 1987).
3. See G. Gissing, *The Whirlpool* (1897, Harvester Press reprint 1984).

Index

INDEX

279